THE CHICAGO RIVER

David Solzman (signature)

THE CHICAGO RIVER

AN ILLUSTRATED HISTORY AND GUIDE
TO THE RIVER
AND
ITS WATERWAYS

DAVID M. SOLZMAN

Wild Onion Books

an imprint of
Loyola Press

Chicago

Wild Onion Books

an imprint of
Loyola Press
3441 North Ashland Avenue
Chicago, Illinois 60657
1-800-621-1008

Wild Onion Books publishes provocative titles on Chicago themes that offer diverse perspectives on the city and surrounding area, its history, its culture, and its religions. Wild onion is a common nickname for Chicago.

Library of Congress Cataloging-in-Publication Data

Solzman, David.
   The Chicago River: an illustrated history and guide to the river and its
waterways/David Solzman.
      p. cm.
   Includes bibliographical reference and index.
   ISBN 0-8294-1023-6
   1. Chicago River (Ill.)—History—Pictorial works. 2. Chicago River (Ill.)—
Guidebooks. I. Title.
F547.C45S65 1998   97-47317
917.73'110443—DC21   CIP

98 99 00 01 02 / 10 9 8 7 6 5 4 3 2 1

DEDICATION

WE ARE, ALL OF US, TEACHERS. Not only those we call teachers, but everyone we meet and interact with in our daily lives. To be a good teacher is the mark of an outstanding person; those who consciously endeavor to teach and teach well are to be very greatly esteemed.

So this book is dedicated, with respect and deep affection, to the great teachers under whose guidance I have been blessed to study: Harold Mayer and his wife Florence who capped outstanding teaching with a lifelong friendship, Chauncy Harris, Norton Ginsburg, and Wesley Calef. Great teachers teach not only their subjects, but the subject of life. And so, in this select company, I must include Margit Varro who taught me so much and so well.

My other great teachers are my children Nancy and Andrea, my parents Pauline and Isel, my uncle Meyer, and my brother Michael. All have been nurturing, loving, and a source of constant learning. My wife Rachel has proved the most formidable, effective, and loving teacher of my life.

In addition, this book is dedicated to all who love, teach about, and care for the Chicago River and the great city upon its banks.

CONTENTS

ACKNOWLEDGMENTS

The task of writing this book was greatly lightened by the assistance and suggestions of a great many individuals. Nowhere was this more evident than in the creation of the maps that accompany the text. The artful and highly legible re-creation of historic maps was the work of Raymond Brod of the Cartographic Laboratory of the Program in Geography, University of Illinois at Chicago. The reference maps of the Chicago River were generously provided by the Friends of the Chicago River. The daunting task of redesigning and creating the maps of Chicago area waterways was assisted by Raymond Brod, David Jones, Jane Lillienfeld, and Victor and Barbara Zaveduk. Victor Zaveduk reworked and computerized the maps provided by the Friends of the Chicago River, David Jones, Jane Lillienfeld, and Raymond Brod, and he created the additional maps of the North Branch tributaries, the south lakefront, the Calumet River system, the Cal-Sag Channel, and the Chicago Sanitary and Ship Canal. Old maps of the Calumet River and the Chicago River were made available by Richard J. Sutphin from his archives. Similarly, additional old maps of the Chicago River came from the collection of William Rossberger. Leith A. Rohr and Cynthia Mathews of the photographic and print library at the Chicago Historical Society offered thoughtful and informed assistance in finding appropriate historical photographs.

Many conversations with David Jones, Jane Lillienfeld, Richard J. Sutphin, Ralph C. Freese, Laurene Von Klan, William Rossberger, and Grant Crowley provided historical background and technical information. David M. Young of the *Chicago Tribune* conferred with the author over a number of years and freely shared his vast expertise on the history and present situation regarding all forms of transportation in Chicago. James Landing of the University of Illinois at Chicago and the Lake Calumet Study Committee was a fountain of information on the Lake Calumet area, and John Gavin of the Chicago International Port District provided much needed information on cargo tonnages and history of the port.

The author is also indebted to Chuck Nekvasil who, when serving in public relations for Acme Steel Company, gave much time and information useful to this project. Tom Kramer of the KCBX Division of Koch Industries gave very generously of his time and knowledge. Matthew Rhead provided a great deal of information on the vexing problem of encroachments on the North Branch of the Chicago River.

Of course, it would be difficult to mention everyone who gave additional advice and assistance. The following list, though incomplete, includes many who provided conversations, criticism, ideas, and information: Rolf Achilles, writer; Harry Arnett, Marsulex Corportion; Fred Axley, McDermott, Will, & Emery, Friends of the Chicago River; Richard Blaylock, Continental Grain Corporation; Frank Bonham, village of Worth; Peggy Bradley, public relations, Metropolitan Water Reclamation District;

David Brent, University of Chicago Press; Edward Budaris, R. Lavin & Sons; Paul Bulow, history graduate student, University of Illinois at Chicago; Wesley Calef, geographer; Jack Carr, U.S. Army Corps of Engineers; Mary Carroll, public relations, Metropolitan Water Reclamation District; Naomi Cohen, Friends of the Chicago River; Alan Crowther, Metropolitan Water Reclamation District, Stickney plant; Gerald Danzer, historian, University of Illinois at Chicago; Leon Despres, attorney; Michael Egan, developer; Phil Elmes, Chicago Maritime Society; Gerald L. File, Trans Trade, Inc.; Charles Fitch, Charles Ringer & Company; Rita L. Freese, Chicagoland Canoe Base; Norton S. Ginsburg, geographer, University of Chicago; Ernest Glenn, U.S. Steel Corporation; Norman Goldring, CPM Corporation; Joe Griffin, Inland Steel Corporation; Michael J. Griffin, chief engineer, Cook County Highway Department; Chauncy D. Harris, geographer, University of Chicago; Nancy Hayes, Friends of the Parks; Sharon Heckman, Ashland Chemical Company; Susan Hedman, Environmental Law and Policy Center, Friends of the Chicago River; Troy Heinzeroth, photographer; Kenan Heise, *Chicago Tribune;* Tim Hildner, Metropolitan Structures, Inc.; Mike Holzer, LEED Council; Mark Horwitz, Environmental Protection Agency; Jeanne Hunt, historian; Michael Iverson, architect; Ray Jacobs, LaFarge Corporation; Glen Johnson, FSC Paper Corporation; Steve Joseph, Reserve Iron and Metal, Reserve Marine and Stevedoring; Adina Kabaker, writer; Stan Kaderback, City of Chicago, Department of Bridges; Louis Kauffman, mathematician, University of Illinois at Chicago; William Koenig, consultant; Leonard Kotin, chemist, University of Illinois at Chicago; Joe Kovac, Reserve Iron and Metal; Gerald Kuecher, geologist, University of Illinois at Chicago; Beverly Kush, Environmental Protection Agency; Christine Kuypers, graduate student in history, University of Illinois at Chicago; Peter Landreth, geography graduate student, University of Illinois at Chicago; Ron Lasew, Forest Preserve District of Cook County; Gary Litherland, City of Chicago, Department of Water; Bill Lowe, R.R. Donnelly Company; Linda Lutz, Evanston Ecology Center.

William A. Macaitis, engineer; Paul Macomas, U.S. Veterans Administration Hospital; Carol Massar, public affairs, U.S. Corps of Engineers; Harold M. Mayer, geographer, University of Wisconsin at Milwaukee; Florence Mayer; William McBride, architect, Friends of the Chicago River; Allan Mellis, Forest Preserve District of Cook County; Donald Miller, historian; Chris Morgan, Arrow Terminal; Elizabeth Morgan, graduate student in geography, University of Illinois at Chicago; Robert Murry, MSI Corporation; Layton Olsen, City Innovations; Jorge Perez, Southeast Chicago Development Commission; Rosemarie Philipowski, public relations, General Mills; Joe Pisano, public relations, A. Finkl and Sons; Rene Prejean, City of Chicago, Department of Water; Jane Pugh, Hyde Park Kenwood Community Council; Dick Race, Hydrographic Survey Company; Andrew Reber, Koppers Industries; Tom Robertson, Cozzi Scrap (Metal Management Corporation); George Ryan, Lake Carriers Association; Jim Sabord, Burlington-Northern Railroad; Tim Samuelson, Chicago Historical Landmarks Commission; Glen Sekus, Environmental Protection Agency; Rick Schleyer, City of Chicago, Department of Planning; Andrea Schuster, Kushner and Wakefield; Deana Schoss, Chicago Park District; John R. "Jack" Sheaffer, Sheaffer International, Ltd.; Diane Slaviero; Arthur Slavi, Centrum Properties; Dale Smyser, PVS Chemical Company; Julia Sniderman, Chicago

Park District; Jay Stanwich, public relations, Ford Motor Company; John Stoeckert, Hannah Marine Corporation; Jack Swenson, City of Chicago, Department of Planning; Deane Tank, Sr., Chicago Maritime Society; Fred Templeton; Irma Tranter, Friends of the Parks; Margit Varro; Shawn Wallace, Chicago Park District; David Weinstein, photographer; Malcolm P. Weiss, geographer, Northern Illinois University; Peggy Weller, public relations, Cargill Corporation; and Tom Wysockey, engineer.

All of the employees of the Mercury Cruise Lines were very considerate and helpful. Special thanks are due to Diane Uczen, Holly Agra, Bob Agra, Kurt Meyer, Rob Davis, Charles Breux, Shareen Pagois, Bob Lund, and Kirsten Lund.

My fellow geographers at the University of Illinois at Chicago, Cliff Tiedemann, Gary Fowler, Albert Larson, Yequiao Wang, and Siim Soot, provided many insights and suggestions. Similarly, the staff of the Friends of the Chicago River were always helpful and supportive. Special thanks to Jim Buccheri, Randall Leurquin, Julia Fabris, Chris Cercone, Chris Parsons, Kathy Hudzik, David Ramsey, Naomi Cohen, and especially Laurene Von Klan.

The book could not have appeared without the energy and understanding of my editor, June Sawyers who provided helpful guidance and good-natured assistance throughout the protracted and sometimes difficult project. Her help is gratefully acknowledged.

Finally, the support and constant assistance provided by my family allowed me to undertake and complete the book. My mother, Pauline Solzman Selner, my daughters Nancy and Andrea, and my son-in-law Jon Goldberg were very helpful. Rachel McKinzie, my wife, offered loving support, suggestions, criticism, and assistance at every stage of the manuscript.

INTRODUCTION

T HIS BOOK EXAMINES THE WATERWAYS OF CHICAGO. The stage is set by reviewing the physical character and natural history of the Chicago area. Then the waterways themselves are described as the earliest settlers found them. This done, the history of the changing form and uses of the waterways is sketched as populations have grown and perceptions, technologies, and economies have changed.

But these changes had environmental consequences as Chicago rapidly burgeoned from a tiny hamlet to one of the world's great cities. Today public awareness of deteriorating waterways has sparked action by governmental and citizen groups. These groups have worked assiduously to reverse the decline of the waterways and bring attention to the importance of these priceless resources. The appendix lists many of these organizations.

The largest part of the book contains a series of waterway tours. Each tour is broken into sections; a map and detailed text describe the history, character, and points of interest of each section.

Increased knowledge and use of Chicago's waterways helps build understanding of the benefits, dangers, and costs that accompany such use. Perhaps, with that understanding, it will be possible to achieve a harmonious balance between human activities and natural processes. Such a balance would improve both the condition and the usefulness of the waterways of Chicago as they flow ceaselessly toward the distant sea.

. . . a branch of the filthy arrogant self-sufficient little Chicago River came into view . . . Here was a seething city in the making. . . .

Theodore Dreiser
The Titan (1914)

Geography of Chicago's Waterways

1673

French Canadian Louis Joliet and Father Jacques Marquette become the first explorers to pass through the area that would become Chicago.

1674

On December 4, Father Marquette and companions build a shelter near the mouth of the Chicago River; they spend the winter at the present intersection of Damen Avenue and the river.

1803

Fort Dearborn is established.

1812

Fort Dearborn Massacre.

1816

The Potawatomi cede a strip of land approximately ten miles wide on either side of the mouth of the Chicago River that extends southwesterly to the headwaters of the Illinois River, giving the U.S. control of the Chicago Portage route.

1822

Congress authorizes construction of the Illinois and Michigan Canal.

1834

Chicago's first movable bridge constructed at Dearborn and the river.

1836

Construction begun on the Illinois and Michigan Canal.

1848

The Illinois and Michigan Canal completed and finally opens to traffic.

1849

Melting ice rushes downriver, crushing small boats, destroying several bridges, and killing six people.

1885

Cholera and typhoid epidemic kills thousands of Chicagoans when a storm carries sewage into Lake Michigan, the city's source of drinking water.

1889

The Metropolitan Sanitary District of Greater Chicago is created to secure the safety of drinking water and to find a suitable way to dispose of wastes.

1892

Sanitary District begins construction of the Sanitary and Ship Canal.

1900

Sanitary and Ship Canal completed, reversing the flow of the Chicago River and diverting sewage away from Lake Michigan and toward the Mississippi River.

1909

The City Club of Chicago publishes Daniel Burnham and Edward Bennett's *Plan of Chicago,* which, among other things, proposes straightening the Chicago River, building a bridge across the river at Michigan Avenue, and protecting the natural resources of the lakefront.

North Shore Channel completed.

1911

Construction begins on Cal-Sag Channel.

1915

The *Eastland* excursion boat, docked near the Clark Street bridge, capsizes in the Chicago River, killing 812 people.

1920

Michigan Avenue Bridge is completed.

1922

The Metropolitan Sanitary District succeeds in reversing the flow of the Calumet River as the Cal-Sag Channel is completed.

1928

Construction begins on September 20 to straighten the Chicago River. The South Branch of the Chicago River is moved a quarter mile west to make room for a railroad terminal and the expansion of downtown Chicago.

1930

River straightening project completed.

1933

Cal-Sag Channel is dredged nine feet to become part of the U.S. inland waterway system.

1951

The Chicago Regional Port District created in June, and construction of port facilities at Lake Calumet started in late September.

1955

American Society of Civil Engineers selects the Metropolitan Sanitary District of Greater Chicago as one of the seven engineering wonders of the United States.

1956

Traffic begins at the International Port at Lake Calumet.

1957

First stage of port construction completed.

1959

First ocean-going ship reaches the Chicago International Port as Saint Lawrence Seaway is completed.

1962

Beginning of local tradition of dyeing the Chicago River green on Saint Patrick's Day.

1975

Tunnel and Reservoir Plan (TARP) begins, a massive project to control stormwater and prevent sewage backup.

1979

Friends of the Chicago River is founded.

1990

The City of Chicago and Friends of the Chicago River develop guidelines for urban rivers.

1992

The Great Chicago Underground Flood creates havoc in downtown Chicago, flooding the old freight tunnels and the basements of many Loop buildings, and producing a transportation nightmare.

1997

The Chicago City Council approves financing for construction of a 1.25-mile pedestrian riverwalk along the South Branch of the Chicago River from Van Buren Street to 18th Street.

Chicago River and Waterways Timeline

CHAPTER 1

WATERS ON THE LAND

I am the mist,

Back of the thing you seek.

My arms are long,

Long as the reach of time and space.

Carl Sandburg, *Chicago Poems* (1916)

WATER MOVING ACROSS THE surface of the earth acts to organize the surface. From tiny rills that run in gutters to giant floods that drain rain forests, to ephemeral streams that, ghost-like, rise and fade away, moving water, both solid (ice) and liquid, is nature's principal arbiter of the shape of the earth's surface.

Surface waters, in addition to organizing and sculpting the form of the land, provide strong divisions and abrupt demarcations on an otherwise generally unmarked surface. Streams cleave the land and separate areas even as the waters bind them together.

In ancient times water was considered one of the four elements out of which the world was created. To this day, streams continue to attract human interest, since they provide water for life, a power resource, a defensive perimeter, a path to distant lands, and a source of inspiration and example for human effort. Indeed, some suggest that humans were

required to form increasingly complex societies in order to manage this precious resource. Zen philosophy advises us to "be like water," following the least resistant path to the goal. And the unwavering persistence of moving water wears away stone. It is little wonder, then, that rivers play such important roles in human activity, organization, and history.

The Chicago River is the key stream in the area and was the principal impetus for the birth and location of Chicago. The river's course includes two branches with a number of forks, and its flow was enhanced by water from a few small tributaries. Although shallow, sluggish, and uninspiring—indeed, "too lazy to clean itself"—the river was nonetheless subtly endowed with remarkable potential.

Of course, the river and its tributaries offered drink, food, and safe harbor for early settlers. But its greatest value for the native tribes of the area was as the key to a system of water routes that connect

Main Stem of Chicago River.

the flowing waters of the midcontinent to the open waters of the Great Lakes.

Near Chicago, a subcontinental divide separates the waters that drain to the Great Lakes from those that flow to the Gulf of Mexico. This low divide is located a scant nine miles southwest of the Chicago River mouth. It was possible, through a portage over the divide, to pass from Lake Michigan and the Chicago River to the Des Plaines River. From the Des Plaines, the traveler could reach the Mississippi River and the Gulf of Mexico.

As master stream of the mid-continent, the Mississippi River provides access to all of the navigable waters of the central United States. These waters include the drainage systems of the Ohio, Arkansas, and Missouri Rivers and their branching tributaries. This network furnishes water routes that stretch from Montana, Wyoming, Colorado, and Texas on the west; near the Canadian border on the north; and east to the Appalachians via the Ohio, Allegheny, and Monongahela Rivers.

The native tribes that occupied or passed through the area were already using the portage when the early explorers and settlers arrived. Thus, Chicago became an *entrepôt* (a connection between routes) as the settlers in turn used this link to the West. As Harold Mayer observed: "Chicago was a port before it was a city."

However, as the distinguished historian William Cronon pointed out, the Chicago River offered intriguing *possibilities*. These possibilities were not fully realized until over the course of a century

settlers translated the stream's potential into physical changes that made it the transport artery they envisioned. These changes allowed for Chicago's subsequent organization of the vast midcontinental commercial hinterland.

Thus, as their technological capabilities evolved, settlers were able to make physical changes to the waterways, reflecting their changing perception and use of them. Major alterations included changes in stream channel shape, depth, width, and orientation, and even in the quality and direction of their flow. When the surface streams were found inadequate for the imagined transport and sanitary uses, a series of canals was constructed.

A canal dug through the Chicago River portage, envisioned in the seventeenth century by Jacques Marquette and Louis Joliet and realized as the Illinois and Michigan Canal in 1848, exploited the advantages and overcame the disadvantages of the Chicago River portage. With the canal, Chicago gained competitive commercial advantage by providing an intervening trade opportunity before St. Louis. The subsequent growth of the Chicago market and the coming of the railroad, led to its usurpation of the north–south trade axis that had existed along the Mississippi River between St. Louis and New Orleans. The ultimate result was a commercial reorganization of the central United States along an east–west trade axis that exists to this day.

Such manifold changes also produced changes in the region's environment. As a result of these changes, the streams we see and use today have been utterly transformed from their original pre-settlement forms. The human changes of the waterways have been so profound that today the waterways are more a human artifact than a natural system.

At the end of the twentieth century the freshwater resources of the Chicago area are still of paramount importance. They supply the region with a virtually inexhaustible source of potable water and provide a path for treated wastewater. They furnish water for industrial processes and for cooling. In addition, the waterways continue to offer paths for waterborne commerce, both for internal trade and export. And, of course, the waters provide homes for wildlife and are themselves a significant recreational resource. The waterways also have aesthetic value. By cutting through the city and creating open space, they offer opportunities to reflect on and enjoy the intermingling beauty of the human and natural world. They are exclamation points in an otherwise undistinguished landscape.

Since the waterways serve important needs of society, they continue to require society's care. The streams demand channel upkeep and improvement, transportation management and control, and water treatment. Their plants and animals require study and conservation. Flood control continues to be important, since the streams swell after major storms. They still flood portions of Chicago's flat surface as if in repeated attempts to return the area to the swamp that greeted the first settlers.

CHAPTER 2

THE PHYSICAL GEOGRAPHY OF THE CHICAGO REGION

. . . the worst harbor and smallest river

any great commercial city ever lived on.

Caroline Kirkland, early Chicago pioneer (1858)

LOCATION

THE CHICAGO REGION IS LOCATED along the southwesternmost shore of Lake Michigan, virtually in the center of the United States. One writer, Joel Garreau (1982), has characterized the city as the capital of the Midwestern heartland. Most of Chicago is remarkably flat. Only a few low ridges interrupt this flatness. However, at the far southwestern portion of the city and in the western and northern suburbs, low rolling hills ring the area. All of these surface features, from the flatness of the terrain to the rolling hills, were wrought by the glaciers of the last ice age.

When the Native Americans held sway, the area was not only flat but decidedly swampy. A few small creeks and rivers oozed across the damp countryside, and many so-called sloughs held stagnant water at the surface. Here and there low ridges rose above the swamp, and surrounding the immediate area was hilly country dotted with small lakes.

BEDROCK

Although the present landscape of the Chicago region is principally the handiwork of continental glaciers that repeatedly surged across it, the surface rests upon ancient bedrock dating from the middle Silurian period some 400 million years ago. At that time tropical seas covered the area that was later to become Chicago. These tropical seas teemed with the aquatic life forms that then dominated life on earth.

In time, as sea creatures died, their shells and other limey parts fell to the ocean bottom and were transformed into limestone. Through the ages this limestone was subjected to heat and pressure and contaminated with magnesium, which eventually changed into a rock

Canoeists glide through serene waters between wooded banks on the upper reaches of the Chicago River North Branch.

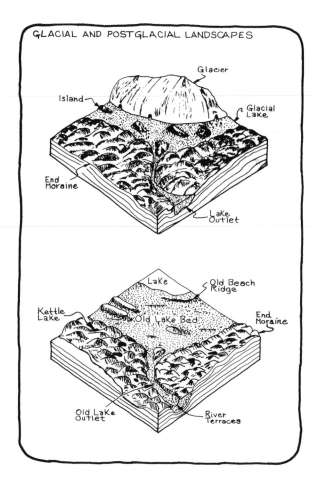

GLACIAL AND POSTGLACIAL LANDSCAPES

Glacier

Island

Glacial Lake

End Moraine

Lake Outlet

Lake

Old Beach Ridge

Kettle Lake

Old Lake Bed

End Moraine

Old Lake Outlet

River Terraces

Glacial action produces a variety of landscape features that linger after the ice has vanished. (Redrawn State of Illinois pamphlet.)

form called dolomite. Dolomitic limestone forms the bedrock of Chicago and is deeply buried under materials deposited by the glacier and the meltwater lakes that followed. Since the buried rock surface is so uneven, it reaches the surface at many places throughout the metropolitan area.

The light-colored dolomite bedrock continues northward and eastward in a great sweeping arc to form the Door Peninsula of Wisconsin and much of the Upper Peninsula of Michigan before continuing as a range of hills in Ontario, Canada. This same rock layer then reenters the United States in western New

York State. Here it forms the rock over which Niagara Falls, falls. Thus its name: the Niagaran formation of middle Silurian dolomitic limestone.

At the southern edges of the Chicago region lie rocks formed more than 300 million years ago in the shallow swamps of the Carboniferous period. Abundant organic residue from these swamps was compressed over time, creating the coal reserves to the southwest of Chicago near Morris, Illinois, and elsewhere.

Despite the antiquity of the local bedrock, most of Chicago's present surface was formed during the last glacial period, which ended twelve to fourteen thousand years ago. With few exceptions, glacial rubble (till) thickly blankets the region's bedrock, often reaching a depth of 150 feet.

WATERS AND SURFACE FEATURES

Lake Chicago

The waters of the Chicago region are, like every other aspect of the area, a legacy from the last ice age. During the Wisconsin period a lobe of glacial ice lay over what we now call Lake Michigan. As this prodigious one-half mile-high mass of ice moved southward it deepened the valleys of some preexisting streams and formed a broad basin. Finally, as the ice began to recede, meltwaters filled this basin. The result was a feature that geologists call Lake Chicago.

At the time of its formation this lake extended beyond the current basin of Lake Michigan to engulf much of the future metropolitan area. Its surface lay some sixty feet higher than the current level of the lake, and all of this water was imponded behind ridges of debris that

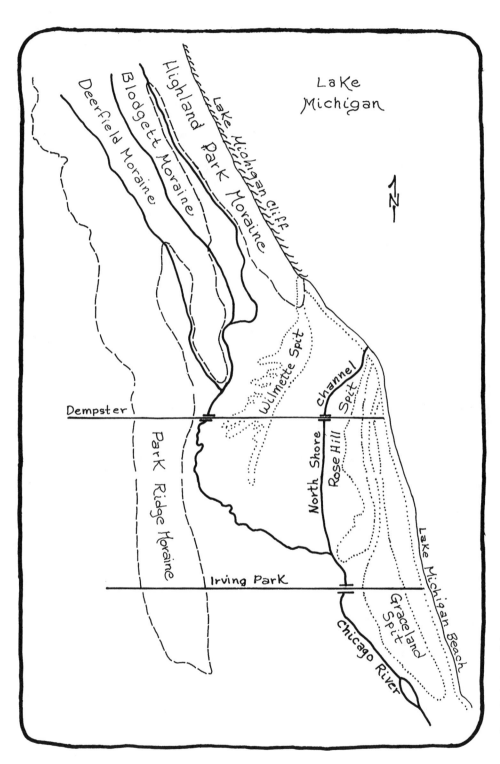

MAP 1.
A reconstruction of vanished sea cliffs and spit connections of the North Shore district. (After Bretz 1955.)

Remnants of Lake Chicago

The draining of glacial Lake Chicago left the area with three sizable remnants of the ancient lake, in addition to Lake Michigan. Shallow Lake Calumet to the south was such a remnant lake. It covered an area of about three square miles with an average water depth of three feet. Close by are two other shallow, and smaller, lakes: Lake George, which is now almost entirely filled, and Wolf Lake, which is of recreational value for boating, fishing, and some hunting.

Turtles and other amphibians abound in Chicago wetlands.

marked out the furthest extent of the now-retreating ice.

Moraines

Moraines are very prominent surface features of the Chicago area. The moraines were formed by the advancing glacier, which carried with it mountains of debris snatched from the land. Although glaciers flow inexorably forward, they may melt back at a rate greater than their forward flow. As a result, the edge of the ice advances and retreats in an irregular fashion, and, like children scuffing their feet in the dust, the back-and-forth motion of the glacier piles up ridges of loose, unsorted material at its edge.

The south end of Lake Michigan is essentially framed by moraines, and the northern portion of the Chicago metropolitan area features a complicated surface of moraine ridges, some of which run along the current lakeshore. The communities of Palos Park, La Grange, and Glenwood; the towns in the rolling country of Lake County, Illinois; the North Shore suburbs of Chicago; and the elevated site of Valparaiso, Indiana, are all situated atop the nearly continuous moraine ridge known as the Valparaiso Moraine.

The Valparaiso Moraine is about fifteen miles wide and generally lies ten to fifteen miles inland from the current shore of Lake Michigan. The height of the moraine varies from less than one hundred feet to more than five hundred feet above the level of the lake plain. Its location thus gives a clear picture of the previous extent of Lake Chicago.

Sags

Though huge, the lake was short lived and underwent numerous significant changes in size and level. Yet during its relatively brief life, finely divided silts and clay materials were deposited on the lake bottom. Then, after one thousand to two thousand years, glacial meltwater formed two drainage channels southwest of the present city, cutting through the moraine bounding the lake. These channels converged and focussed the outrushing water as it poured southwestward toward the Mississippi. The old channels appeared as low-lying ground to the early settlers, who called them *sags,* or low places in the landscape. The converging drainage channels joined at Sag Junction near the present town of Lemont.

Their focussed converging waters made a stream that would rival the most awesome rivers of today. Indeed, the flow appears to have exceeded even that of today's largest stream, the Amazon River. This all-but-unimaginable torrent carved out the valley now occupied by the Illinois River. But since the flow of the Illinois is so small relative to the titanic stream that preceded it, the Illinois occupies a much larger valley than it could have created. Because of this mismatch, geologists call the Illinois an underfit stream.

Beach Ridges

As the waters of glacial Lake Chicago drained westward the lake level fell gradually and paused in stages, falling about twenty feet each time. The result is that the lake plain on which Chicago is located is ringed by old beach ridges that show the gradually dropping level of the glacial lake. The three most important stages were Glenwood Beach, sixty feet above the current lake level; Calumet Beach, forty feet above the current level; and Toleston Beach, about twenty feet above today's lakeshore.

It is still possible to see these old beach ridges by driving west along either Devon Avenue on the city's North Side

or 95th Street on the South Side. As one drives west the road rises in stages over the old beaches. Then, as on 95th Street, one reaches the oldest lakeshore at Beverly Hills, the city's highest elevation, sixty feet above the current lake level.

In addition to these old beach ridges, several islands stood above the glacial flood. These included Stony Island and Blue Island.

Now Chicago's sprawling suburban development extends more than thirty miles and so has come to occupy positions on the Calumet and Glenwood beach ridges; and beyond to the morainic uplands north and west. Some of the newest suburbs are so remote they lie on the plains far beyond the glacial hills.

Soils

The soggy terrain of the lake plain gave rise to a variety of wet soils, including a good deal of sand and/or clay. The soil pattern is complex, with heavy soils in the low areas, and lighter stony soils on the morainic uplands.

LAKE MICHIGAN

Lake Michigan, third largest of the Great Lakes, is the only one located entirely within the United States. Its surface sits about 582 feet above average sea level at New York, and, at its deepest point, its bottom lies 341 feet below sea level. This vast lake has a maximum length of 307 miles and a maximum width of 118 miles, with a volume of about 1,180 cubic miles of water.

Lake Michigan is made up of two main basins. The northern basin begins just north of Milwaukee. It is deep with a rugged bottom swept by fast-moving currents. By contrast, the southern basin is shallower, with a relatively flat bottom and slow-moving currents. Unfortunately, since most of the industry surrounding the lake lies around the southern basin, pollution tends to remain for extended periods because of the slow-moving currents. Remarkably, the drainage basin supplying Lake Michigan with water is very restricted by the ringing moraines, and it now appears that the lake's water is replenished mainly by rainfall.

The level of the lake rises and falls about six feet over periods of about eleven and one-half years, and there are slight tides on the lake surface due to the gravitational pull of the sun and the moon. These tides cause the lake levels to rise and fall just an inch or so.

Moraine Lakes

Besides the vast inland freshwater sea that is Lake Michigan, the rolling uplands of the moraines are dotted with small lakes that were formed when chunks of ice from the retreating glaciers melted, leaving lakes in undrained depressions between hills. These small lakes now provide scenic and recreational benefits and are appealing sites for suburban homes.

Area Fish and Fowl

Lake Michigan and surrounding streams are host to about seventy species of fish, including lake trout, sturgeon, muskellunge, pike, whitefish, salmon, grayling, sculpin, sunfish, bass, perch, and buffalo. The lake is home also to many species of birds, including several varieties of gulls. In addition, hosts of waterbirds nest and breed in and around Lake Michigan and nearby wetlands.

Canada geese competing for territory in the spring.

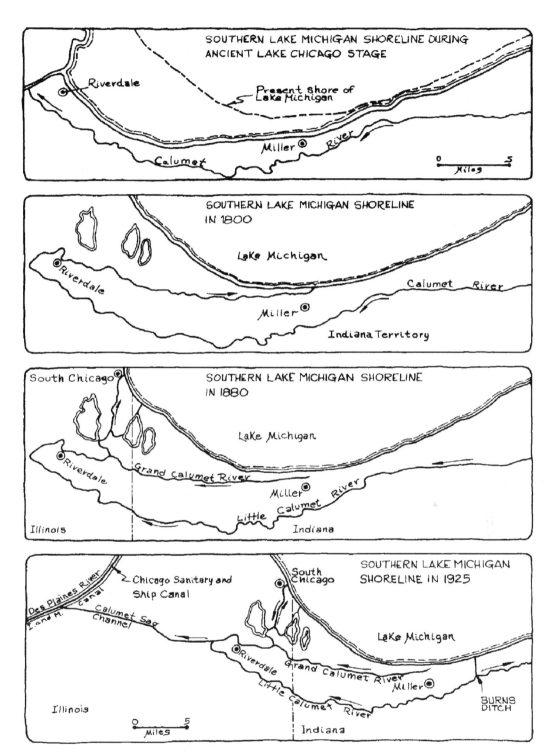

MAP 2.
Changes in the flow of the Calumet River as Lake Chicago retreated and as new artificial channels and canals were dug during the nineteenth and twentieth centuries. (After Fryxell 1924.)

Rivers

The Chicago River

The rivers of the Chicago region had the most influence on the human population, organization, and use of the area. Of these, the Chicago River was the primary stream. Its winding course shifted between sand dunes and connected some of the sloughs that lay on the surface of the swampy old lake bed. In its natural state, it drained directly into Lake Michigan.

The river originated from three main source areas: one to the north, one to the southwest, and the other to the south. The stream's three main northern tributaries dribbled out of springs and wetlands, the west fork oozed out of Mud Lake to the southwest, and the south fork flowed out of the southern wetlands. Numerous other small tributaries joined the river before it emptied into shallows and swamps east of Michigan Avenue near Monroe Street.

A south-flowing current along the lakeshore built up a large obstructing sandbar that blocked direct flow of the river into the lake. Early settlers found the rivermouth so clogged with sand that the water was only one to two feet deep. A small hill on the south bank overlooking the rivermouth was the site where Fort Dearborn was built in 1803.

The Calumet River

To the south, near Lake Calumet, lay the channels of the Calumet River system, including primarily the Grand Calumet and Little Calumet Rivers. But these two streams were really one, for the Calumet had a course rather like the flight of a boomerang. It rose in northwest Indiana among the sand dunes at the south end of Lake Michigan. From there it flowed northwestward between the dunes for perhaps thirty miles before turning back to the east. Altogether, the river's winding course covered about sixty miles, ultimately emptying into Lake Michigan near Miller, Indiana, relatively close to its source. Its remarkable history is illustrated in the accompanying diagrams (Map 2).

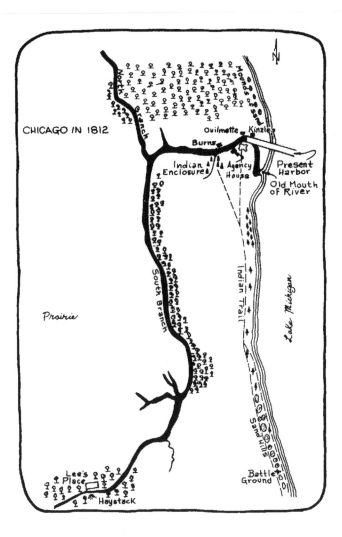

"The Calumet River is a curious and interesting stream that drains the part of the lake plain south of Chicago and in northern Indiana. At one time this river entered Lake Michigan near Riverdale. . . . " Throughout the forty-five mile stretch between its source in La Porte County and Riverdale it flowed parallel to the lakeshore and only a few miles from it. Two well-developed parallel beach ridges held it to this very unusual course. But the constant wave action kept building up sandbars from the north across the mouth of the river, steadily shifting the mouth southeastward. At times of high water the river would break across the bar obstructing its mouth, but a new bar would again form at the mouth and the whole process would be repeated. Thus there developed a series of alternating sandbars and lagoons, the lagoons representing channels formerly occupied by the river (Fryxell 1924, 15).

By the time settlers had arrived, the Calumet had shifted fourteen miles eastward to a point north of Miller, Indiana. The upper and lower sections of the river then flowed parallel to each other but in opposite directions, separated by a narrow barrier of alternating sand ridges and lagoons, only two or three miles wide. Frequently, the river mouth north of Miller was nearly closed by sand.

Today the Calumet River has been completely rearranged by human action. It now flows westward out of Lake Michigan through a canal and ultimately into the Des Plaines, Illinois, and Mississippi Rivers. A new river mouth and an artificial channel were cut from Lake Michigan through some preexisting sloughs toward Lake Calumet. From there,

water from the Grand Calumet River—the formerly eastward-flowing, curled-back portion of the stream—mixed with water from Lake Michigan and Lake Calumet and flowed westward to be joined by the west-flowing waters of the Little Calumet River. Yet even these massive changes have been further altered through widening, straightening, and deepening the channel and through dredging and filling in Lake Calumet.

The Des Plaines River

After the glaciers melted away, the Des Plaines River flowed southward and then to the southwest on the west side of the continental divide. The southwestward course of the river lay along the northern sag of the two that remained after glacial Lake Chicago drained to become Lake Michigan. As a result, the Des Plaines is a part of the Mississippi River drainage, and it is the stream to which the Chicago River portage gave access. Near the town of Lemont, the Des Plaines turns more to the south and flows about twenty miles before joining the west-ward-flowing Kankakee to form the Illinois River.

About one-quarter mile north of Interstate 55 (the Stevenson Expressway), the Des Plaines lies just a few hundred yards west of Harlem Avenue. This was the western end of the Chicago River portage.

Other Streams

Numerous small tributary streams also existed after the glacial period. They were short and of little special importance. However, some of their channels were later incorporated into canals or the altered channels of the main streams.

CLIMATE

Temperature

Most of the Chicago metropolitan area experiences a humid continental climate with cool to cold winters. Such climates are characterized by rapid heating and cooling and sizable daily and seasonal temperature swings. Chicago's temperature extremes, which range from 106°F to –26°F, illustrate this principle. July is usually the warmest month, with an average temperature of 73°; January tends to be coldest, with an average temperature of about 21°.

Chicago's climate is altered somewhat by its lakeside location. Close to Lake Michigan, summer temperatures are cooler than surrounding areas, while winter temperatures tend to be warmer, resulting in a more temperate microclimate near the lake.

Rainfall

Most of Chicago's rainfall comes in the growing season, with a peak of about four inches in June. Overall, the city experiences 34 1/2 inches of precipitation annually, although the actual amount in a given year may vary considerably.

Occasionally, thunderstorms produce unusually large amounts of rainfall, often leading to flooding and contamination of the waterways. In August 1987, for instance, Chicago experienced a downpour of almost 9 1/2 inches in a twenty-four-hour period. Almost one hundred years earlier, a similar torrent of rain in 1885 led to sewage contamination of Lake Michigan. In the cholera epidemic that followed, nearly three thousand people died. The Sanitary District of Chicago was created after this tragedy, charged with providing, maintaining, and safeguarding the city's water supply.

Today, because the Chicago metropolitan area is so large, different sections experience slightly different climates and rainfall amounts. Since this is the case, the temperature and precipitation measured at O'Hare Airport, the official recording station for the city, often differ from those along the lake and elsewhere.

Although extreme cold usually causes an accumulation of ice along the lakeshore, only rarely is Lake Michigan frozen to any great extent. Farther to the north the Great Lakes are often blocked by winter ice, limiting the shipping season to about ten months. On the other hand, the ice that forms on the rivers and canals near Chicago tends to be thin, rarely inhibiting navigation. River traffic breaks up the forming ice, and the use of river water as a coolant for power plants raises stream temperatures somewhat.

Winds

Chicago bears the nickname the Windy City, but it is not particularly windy. The popular name actually refers to the "windiness" of nineteenth-century Chicago politicians, whose uninhibited bragging earned the city its moniker. In general, Chicago experiences winds similar to those of the surrounding areas. The strongest winds tend to come in late winter and early spring, when temperature and pressure contrasts are greatest.

Temperature contrasts between Lake Michigan and the rest of the region often produce lake breezes during warm summer days and offshore breezes on summer evenings. Cooling breezes attract crowds to Chicago's lakefront parks. Because of these breezes and attractive lakefront vistas, Lake Michigan's shoreline is highly valued for residences. Particularly along the city's North Shore, a virtually unbroken line of high-quality apartments and homes stretches along the lake.

Thunderstorms are the most common violent storms characterizing the local climate. However, spring thunderstorms occasionally spawn tornadoes. Curiously, although tornadoes have ravaged sections of the Chicago metropolitan area, especially southwest of the city, no major tornado has ever been recorded in the city's central area. The reasons for this are unclear and are a continuing subject of study and debate.

FLORA AND FAUNA

Vegetation

The variety of vegetation at the south end of Lake Michigan is among the most complex in the United States. Here arctic plants such as the jack pine were imported by glacial ice. They mingle in close proximity with plants from the desert Southwest whose seeds were borne by the winds to the sandy lakeshore. One reason for the establishment of the Indiana Dunes National Lakeshore was the extraordinary variety of plants that the area contains.

Chicago's native vegetation was just as varied, for this area is the meeting place between the virtually uninterrupted deciduous forests to the east and the immense prairie lands to the west. Shrubby growth and tough grasses helped secure dune sands against the wind. Nearby, wetland vegetation lined the watercourses and filled the sloughs. Forest vegetation appeared principally along waterways and in small, isolated stands.

Most agree that the Indian word *Chicagou* means "place of wild onions or garlic."

Lake Michigan Storms

Today, Lake Michigan seems docile. So many people swim in it or boat on it that it seems to be a gentle and almost domesticated part of our park system. But early sailors on the lake had quite a different view. For them, a passage down Lake Michigan was a serious and often dangerous venture, and it is our view today that is unrealistic and romantic. The Chicago River shows persistence, but Lake Michigan demonstrates power, and the Great Lakes have been known to experience storms described as virtual hurricanes although such tempests are fortunately uncommon. Nonetheless, major storms do occur about once every twenty years, taking a heavy toll on lives and ships. These storms often occur in late autumn.

Because the Great Lakes are virtually inland seas, heavy storms may occur at any season. Such was the case in May 1894 when a storm blew for three days on Lake Michigan off Chicago. An estimated one hundred thousand spectators watched as the schooner *Jack Thompson* was blown into the *Rainbow*, the *Evening Star* rammed the *Myrtle*, and all were destroyed. All told, thirty-five schooners and twenty-seven lives were lost.

Of all the serious storms over the lakes, the worst is generally considered to be the near-hurricane that raged for four days in November 1913. In this fearful tempest, gales of at least sixty miles per hour generated forty-foot waves. Nineteen ships were demolished, many with the loss of all hands, and fifty-two more were damaged. By the time the tumult subsided, a Chicago lakefront park that had taken eight years to build had been ruined, millions of dollars in damage had been done, and 248 lives were lost.

Modern steel-hulled ship designs and greatly improved weather forecasting have lessened but not removed the danger of lake storms. Grim confirmation of this came in November 1958, when the *Carl D. Bradley*, then the largest lake vessel, went down with all hands. Then came the legendary loss on Lake Superior of the 729-foot *Edmund Fitzgerald* on November 10, 1975. When it sank in 530 feet of water it, too, was the largest ship on the lakes. It broke up so suddenly that, despite more than enough lifeboats and life preservers for the crew, not a man among the twenty-nine hands was saved.

The Chicago area marked the western limit for many eastern varieties of trees such as the tulip tree and the beech, chestnut, sassafras, and sycamore. However, trees from the north woods were also present and included jack pine, tamarack, white pine, arborvitae, and paper birch. Further inland, tall-grass prairie predominated. The swampy lands near the mouth of the Chicago River were covered with rank grasses, among which were the wild garlic and onion that probably gave the region its Indian name of Chicagou, supposedly "the place of wild onions."

Animals

At the beginning of the nineteenth century, the Chicago region teemed with a vast array of animals. These included large predators such as black bear, cougar, gray wolf, Canada lynx, wildcat, weasel, badger, gray fox, red fox, marten, fisher, and coyote. Bison, elk, and white-tailed deer were abundant, as were many smaller animals such as opossum, otter, mink, beaver, muskrat, woodchuck, skunk, fox squirrel, red squirrel, rabbit, varieties of snakes, frogs, crustaceans, and a host of others.

Because the habitats at the south end of Lake Michigan are so diverse, they also supported a great variety of birds. Huge numbers of them thronged the wetlands, prairies, and lakeshores of the Chicago area. The wetlands near Lake Michigan also provided important links in the migration pattern in the so-called central flyway. Golden and bald eagles were present, as were osprey, five kinds of owls (including snowy owls and great horned owls), and turkey vultures. Birds of the prairies featured vast flocks of passenger pigeons as well as smaller numbers of chimney swallows, horned larks, cardi-

nals, magpie, raven, pileated woodpecker, woodcock, Carolina parakeets, quail, willow grouse, sharp-tailed grouse, prairie chickens, and many others.

Shorebirds and waterfowl were similarly abundant. Innumerable swans, geese, egrets, great blue herons, black-crowned night herons, green herons, many kinds of wild ducks as well as other waterfowl inhabited and nested or passed through the region.

CHICAGO'S ORIGINAL WATERS

In addition to Lake Michigan, early settlers found a host of smaller lakes dotting the uplands around Chicago. But water was everywhere present on the land. Surface streams wound their way sluggishly between sand dunes and in some places formed broader expanses of water called *sloughs*. Here and there along the streams were small stands of oaks and other trees that broke the monotony and that today are memorialized in names such as Cottage Grove and Oak Park.

The accompanying map on the following page shows a close approximation of the original waterways. In addition, it depicts the shoreline of the lake as it appeared at the beginning of the nineteenth century. It is fascinating to see how much human activity has changed the lakeshore as well as the courses of the streams. In fact, when the Fine Arts Building was built in 1886 on Michigan Avenue near Van Buren, the shallows of Lake Michigan lay just a few paces from the eastern edge of the road.

Swampland

Most of the city of Chicago lies a few feet above the level of Lake Michigan.

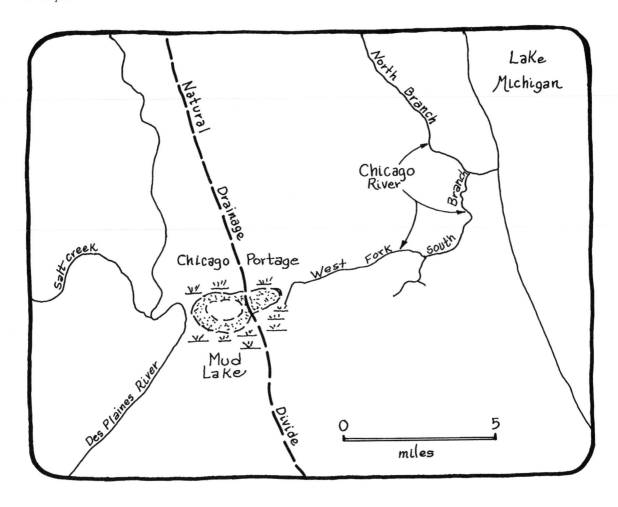

MAP 4.
The original Chicago portage crossed the low divide that separated the Mississippi drainage from the drainage to Lake Michigan. (After Solzman 1966.)

Because of it flatness and low-lying position, the original area was basically a swampy, miserable land.

It was this less-than-enchanting scene that greeted William B. Ogden, an early settler destined to become Chicago's first mayor, when he arrived to oversee the land speculations of his brother-in-law. He found most of the land underwater.

Ogden wrote his brother-in-law: "I am sorry to inform you that [you have] been guilty of an act of great folly in making [this] purchase." Yet despite his personal belief that "there is no . . .

value in the land and won't be for a generation," Ogden soon recovered his brother-in-law's original purchase price by draining and selling just one-third of the land. Even today, Chicago must operate an extensive pumping system to keep the area well drained. (Miller 1996, 70; Mayer and Wade 1969, 18).

Mud Lake

Of special interest is Mud Lake, a geographical feature no longer existing but historically significant nevertheless. This so-called lake was in reality a very large slough or swampy area of varying water depths at different times and seasons. Mud Lake stretched from just west of Damen Avenue on the east to Harlem Avenue on the west.

In dry weather, when Mud Lake was too shallow for canoes, it was necessary to portage from the lake's eastern end all the way to the continental divide near Harlem Avenue. About one-half mile beyond lay the Des Plaines River. Today motorists speed along Interstate 55 just a few yards south of the old portage route, traveling its five-mile distance in five to eight minutes. But in 1818, when influential Chicago pioneer Gurdon Hubbard used the portage, it took him and his companions a hellish three days to make the passage.

In wet weather, however, Mud Lake filled up, making it possible for travelers to reach the divide without having to carry their canoes. In very wet conditions Mud Lake was even known to top the divide, temporarily causing it to drain westward directly into the Des Plaines River. Thus, on occasion, the Chicago River reversed its flow. This peculiar behavior pointed the way for the engineering feats that were to follow. Now the Chicago River pulls water from Lake Michigan and drains westward toward the Mississippi.

Chicago River Branches

The original courses of both the North and South Branches of the Chicago River were quite different from those of today because of channel straightening, widening, and deepening. William B. Ogden dug a canal that still exists on the North Branch and created an island. Four other canals described in chapter 3 were also added to area waterways. They were the Illinois and Michigan Canal, completed

in 1848; the Sanitary and Ship Canal, completed in January 1900; the North Shore Channel, in 1909; and the Cal-Sag Channel, finished in 1922.

Calumet River System

The natural Calumet River system was unlike the stream that today drains the southern portion of the Chicago area. Engineering produced a new rivermouth and reversed the drainage. The next chapter describes these and other changes to Chicago's waterways.

CHAPTER 3

CHANGING USES, CHANGING WATERWAYS

Manny's th' time I've set on th' bridge . . . watch'n th' light iv th' tugs dancin' in it like stars . . . Twas th' prettiest river f'r to look at that ye'll iver see . . . th' Chicago river niver was intinded as a dhrink. It didn't go ar-round advertisin' itself as a saisonable beverage! . . . It had other business more suited to it.

Finley Peter Dunne (1900)

THE GROWTH OF CHICAGO WAS ONE of the wonders of the age. At the time of its incorporation as a village in 1833, Chicago was a squalid frontier outpost of a few hundred people that mushroomed to a city of about four thousand in just four years. By the time the city reached the venerable age of sixty in 1893, it was home to more than one million people. This explosive growth caused massive changes in the landscape: most of the surface water was drained, the center of the city was lifted five to twelve feet out of the muck, the lakeshore and surface streams were rerouted or otherwise altered. Louis Joliet's seventeenth-century dream of a water route to the West was realized two centuries later by the completion of the Illinois and Michigan Canal in 1848.

Commerce and population kept pace with these changes. Propelling the commercial development was the area's strategic water transportation, which brought grain from the interior—downstate Illinois and the Mississippi Valley—via canal barges and lumber from the northern lakes by three-masted schooners and steam-driven side-wheel propeller vessels. Lake vessels also helped move goods toward eastern markets, although the railroads became ever more dominant. Giant warehouses and steam-powered grain elevators lined the Chicago River and the Union Stockyards surrounded the southernmost portion of the south fork of the river's South Branch (now known as Bubbly Creek).

By 1871, the year of the Great Chicago Fire, more vessels arrived at Chicago than at "New York, Philadelphia, Baltimore, Charleston, San Francisco, and Mobile combined" (Miller 1996, 33); by 1883, twenty-two thousand ships called at Chicago. Starting in 1880, new port facilities began to be developed along the Calumet River. The emerging steel industry in particular found the large areas of cheap land and ready water access to be attractive.

Early morning rowers ply the Chicago River near the Chicago Lock and Ogden Slip. The river is used increasingly for recreation as its water quality slowly improves.

The alteration and virtual reconstruction of Chicago's waterways began almost immediately. More than 150 years of such pervasive and continuous change has produced a landscape that today bears little resemblance to that which nature presented to the first settlers.

LAKE MICHIGAN SHORELINE

The twenty-nine-mile Lake Michigan shoreline in Illinois has undergone constant change throughout Chicago's history. The accompanying map on page 31 (Map 5) indicates the steady advance of "made land" into the lake. The shoreline has been pushed so far eastward that most of today's lakefront parks, Lake Shore Drive, and portions of the central city rest on filled sections of the lake.

Streeterville
On the north side of the Chicago River, sand buildup and landfill angled outward and extended toward the pier, which by from 1834 bounded the river mouth on the north side. Eventually this fill engulfed a sizable sandbar that had built up around the grounded schooner of one of Chicago's most colorful characters, Captain John Wellington Streeter, in 1886:

> Streeter, a circus and show promoter, ran aground on a sandbar just east of the elegant mansions on North Michigan Avenue. (He). . . took up residence aboard his little ship, and when the lake currents and the garbage wagons had filled in the area around his sandbar, "the Barnum of Michigan Woods" laid claim to 168 acres. He based his right on an 1821 shoreline survey which indicated that his land was not part of the original Federal grant of land for settlement. Streeter soon established a "District" yielding allegiance to none but the Federal government . . . he built a shack . . . and began selling lots to gullible investors. . . . the owners of the mansions to the west of him, including Potter Palmer, considered him "a rude, blasphemous, drunken thief" (Mayer and Wade 1969, 305).

After years of struggle during which "events both spectacular and ludicrous" ensued, control of the land was wrested from Streeter in 1918 when he was sent packing for selling liquor on Sundays. Interestingly, Streeter's shipwreck occurred roughly at the spot now occupied by the northeast corner of the John Hancock Building.

Virtually all of the land between Michigan Avenue and the lakeshore north of the river is thus either artificially filled in or the result of sand deposited by the lake's southward-moving currents. We still call this huge area, now among the wealthiest in the city, Streeterville.

In fact, the method of making such filled-in land was developed in Chicago. A type of corrugated, interlocking sheet-steel piling was invented that could be driven into the lake or river bottom as required. The design of these pilings allows them to "lock" together to form a virtually impervious wall, behind which fill may be dumped. Successive lines of such pilings marked out the lakeward edge of the new land. In the early 1990s such a procedure created new land for rerouting the portion of Lake Shore Drive approaching the river from the south, allowing the removal of the drive's infamous S curve.

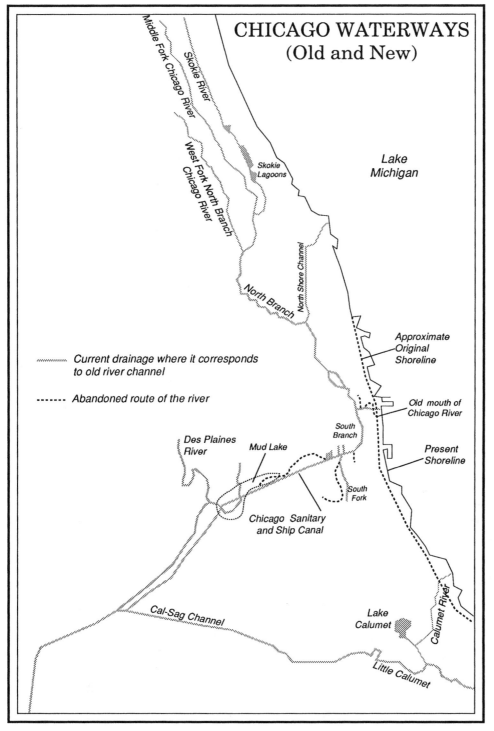

CHICAGO WATERWAYS
(Old and New)

Middle Fork Chicago River

Skokie River

West Fork North Branch Chicago River

Skokie Lagoons

Lake Michigan

North Branch

North Shore Channel

.... Current drainage where it corresponds
to old river channel

------- Abandoned route of the river

Des Plaines River

Mud Lake

Approximate Original Shoreline

Old mouth of Chicago River

South Branch

Present Shoreline

South Fork

Chicago Sanitary and Ship Canal

Cal-Sag Channel

Lake Calumet

Calumet River

Little Calumet

MAP 5.
This rough map suggests the many changes the waterways have undergone through time. The cutting of a new rivermouth and the straightening of the South Branch are indicated as is the filling-in of the old West Fork. The I & M Canal, the North Shore Channel, the Sanitary and Ship Canal, the North Branch Canal (which created Goose Island), and the Cal-Sag Channel are all shown. The artificial course and new mouth for the Calumet River are also included. Major changes to the lakefront are suggested.

Lakefront Parks

In the late 1850s Lake Michigan's shoreline lay just a few paces east of Michigan Avenue, and it was quite an eyesore. Political maneuvering by Senator Stephen A. Douglas forced the Illinois Central Railroad and the Michigan Central to enter the city from the south along the lakefront. An offshore trestle carried the Illinois Central Railroad to the station and roundhouse at the northeast corner of Randolph Street and Michigan Avenue, and created a cut-off, swampy lagoon. "Rude temporary piers and wharves jutted out into the shallows and piles of lumber and rock littered the dirt beach" (Mayer and Wade 1969, 40; Miller 1996, 102).

The dirt beach gradually was transformed into an esplanade, and after the Great Fire of 1871, much of the debris was pushed into the shallow lagoon. This set the stage for the battle that led to the creation of Chicago's lakefront system of parks.

The parks gracing Chicago's lakefront are constructed almost entirely on landfill. Among the city's most unique

A bird's-eye view of the mouth of the Chicago River in 1857.(From a lithograph by Charles Inger after a drawing by I.T. Palmatary. Courtesy, Chicago Historical Society.)

and beautiful elements, their full value to Chicago is being understood only today as visitors from around the world come to the city to see and use them. In the global economy, such tourism is a leading economic force and element in any world city's economic base.

Lakefront parks frame views of the city and Lake Michigan and they provide unique and beautiful spaces for activities of many kinds. The parks stretch nearly unbroken for twenty-nine miles from the Indiana state line to Evanston, Illinois. They came into being because of the almost obsessive drive of retail magnate A. Montgomery Ward, who worked tirelessly to prevent development along the lakefront.

In this fight Ward was following the lead of Gurdon S. Hubbard, William F. Thornton, and William B. Archer, Illinois and Michigan Canal commissioners who in 1836 refused to sell some valuable lakefront land so that the area could remain "forever open, clear, and free" as public space. Ward invested his enormous energies, his fortune, and his time to further this goal, though his associates derided his actions and urged him to help promote the lakefront for "productive purposes." Clearly, his vision was the greater, for few cities in the world today can boast such a beautiful and spacious front yard.

The few interruptions to the nearly continuous lakefront parks include some commercial land use at the mouths of the Chicago and Calumet Rivers; small sections of privately owned lakeshore on the city's extreme North and South Sides; and, between 79th and 93rd Streets on the South Side, an artificial peninsula constructed of slag and landfill. This peninsula served until 1992 as the home of the United States Steel South Works.

Length: The Chicago River System is more than 150 miles long.

Northernmost point: Park City in Lake County.

Southernmost point of Sanitary and Ship Canal: Lockport, Illinois in Will County.

Tributaries, branches, and canals: North Branch: West Fork, Middle Fork, and East Fork (Skokie River and Skokie Lagoons), North Shore Channel, North Branch Canal. South Branch: South Fork (Bubbly Creek), Sanitary and Ship Canal. Other adjacent waterways include the Grand Calumet River, the Little Calumet River, and Cal-Sag Channel.

Deepest point: 20 to 21 feet in the Main Stern.

Widest point: 800 feet at the North Avenue Turning Basin and Grand Avenue.

Water quality: Upgraded from "toxic" to "very polluted" (but slowly improving).

Cleanest point: Main Stem.

Dirtiest point: The North Avenue Turning Basin and Grand Avenue.

Number of movable bridges: At one time there were 52 movable bridges over the Chicago River, but today many are being changed to fixed bridges.

Species of fish: More than 50, including carp, goldfish, darters, minnows, bass, and the occasional trout and salmon.

Plant life: An enormous variety of plant life from wetlands, prairies, and forests borders the river and lakeshore.

Animal life: Deer, beaver, coyote, and other large mammals; a large number of birds, including many waterbirds.

Number of prairies: 2.

Number of islands: 1 (Goose Island).

Number of neighborhoods along the river: 24.

Number of suburbs along the river and tributaries: 42.

Number of golf courses along the river: 16.

Number of colleges along the river and its tributaries: 2 (Trinity College and North Park).

Number of high schools along the river and tributaries: 3 (Deerfield, Von Steuben, and Gordon Tech).

Number of waterfalls on the river: 1.

Number of cemeteries along the river: 2 (Saint Lucas and Bohemian National).

Major disasters on the river: Ice dam collapses destroying bridges and boats, killing 6, March 1849; capsizing of steamer *Eastland*, July 1915; the great subterranean flood, April 1992.

The Chicago River

THE CHICAGO RIVER

Rivermouth Improvements

Although the Chicago River served as a port for the canoes of traders and Native Americans, its mouth was usually blocked by an extensive accumulation of sand that prevented large lake vessels from entering. Thus, for trading vessels, the Chicago harbor was what is termed an open roadstead—that is, it offered virtually no protection from storms. Indeed, many vessels did run aground or were destroyed by storm. In 1813, for example, "the schooner *Heartless*, in an attempt to reach the Chicago River, ran aground, possibly on the bar that blocked the river's mouth, and was a total loss" (Young, in press).

To enter the protected waters of the river, "even small ships had to be off-loaded to reduce their drafts to clear the bar. The practice produced a fleet of small boats, called 'lighters' that were sent out to unload ships anchored . . . just outside the river's mouth." In the 1830s vessels such as the topsail schooner *Illinois* were especially designed to be hauled across the Chicago bar after they were unloaded (Ibid.).

Because of these conditions, numerous harbor improvements were necessary before the river could become a true port. The first such effort came in 1831, when a federal appropriation of $5,000 was used to construct a lighthouse to mark the river entrance. Unfortunately, the fifty-foot structure collapsed before it could be used, and a new tower forty feet high was built in its place the following year (Andreas 1884–86, 240).

Nonetheless, the primary difficulty afflicting the would-be port continued to be the offshore sandbar. Many ideas were considered by the townspeople, the military, and sailors, but nothing came of them until engineers, brought to the area to plan the Illinois and Michigan Canal, provided guidance. In 1830 William Howard was among a group of young army engineers who made surveys for the canal route. He proposed a plan for improving the mouth of the Chicago River: close the original outlet, cut a channel through the sandbar blocking the river's mouth, and construct long piers extending into the lake to prevent additional sand buildup (Ibid., 234).

A federal grant of $25,000 funded the dredging of the sandbar and the construction of the piers. By 1834 soldiers from Fort Dearborn completed the rechanneling; with the addition of two long piers, the rivermouth began to resemble the area as it appears today. "On July twelfth, the schooner *Illinois* sailed up this channel into the sheltered river harbor, instantly establishing Chicago as one of the leading ports on the lake, its major enterprises . . . hugging the banks of the sluggish river. . . ." (Miller 1996, 68). Thus began what one author has called "the battle of the bar" (Young, in press).

The two piers were of different lengths. The southern pier, about 500 feet long, was finished in 1833. After the 1,260-foot northern "weather pier," which holds off the lake's largest waves from the northeast, was completed in 1835, more than two hundred ships used the improved river harbor that same year. Chicago's river harbor thus became one of the few sheltered spots along the west shore of Lake Michigan, and the rapid rise of shipping soon produced massive congestion in the river port. It became necessary to enact laws preventing vessels from anchoring where they would block the free passage of other craft.

But the sand buildup was not so easily thwarted, and a new bar immediately began to form. As a result, federally funded dredging and pier extensions would continue off and on for decades. The noted Chicago historian A. T. Andreas was moved to remark:

> . . . It would seem, unless the direction of the work was changed, that the task of protecting the harbor entrance would be an indefinite contest between the governmental purse and the natural forces of wind, wave, and current (Andreas 1884–86, 235).

Despite these ongoing problems, Chicago's water commerce continued to increase. By 1869 the river port became horribly congested when more than thirteen thousand ships called. By this time the north pier had reached a length of about 2,310 feet and the channel had been dredged to a depth of 14 feet. Despite these efforts, the obstinate sandbar continued to reappear, causing the resulting shoreline to march steadily eastward by hundreds of feet.

Harbor Expansion

Around this time, the city proposed widening the main branch of the Chicago River to 250 feet and its two branches to 200 feet (Young, in press). Nonetheless, the first real expansion of the harbor capacity was

Young city dwellers from nearby apartments relax at the head of the old Ogden Slip.

accomplished in 1869, when the Chicago Dock and Canal Company run by William B. Ogden was allowed to build a slip just north of and parallel to the river. This Ogden Slip still exists, though its west end is filled, and the slip and adjacent North Pier Terminal Building have been adapted to new uses. Now retail stores, nightclubs, and restaurants and expensive townhouses line the Ogden Slip, and recreational boats ply the waters where formerly large lake vessels served waterside industries.

By 1869 the rise in water traffic necessitated a more-or-less global solution to the problem of sand drift. The U.S. Army Corps of Engineers advanced a plan to construct a four thousand-foot breakwater that would create a ringing harbor, that would limit sand buildup and shield vessels from the full force of the lake's largest waves from the northeast. The construction of the inner breakwaters began in 1870, and ten years later construction began on the outer breakwater.

Burgeoning water traffic in the Chicago River harbor peaked in 1889, when more than twenty-two thousand ships called and handled more than eleven million tons of cargo. Additional federal appropriations in 1894 made it possible to deepen the main channel of the river to twenty-one feet and the South Branch to seventeen feet.

However, the rebuilding of central Chicago for commercial rather than industrial use after the Great Fire of 1871 led to greatly increased land values along the Chicago River. Manufacturers, including the fledgling steel industry, then moved away from the river to huge tracts of undeveloped cheap land adjoining the Calumet River, eleven miles to the south.

Navy Pier Construction

In 1908 the Chicago Harbor Commission was established. Its first report the following year paralleled proposals of the Burnham Plan of 1909. Like this plan it called for building two giant piers three thousand feet long at the mouth of the Chicago River; widening the Calumet River; creating an inland harbor at Lake Calumet; removing obstructions in both rivers; and replacing the swinging "center-pier" bridges, which impeded river traffic.

The first pier, today known as Navy Pier, was completed in 1916, and was designed to handle both passenger and freight traffic. Passenger vessels continued to call at the pier into the 1920s, but cargo vessels were less well served. The design of the pier for cargo handling was outmoded almost immediately by the changing design of large vessels. In addition, its landward access proved too restrictive for efficient use by modern freighters (Mayer 1957, 221–26). As a result, when passenger traffic declined, package freight activity was only sporadic. "Navy Pier was abandoned for vessel traffic between the beginning of World War I and 1956 when it experienced a brief revival. By the end of 1978 the pier was again idle"(Young, in press).

Nontransportation uses were conceived for the pier. During World War II (from 1942 to 1946), it was used to train naval personnel, and from 1946 until 1965 it was the home of the Chicago branch of the University of Illinois. Ultimately, the pier's old transit sheds proved an impediment to other uses. As a result, beginning August 25, 1992, the old superstructure was removed and a totally new set of facilities constructed.

These facilities include a glass-enclosed winter garden that connects with garages, retail stores, and restaurants. The newly configured pier also houses a 1,500-seat theater, an Omnimax theater, and a 170,100-square-foot exhibition hall. Only the pier's entrance and the grand ballroom at the far eastern end of the pier remain from the original construction.

On the west end of the pier is a large carousel. The west end also sports a 150-foot-diameter Ferris wheel that recalls the very first 250-foot Ferris wheel exhibited at the World's Columbian Exposition in Jackson Park in 1893 (Petroski 1993, 216–21).

Lock Construction

In addition to the many extraordinary changes to the Chicago River mouth, the river, which originally emptied into Lake Michigan, was ultimately closed off from the lake by the Chicago Lock. This facility was built at the river mouth in 1938–39. The lock now functions primarily to meter the flow of lake water into the Chicago River.

The original diversion from Lake Michigan, authorized by the Secretary of War on May 8, 1889, was basically unrestricted, with a total flow of ten thousand cubic feet per second or more (Solzman 1966, 20). Because of the unrestricted flow, the level of the Chicago River was about two feet higher than it is today. It remained at this level until 1934. Then, because of suits brought against the city of Chicago by other Great Lakes states, the diversion was

Navy Pier and the Near North Side. The newly reconstructed pier sits in front of the buildings of Streeterville.

restricted by a decision of the U.S. Supreme Court to fifteen hundred cubic feet per second plus domestic pumpage. Today, after continuing legal wrangles, the allowed diversion is thirty-two hundred cubic feet per second for all purposes. New methods for measuring this flow have been implemented to overcome the weaknesses plaguing earlier measuring efforts. Besides helping to limit the diversion of lake water into the river, the locks also prevent the backup of river water into the lake during heavy rains.

The Chicago Lock was the final step in the great river reversal project (discussed later in this chapter) begun with the Sanitary and Ship Canal, which opened in 1900. However, the changing scale of transportation technology in the late twentieth century has rendered the sixty-by-eight-hundred-foot lock too small to handle modern lake vessels.

Main Stem Improvements

Originally the Chicago River's main stem, the confluence of its North and South Branches, carried water eastward, where it emptied into Lake Michigan. This flow has been reversed so that the main stem now serves as a conduit through which lake water is carried westward to join with the flow of the North Branch. At "the forks," this combined flow then moves south and westward through the channel of the South Branch, toward the Sanitary and Ship Canal, and across the continental divide to the Mississippi River.

As noted earlier, the main stem has been successively widened and deepened over time. Its small tributary creeks have disappeared, their flow assumed by a system of combined sewers that carry not only sanitary waste but also storm runoff. In its natural state, the eastern end of the main stem was marked by a small, sandy hill on its southern bank, where the original rivermouth was diverted southward by accumulated sand. This elevated site, rising just thirty feet above the flat and swampy terrain, became the location of both the original and the rebuilt Fort Dearborn. Today bronze markers mark the site on the west side of Michigan Avenue at the corner of Wacker Drive.

"Raising of the Grade"

The sandy hill, one of very few elevations above Chicago's extraordinarily flat terrain, is, alas, no more. Its sandy soil ultimately became part of the fill used to raise the downtown section of the city from five to twelve feet. This "raising of the grade," began in the 1850s, created a very much altered aspect for the river. Now the stream runs between banks elevated not by nature, but by engineering.

The need to raise the grade arose from the swampy condition of the area. Poor drainage impeded the provision of sewers and placed the young town alternately in a sea of mud in wet weather or in clouds of blowing dust in dry. Early records are replete with references to frontier humor developed by citizens attempting to make light of a miserable situation. For example, a sign proclaiming "No Bottom" graced a wagon stuck up to its wheel tops in the mire. A joke passed around the young town featured an onlooker who saw a military officer up to his boot tops in mud. "You're in pretty deep this time," says the onlooker. "Deep, hell," the officer responds, "there's a horse under me."

These drainage problems led to difficulties with waste disposal, which in turn caused disease. By the 1850s recurrent epidemics of cholera and typhoid struck the burgeoning city with terrifying effect. Outdoor privies polluted shallow wells, yet the city could offer no sewage system, since the level of the land surface lay very near the level of standing water. Roadside ditches diverted waste of all kinds directly into the Chicago River, which was also used as a common sewer by the industrial firms lining its banks. "The river is positively red with blood under the Rush Street bridge and down past our factory," complained William McCormick in a letter to his brother (cited in Miller 1996, 123).

William B. Ogden, the prime mover in Chicago's early history, brought engineer Ellis Chesbrough from Boston to overcome the escalating health crisis. Chesbrough oversaw the construction in Chicago of the nation's first comprehensive sewer system. But even this system of brick sewers merely diverted the waste directly into the river.

The only way Chesbrough could build the sewers was to place them in the middle of the existing streets and then cover them over with earth. Constructing them required that the level of the entire street be raised and that the adjoining buildings be similarly elevated. This set off two decades of chaos in which many buildings and sidewalks were raised while other buildings, whose owners refused the expense, sat at lower levels. The result was that for about twenty years downtown Chicago was a pedestrian roller coaster of hills and valleys created by the uneven progress of the grade raising.

Grade-raising efforts brought to town a man who was to become one of its richest, most influential, and most controversial citizens. A young house mover, George Pullman arrived in 1859. Pullman's firm was among those raising large buildings and entire blocks. In one especially celebrated episode, the Pullman

brothers raised the city's largest hotel, the Tremont, while it remained open, amazingly without "breaking a pane of glass or cracking a plaster wall" (Ibid., 126).

Bridge Building

Many other changes came to the main stem of the Chicago River with the explosive growth of the new town. At first, connections across the stream were made by canoe and then in 1829 by a rope-pulled ferry crossing the South Branch roughly at Lake Street.

> When Chicago became a city . . . shipping was the main business and the Chicago River . . . was the principal thoroughfare, . . . it was also a barrier between the communities on both sides. There was talk of the need for a bridge, but the idea was opposed by the shipping interests on both sides of the river, fearing that they would lose trade to competitors on the opposite side (Chicago Department of Public Works 1979, 3).

In spite of this short-sighted opposition, the mushrooming growth soon required that the stream be bridged. Many types of bridges were built and destroyed over the years. As the city grew and new problems appeared, new types of bridges were developed and placed in use. The result is that today Chicago is home to the greatest number of movable bridges of any city in the world. Thus, along with its architectural splendors, Chicago truly displays a "museum of bridges."

The first primitive log drawbridge over the Chicago River was built in 1834 at Dearborn Street. It was ten feet wide, with a sixty-foot center section that could be opened to allow river traffic to pass

In former times, large ships entered the Chicago River which, until 1906, was the city's principal port. In this photograph the steamer *Pere Marquette* is being towed through the river's Main Stem. (Courtesy, Chicago Historical Society.)

through (Ibid., 4). This bridge was poorly engineered and often in need of repairs. After the Chicago Common Council ordered it removed in 1839, apparently exasperated citizens brought down the structure with axes to prevent any chance that it could again be placed in service.

Since that inauspicious beginning, the evolution of bridge construction technologies caused a parade of new types of bridges. In the 1830s and 1840s **float bridges** were constructed. These primitive bridges were operated by winding a chain on a capstan to open or close the draw. The first bridge of this type was built at Clark Street, and similar floating bridges were built at Wells, Randolph, and Kinzie Streets.

One of the more extraordinary events in the young city's history occurred on March 12, 1849. After several days of heavy rain, ice which had clogged the river suddenly broke loose. When this gorge or "ice dam" gave way, it was swept downstream by the swollen stream with violent and amazing effect. Vessels picked up by the racing waters were flung against the Randoph Street Bridge. The bridge was "torn from its moorings in a few seconds" (Ibid., 5).

The rapidly growing mixture of ice, water, and debris raced onward, smashing every vessel and every bridge on the main stem of the river before hurling the debris into Lake Michigan. To accommodate Chicago's growing population, all the destroyed bridges were replaced within a single year.

Swing Bridges

In the 1850s **swing bridges** were constructed to appease shipping interests, which demanded removal of the obstructions caused by floating bridges. The swing bridges were built of wood or wood and iron, resting and rotating on piers set in the center of the channel. When necessary, these hand-operated bridges were rotated on the piers so that vessels could pass on either side.

Prior to the construction of the swing bridge at Madison Street in 1856, bridges were financed by landowners who stood to benefit from their presence. A proposal to build the Madison Street Bridge at public expense was strongly opposed initially. However, it was eventually supported by the electorate, which ushered in a new era of public financing for the city's infrastructure.

The first iron swing bridge was built at Rush Street in 1856. It, too, came to an unhappy end. In November 1863, a herd of cattle, caught on the bridge when it opened, apparently stampeded to one side, causing the bridge to buckle under the uneven load. Bridge parts and cattle plunged into the river. Like the earlier floating bridges that were destroyed, this bridge, too, was replaced within a year.

The view eastward from the Rush Street Bridge in the late 1880s suggests the bustling river traffic when 22,000 vessels called at the Port of Chicago. Sailing schooners jostle with steam tugs, large steamships, and even sidewheelers. A dredge operates in mid-river. (Courtesy, Chicago Historical Society.)

The view westward from the Rush Street Bridge in 1908 shows the industrial activity along the river. Kirk's soap plant sits on the north (*right*) bank. The Clark Street Bridge is in the middle distance. (Courtesy, Chicago Historical Society.)

Hand-powered swing bridges were ultimately supplanted by other types of bridges and by larger, mechanically operated swing bridges made of steel. Four such bridges still exist on the Sanitary Canal.

The older swing bridges over the Chicago River's main stem were destroyed by the Great Fire of October 1871. The bridges at Rush, State, Clark, and Wells Streets vanished in a holocaust of flame, as did the Chicago Avenue Bridge over the North Branch and the South Branch bridges at Adams, Van Buren, and Polk Streets. All were re-placed within six months by larger, sturdier swing bridges.

The number of bridges continued to multiply as the city expanded. By the 1880s, thirty-five bridges connected the central city with its North and West Sides. Newer bridge designs were larger and wider and operated more smoothly and rapidly to accommodate the large steam-powered vessels that had begun to appear. However, the center piers of the old swing bridges were themselves obstructions to navigation, so new bridges were designed to allow use of the entire channel. This necessity spawned many innovations in bridge technology that were developed in Chicago.

Jackknife Bridges

In 1891 a new bridge design appeared. It required no pier in the channel and lifted by rotating on a single pivot on or near the riverbank. The first such "**jack-knife**" bridge was built at Weed Street. This design subsequently was used for a new bridge at Canal Street over the South Branch. The 1890s also saw construction of **vertical lift bridges (center-span lift bridges)**, of which a number remain over area waterways. In such bridges the entire center span lifts vertically by cables hung from towers on either side of the stream.

Scherzer Rolling Lift Bridges

The pace of mechanical innovation quickened as larger steamships penetrated the waterways and heavier railroads were constructed. New bridge types also proliferated. By 1900 so-called **Scherzer rolling lift bridges** had been put into use on the South Branch at Van Buren Street. (The Cermak Road Bridge over the South Branch is also of this type.) In this design the bridge opened by rocking or rolling back along a rocker, which had openings that engaged teeth in the bridge abutments. These teeth kept the rolling bridge leaves from slipping as they opened.

Bascule Bridges

In 1910 a major advance in bridge-making technology was achieved in Chicago and introduced at Cortland Avenue. It was the city's first bridge featuring a **trunnion bascule** design. In this design the two bridge leaves open by turning on giant trunnion bearings on the riverbanks. The great weight of the leaves require a counterweight to balance the load (*bascule* is French for seesaw). Each such bridge must be designed specifically for its location, so no two are identical. Chicago engineers modified and perfected this general bridge type and used it so widely that today such bridges are said to be built in the "Chicago style."

Chicago's bascule bridges are meticulously designed to ensure that they will withstand "dead load, vibration and impact as well as . . . ice and snow loads" when closed. When open, the bridges "must be able to resist a wind load up to one hundred miles per hour from any direction." To meet these requirements, each bridge structure rests directly on bedrock. Its machinery is designed precisely to ensure that the bridge "can be opened, . . . closed, (or) held in any desired position regardless of extremes of wind, weather and temperature" (Ibid., 12).

Subsequent improvements to the basic bascule design produced the first **double-deck trunnion bascule bridge** at Michigan Avenue in 1920. The Michigan Avenue Bridge is considered by many to be a Chicago landmark. This huge structure carries passenger autos and pedestrians on its upper deck and, cars, trucks, and pedestrians on its lower level.

Each of the bridge's two leaves weighs 3,340 tons, and the foundations reach down more than one hundred feet to bedrock. Each giant leaf rests on four 26 1/2-inch-diameter trunnion bearings so that each trunnion supports a load of more than 800 tons. Yet because the entire enormous weight of the structure is very delicately balanced, the bridge may be opened or closed in less than one minute, powered by just four 100-horsepower electric motors.

A turn-of-the-century view from the top of the Lake Street Bridge. The Saint Paul elevator sits on the west bank. (Courtesy, Chicago Historical Society.)

Double-deck bascule bridges are also located at Lake Shore Drive and at Lake and Wells Streets, where they carry the elevated rapid transit lines across the Chicago River on their upper deck. "In recent years as many as 73,000 vehicles per day pass over the [Michigan Avenue] bridge, and the average number of openings for the Michigan Avenue, and the other eight typical drawbridges over the Main Branch of the Chicago River, is 450 times per year with an average elapsed time of 7 minutes for each opening" (Ibid., 14).

In 1977 Chicago opened a shop-welded and field-bolted bascule bridge at Loomis Street on the Chicago River's South Branch. It "was voted the most beautiful movable span bridge in the United States built during 1976–1977. . . (by) the American Institute of Steel Construction" (Ibid., 17).

The second-longest bascule bridge in the world currently graces the main stem of the Chicago River at Columbus Drive. Built in 1982 at a cost of $33 million, this giant span carries a roadway 111 feet wide over two leaves, each 269 feet long. It is exceeded in size only by the bascule bridge over the Bay of Cadiz in Spain.

Eight box girder trusses are required to support each leaf, and the leaves are aligned by laser. The bridge has very clean lines and a relatively smooth appearance due to its modern, all-welded construction. This structure was especially designed to allow construction of a riverwalk along the banks beneath the bridge.

The process of bridge construction and reconstruction continues to this day. In the 1990s, a large federal grant is being used to renew Chicago's infrastructure, build new bridges at Randolph Street, Lake Street, and Cermak Road, and repair virtually all the other downtown bridges.

Riverwalk and "River–Friendly" Developments

In 1990 the City of Chicago, Department of Planning and Friends of the Chicago River developed a set of guidelines for urban rivers intended to promote the appreciation and multiple-use of streams in downtown areas. They specify setbacks for new construction so that citizen access to waterways may be improved, and they suggest methods of securing the stream edge against slumping and erosion. The increasing use of the river as an amenity with landscaping and an emerging riverwalk are examples of the positive effects of these guidelines. One of the most attractive downtown riverwalks begins in Pioneer Court, steps away from the Michigan Avenue Bridge and continues along to Columbus Drive.

The north bank of the river east of Michigan Avenue has shifted from industry to commercial and residential development. The Gleacher Center (*shown here*) is the new downtown home of the University of Chicago. In the foreground is a portion of the new riverwalk designed by Dirk Lohan and Associates.

Chicago has long boasted the greatest collection of movable bridges of any city on earth with fifty-two. However, many of the moving bridges are now fixed and have had their machinery removed. Nowadays towboats are fitted with pilothouses on pneumatic pistons, so they can be lowered as necessary to clear the fixed spans. In addition, the river has now shoaled to a depth too shallow for the large lake vessels that required bridge openings.

This shoaling occurred because severe pollution of river bottom sediments has prevented the U.S. Army Corps of Engineers from dredging the channel. The extreme pollution stems principally from earlier times, when the river was the outlet for the city's sewage and runoff from tanneries, steel mills, soap plants, and stockyards. Recently, the pollution levels of the river bottom sediments have been upgraded from toxic to severe so that, theoretically, dredging is once more an option.

The North Branch
The North Branch of the Chicago River was originally called the Guare River after an early settler because it was considered a separate stream from the river's South Branch. It wound its way south-ward from its origins some twenty-five to thirty miles north of the rivermouth, at the heads of its three principal tributaries: its west and middle forks and the Skokie River. It was thus distinct from what we now call the South Branch, which was originally named the River of the Portage. The North Branch continues to flow southward and was not reversed.

Even so, the natural course of the North Branch has been significantly altered, especially in the area south of its confluence with the North Shore Channel. Here its winding course has been straightened, and the river has been widened and deepened to accommodate the flow of lake water coming in from the North Shore Channel.

North Branch Canal and Goose Island
The North Branch Canal was dug by William B. Ogden in order to obtain blue clay for brick making and also to develop additional valuable riverfront land. This canal created an artificial island on the North Branch that was originally called Ogden Island, but Goose Island is the nickname by which it is known today. It is generally believed that the name derived from the presence on the island of Irish slums, where many geese were kept. The island later became a center of heavy industry, with metalworking, grain elevators, slaughterhouses, and tanneries nearby.

There is some evidence that after the North Branch Canal was completed in the 1850s, portions of it may have been filled. Whether or not this is correct, it is clear that the channel was complete in the 1870s.

Now, as the twentieth century draws to a close, some groups working to keep industry and jobs in the area have

CHICAGO RIVER FACT: THE CHICAGO RIVER HAS THREE NORTHERN BRANCHES: THE WEST FORK, THE MIDDLE FORK, AND THE EAST FORK (AKA THE SKOKIE RIVER).

suggested that this old canal be filled in. It appears, though, that this will not be done since many industries use the river as a moat to protect their property. Friends of the River has taken a position calling for "no net loss"—any loss of surface water must be compensated with a similar-sized area of open water or wetland. As of this writing, there is heavy pressure from developers who want to convert the area from industrial to residential and commercial use. The resulting conflict between these competing groups requires an examination of Chicago's land-use policy objectives for the future.

North Shore Channel

The North Shore Channel which runs from Wilmette Harbor to the Chicago River North Branch near Lawrence Avenue was completed in 1909 to divert sewage from the North Shore away from Lake Michigan. It was thus an integral part of the great chain of projects that rerouted the Chicago River system flow away from the lake and westward into Mississippi River drainage. The channel is eight miles long, one hundred feet wide, and nine feet deep—large enough to be navigated by barges, but the sluice gate at Wilmette now blocks the channel and prevents navigation. Now only

Starting in 1926, the City of Chicago undertook a massive, river-straightening project to eliminate an eastward bend and to open up access to the Loop from the south. (Courtesy, Chicago Historical Society.)

canoes or other small craft use this waterway. An artificial waterfall is located
at the confluence of the North Shore
Channel and the Chicago River
North Branch.

South Branch

Originally called the River of the Portage,
the South Branch of the Chicago River
was the key water link between the Great
Lakes and the Mississippi River. Because
of its value to explorers and traders, it
was primarily responsible for the development of the city.

The South Branch flowed from the
southwest, where it originated in a large,
swampy area called Mud Lake. A channel that appeared when Mud Lake was

drained was subsequently called the West
Fork, which joined the South Branch
just west of Damen Avenue. For a time
this channel was used by small canal
boats, but then its eastern section and
later its western portion were placed in
the city sewer system, and the channel
was filled. Today scars of this old river
channel appear on the West Side of the
city, indicated by irregular fence lines
and a few remnants of walkways from
vanished bridges.

The South Branch underwent a
major episode of channel straightening
beginning in 1926. A large eastward
bend of the channel was removed by
digging a new channel straight through
it and filling in the old riverbed. The

Slips

Among other changes, the South Branch had many slips cut into its banks to provide wharfage and ease congestion in the main channel of the river. Most of these slips were on the north bank of the stream between Halsted Street and Damen Avenue, although a few were on the south bank east of Halsted and west of Damen.

One of the slips cuts into the bank of the Chicago River. This slip, although similar to those on the South Branch, was located on the Main Stem near the rivermouth. Schooners, which were the backbone of water trade into the 20th century, crowd the slip. Elevator A sits in the background. (Courtesy, Chicago Historical Society.)

straightening required moving a huge railroad bridge seven hundred feet west to the new channel.

The South Fork

As the Chicago River flowed toward Lake Michigan, it was joined by another major tributary from the south; the south fork, or Bubbly Creek, so named because bubbles caused by decaying animal parts from packinghouses rose to its surface. This relatively long tributary flowed into the South Branch from the south after following a wriggling path through swampy terrain. It was along the east arm of this portion of the river that the Union Stockyards was constructed in 1865. The use of this channel for the disposal of packinghouse wastes led to such intense pollution that the only solution was to fill in first the east arm—a canal—and then the west arm as well.

West Fork

The West Fork was the main continuation of the South Branch westward into Mud Lake. More of this channel appeared as Mud Lake was drained by a ditch dug by Ogden and Wentworth. Their drainage ditch was intended to dry out land they owned so it could be subdivided and sold, but it had the unintended effect of silting portions of the Illinois and Michigan Canal, which reduced the canal's flow and subverted the first efforts to reverse the Chicago River through the canal.

Illinois and Michigan Canal

The notion of a canal between the South Branch of the Chicago River and the Des Plaines or Illinois River drainage was first suggested in 1673 by Louis Joliet on his portage from the Des Plaines to the Chicago River. He wrote to Father Dablon of Quebec on the first of August 1674:

> We could go with facility to Florida in a bark, and by very easy navigation. It would only be necessary to make a canal by cutting through but half a league of prairie, to pass from the foot of the Lake of the Illinois (Lake Michigan) to the St. Louis (Illinois) River, which empties into the Mississippi (Larson 1979, 5–6).

Joliet's exuberant prediction may have been influenced by the weather at the time he made the portage. There were occasions, during wet weather, when the Des Plaines River overflowed its banks and the low divide that separated it from Lake Michigan drainage. At that point, there was little if any portage to be overcome.

On the other hand, in dry weather, the portage could be long and formidable. One has only to read Chicago pioneer Gurdon Hubbard's account of his portage with several large, heavy canoes of supplies to realize what a daunting prospect it could be. Hubbard and his companions labored for three horrific

CHICAGO RIVER FACT: THE NORTH BRANCH OF THE CHICAGO RIVER JOINS THE MAN-MADE, EIGHT-MILE LONG NORTH SHORE CHANNEL, WHICH PULLS WATER FROM LAKE MICHIGAN AT WILMETTE HARBOR, IN RIVER PARK, JUST SOUTH OF FOSTER AVENUE.

The Human Cost of the Illinois and Michigan Canal

Construction of the Illinois and Michigan Canal gave employment to many Irish who had arrived from the old country with few skills and little education. Because their Roman Catholic religion and manner of living conflicted with that of many Protestant Yankees who had established an economic and social presence in the developing town, they were little appreciated and virtually unemployable except for the harshest manual labor.

Many Irish laborers worked on the canal, often digging the ditch by hand. It is said that such men were virtual human digging machines who labored six days a week for whiskey and a dollar a day. After church on Sunday, they spent hours more digging in the backyards

of their shanties so that their muscles would not tighten up and prevent them from working. Many died from exhaustion, malaria, and waterborne diseases digging the ninety-six-mile canal, and

many are buried at Saint James of the Sag Church near Lemont.

days, bitten by mosquitoes, set upon by leeches, and sinking above the knees in mud resembling wet concrete as they struggled to move their heavy loads six miles between navigable streams.

Eventually, Joliet's idea took firm hold of the imagination of the young republic, and by 1816, Major Stephen Long was already in the area to reconnoiter a possible canal route. Six years later Congress authorized the State of Illinois to construct an Illinois River–Lake Michigan canal, and in February 1823 the state legislature passed a bill providing for five commissioners to lay out a canal route.

The canal commissioners were "urban strategists" who laid out plans for towns along the canal, including Chicago at its eastern end. In effect, the canal spawned Chicago even though Chicago had already been established before the canal was dug. Successive groups of army surveyors helped fix the route, and the platting of Chicago by James Thompson in 1830 officially placed the town at the Lake Michigan end of the proposed canal.

The Illinois and Michigan Canal followed the route suggested by Joliet in the seventeenth century. Although it was surveyed during the presidency of Thomas Jefferson, construction did not begin until 1836. A financial panic the following year stopped all payments from the federal government to Illinois, even when William Ogden and others made heroic efforts to keep canal construction going. Finally, in 1841, it became impossible to continue. Work was suspended until 1845. At that point Ogden and his fellow canal commissioners were able to develop a bond and loan program to finance the project. When the roughly one-hundred mile canal was completed

in 1848, it ran sixty feet wide and six feet deep from its origin at Ashland Avenue on the Chicago River South Branch to its entrance into the Illinois River near LaSalle-Peru, Illinois. Along the way it crossed a number of surface streams, requiring the construction of slack-water pools such as one near Channahon, Illinois, where the canal crossed the Du Page River. In other places, water-level differences between the canal and the natural streams called for water bridges (aqueducts) in order to continue the canal. Another challenge was providing enough water to keep the little canal open, so feeder canals had to be cut from the Calumet River, the Des Plaines, and the Fox.

Yet despite the many construction difficulties, this little ditch established Chicago as an alternative trade market to St. Louis, thereby bringing about the rearrangement of Midwestern trade from a north–south axis along the Mississippi River to an east–west axis focusing on Chicago.

The Sanitary and Ship Canal and the Reversal of the Chicago River

Chicago's production of waste was as prodigious as its growth. Human waste mingled with factory pollutants that continually flowed out of the Chicago River into Lake Michigan, fouling the city's water supply. The result was recurrent epidemics of typhoid, cholera, and other waterborne diseases that, in some years, killed more than 5 percent of the burgeoning city population.

When plans were first considered for the Illinois and Michigan Canal, a deep cut was proposed that would have allowed the canal to draw its flow directly from Lake Michigan—that is, reversing the flow of the Chicago River.

Unfortunately, the financial panic of 1837 put an end to these plans. The canal commissioners had to fall back on a cheaper, shallow-cut approach, which required pumps to fill the canal instead.

As cholera epidemics continued to ravage the city, an effort was made to deepen the canal, and additional pumps were installed in an attempt to reverse its flow. Ellis Chesbrough, the Boston engineer William Ogden had hired to create a sewer system, proposed reversing the Chicago River in this manner. When the deepened canal was opened, a great hullabaloo and celebration ensued. But the river's reversed flow, to the extent that it occurred at all, was barely perceptible.

To make matters worse, Ogden and his business partner John Wentworth dug a ditch of their own to drain land they held near Mud Lake. This project unwittingly short-circuited the reversal effort. When spring deluges flooded the Des Plaines River, the Ogden-Wentworth ditch poured floodwater directly into the Illinois and Michigan Canal, which promptly backed up, causing the Chicago River to resume its original course to Lake Michigan. Sewage and filth carried by the river flooded back past the water intake crib in the lake, and once again cholera ravaged the city.

To the extent that the reversal plan worked at all, it succeeded in enraging the citizens of Joliet and other communities downstream. At one point they "threatened to block the canal with dirt, forcing it to back up and causing Chicago to 'stink itself to death.' " But apparently there was no need for such drastic action because silt from the Ogden-Wentworth ditch quickly reduced the meager flow, and the much-heralded reversal came to a virtual standstill within one year.

Additional means were employed. A conduit was dug along Fullerton Avenue in 1876 to bring additional water

The Sanitary and Ship Canal during construction in 1895. This view shows activity in a rock-cut section of the huge canal. (Courtesy, Chicago Historical Society.)

into the Chicago River system, and when this failed to generate the required flow, new pumps were installed in 1884.

Then on August 2, 1885, one torrential storm dumped more than six inches of rain on the city. The resulting backup of the Chicago River triggered an explosion of waterborne diseases that killed approximately 12 percent of the population. Repeated outbreaks of epidemic diseases and public panics finally compelled the state legislature in 1889 to create the Sanitary District of Chicago. This regional agency was charged with finding a comprehensive solution to the dual problems of water supply and sewage disposal. The Sanitary District proposed a combination sanitary and ship canal to remedy the predicament, and local voters approved the scheme by the unprecedented vote of 70,958 to 242. The canal project was the largest municipal project in the United States at the time it was built, and its scale and importance attracted many of the top young engineers in the country. After the canal was finished, some of these people remained in the area and designed Chicago's subway system.

The new drainage canal was constructed between Damen Avenue on the South Branch and the town of Lockport north of Joliet. This twenty-eight-mile canal had a project width of 160 feet and a project depth of 21 feet.

The canal project was a gigantic undertaking; construction required digging out more rock, soil, and clay than was removed to make the Panama Canal. In fact, General George Goethals, who oversaw construction of the Chicago project, later moved to Panama and applied the lessons learned in Chicago to supervise the final phases of the Panama Canal project.

Although the diversion of water from Lake Michigan into the Sanitary Canal was authorized by the Secretary of War in 1889, as the canal completion approached, other communities began to have second thoughts.

> Late in December, 1899, with the end of the mammoth task in sight, the Board of Trustees learned that the State of Missouri had decided to seek an injunction in Federal Court to prevent the opening of the canal.
>
> The Missouri objection centered chiefly around the contention of St. Louis that the proposed dilution system of sewage treatment at Chicago would flush the wastes into the Mississippi River and imperil the St. Louis water supply.
>
> The Board of Trustees regarded such an argument as academic. Reasoning that once started the flow would be hard to stop, the Board quietly ordered a needle dam knocked out on January 2, 1900, which turned the waters of the Chicago River into the channel.
>
> On the night of January 16, 1900, the Board went to Lockport and early the next morning—minutes before the suit for injunction was filed in the United States Supreme Court—the controlling gates were lowered and the water from Lake Michigan flowed toward the Mississippi (Walker 1960, 17).

The suit, filed subsequently by the State of Missouri, was the first of a long series of legal battles that continues to this day. Nonetheless, although the diversion has been reduced since the canal was first opened, the flow of the Chicago River has been permanently reversed. In 1955 the American Society of Civil Engineers named the river reversal and

Commerce along the Sanitary and Ship Canal Today

Water transportation is not dead. On the contrary, even though water transport is no longer necessary for most industries, it is vital for the transportation of heavy, low-value bulk commodities. Therefore, the principal commodities moved along the Sanitary and Ship Canal include crushed stone and gravel, coal, sand, portland cement, fuel oils, pitch (asphalt), light oils, coke, salt, soda lye, calcium chloride, maize (corn), gasoline, lube oils, and medium oils.

So many tank farms line the Sanitary and Ship Canal that for years this stretch of the waterway was known as Gasoline Alley. The presence of these storage facilities underlines the use of water transportation for high-bulk liquid cargoes.

the combined facilities of the Sanitary District (now the Metropolitan Water Reclamation District) one of the seven engineering wonders of the United States.

When the new canal was opened, the Sanitary District published advertising brochures seeking industrial customers to locate along it. One brochure, "Building Sixty Miles of Industries," predicted a corridor of industry stretching on both sides of the canal all the way to Lockport. Clearly, this vision was flawed. Waterways lost some of their importance as, first, railroads and later trucks provided faster, more flexible transportation.

But this effort, the largest ever undertaken by any U.S. municipality up to that time, did accomplish its original intention. The Chicago River was reversed, the city's water supply was safeguarded, and the mushrooming growth that had characterized Chicago's early history continued unabated into the twentieth century.

THE CALUMET RIVER SYSTEM

Changes to the Calumet River, a boomerang stream that today drains the southern portion of the Chicago area, have made it far different from its natural state. This strange stream, which had no real mouth in the Chicago area leading to Lake Michigan, was rearranged and a new mouth created starting in 1869, when several sloughs in the Calumet region were dredged. The result was a safe harbor for shipping and water access to large, inexpensive industrial tracts of land that were developed into the world's greatest concentration of heavy industry.

Lake Calumet, Wolf Lake, and Lake George

In 1959, ninety years after development began in the Calumet River area and just before the opening of the Saint Lawrence Seaway, Lake Calumet was partially dredged and partially filled to create the International Port of Chicago at Lake

CHICAGO RIVER FACT: In 1900 the Chicago Sanitary District finished the twenty-eight-mile Sanitary and Ship Canal to connect the Chicago River to the Des Plaines and Illinois Rivers. The Main Branch and the South Branch (except for Bubbly Creek) were reversed so that today the river flows away from Lake Michigan, the city's drinking water supply, and into the Sanitary and Ship Canal.

Calumet. This deep-water port with a project depth of twenty-six feet accommodates any vessels able to pass through the Saint Lawrence Seaway on their way into the Great Lakes, "the Fourth Seacoast."

A 3,000-by-670-foot section of the old lake was dredged to achieve the required harbor area; prior to this, Lake Calumet had a surface area of about three square miles and an average depth of three feet. For many years the port drew foreign and domestic vessels, leading to the creation of a free-trade zone deep in the heart of the United States. It continues today as an important element of the Port of Chicago, although the number of foreign cargoes is down considerably from its heyday.

Like Lake Calumet, Wolf Lake and Lake George are remnants of glacial Lake Chicago, which formed when the last of the glaciers melted back from the Lake Michigan basin. Lake George has been drained, while Wolf Lake continues to exist as a shallow body of water that offers important recreational uses. The western arm of Wolf Lake, called Hyde Lake, contains the William W. Powers State Conservation Area.

The Cal-Sag Channel

Digging for the Calumet-Sag Channel, commonly known as the Cal-Sag, began in 1911 along the line of an old feeder canal that had furnished water to the Illinois and Michigan Canal. Originally, it was conceived of principally as a drainage canal that would draw polluted water away from Lake Michigan and into the Illinois River system. The resulting canal was small, only sixty feet wide, but it became an important transport route after 1930 when it was dredged to a depth of nine feet and connected to the Sanitary and Ship Canal.

The extreme concentration of heavy industry along the Calumet River made the Cal-Sag a potentially vital shipping link. However, the narrowness of the channel inhibited its full use. After all, most standard barges are about thirty-five feet wide so only one barge at a time could pass through. Were it not for especially widened passing points two-way traffic would not have been possible. Shippers called the Cal-Sag "sixteen sad miles" because of the slowness and difficulty of taking barges through the restricted channel.

The Rivers and Harbors Act of 1946 relieved this situation by calling for a channel width of 225 feet at the standard 9-foot depth. To make this change in the Cal-Sag, seventeen rail bridges had to be removed or replaced at an average cost of about $18 million each (1965 dollars). Since project completion in 1965, barge traffic into the Calumet has moved steadily upward, carrying cargoes of coke, fuel oils, gasoline, ethylene glycol, light oils, jet fuel, soda lye, and ethyl alcohol.

CHICAGO RIVER FACT: THE CAL-SAG CHANNEL IS A SIXTEEN MILE WATERWAY THAT EXTENDS WESTWARD FROM THE LITTLE CALUMET RIVER AT BLUE ISLAND TO THE SAG JUNCTION ON THE SANITARY AND SHIP CANAL.

We went in canoes to the River Chicagou . . .

Henri de Tonti,

early explorer (1681)

Guide to Chicago's Waterways

CHAPTER 4

TRIPS ON AND AROUND CHICAGO'S WATERWAYS

It is a river of contradictions.

It flows past great modern buildings and ugly makeshift structures.

It sees the opulence of Chicago's market place and the filth of its

back yards.

Henry Hansen, *The Chicago* (1942)

THIS PART OF THE BOOK SERVES AS A guide to the waterways in the Chicago area. The maps that accompany the text on the Chicago River were adopted from those developed by Friends of the Chicago River, whose generosity is gratefully acknowledged. Additional maps are included in each section to detail other waterways.

Although most of the waterways are accessible by canoe, it is also possible to visit many sections by boat, by walking, or even, in some areas, by car.

Please keep in mind that it may be hazardous to operate small craft near larger vessels or barges and on the rough waters of Lake Michigan. Various canoeing organizations offer equipment, guided tours, and instruction in safe canoeing practices. These organizations are listed in appendix A.

A major challenge in producing this guide is that a book could be written about nearly every major waterway section. The goal here is to be general

enough to be interesting, but specific enough to be useful. In addition, large and small changes continually occur throughout the waterway system. There are blank pages in the back of the book for interested explorers of the Chicago waterways to record some of the changes that they observe.

The Chicago River is the thread that binds together virtually all elements of Chicago's history. Its presence is chiefly responsible for the city's existence. Changing patterns of settlement, trade, manufacturing, and technology are reflected in the river. It has been the city's main thoroughfare, its sewer, and its key to a commercial empire. The river has seen it all, done it all, carried it all. Its current whispers of the past even as it rushes into the future. Those who know the river and its connected streams know Chicago in an elemental way. In a strong sense, the river is Chicago. Follow the river and travel into the soul of the city.

The Chicago Light guards the main entrance to Chicago's outer harbor. Though fully automated, it was staffed by the Coast Guard for 100 years.

THE CHICAGO RIVER SYSTEM

The Chicago River, although known to everyone, is well understood by few. It is a much larger stream system than many are aware—its combined channels stretch for more than 150 miles through the Chicago metropolitan area. The river and its major tributaries link twenty-four highly diverse Chicago neighborhoods and touch forty-two suburbs. Because the stream system lies entirely within one of the world's major metropolitan areas, its tributaries include not only its branching forks but also the runoff from parking lots, storm drains, and sewers ". . . Even homes are tributaries, drawing water from Lake Michigan and discharging it ultimately into the river" (Cohen 1996).

Early settlers distinguished the river's two main branches, calling the North Branch the Guare (or Guarie) River after a French trader who lived along its banks, and the South Branch the River of the Portage (Currey 1908–12, 47). The Potawatomi Indians who lived near the stream had a keen appreciation of its geographic importance, so they called it *Rora,* a term meaning "confluence." Eventually, when traders and settlers came to the area, it was the stream's function as a link to the Mississippi River system that was the principal force that directed first the location of the settlement and later the growth of Chicago.

The commercial value of the Chicago River was enhanced after it connected to the Illinois River by the Illinois and Michigan Canal. The rivermouth became a safe port on the western shore of Lake Michigan, which served thousands of ships each year.

Sadly, the river became also the catchall for human and industrial wastes, turning into a reeking open sewer that dumped poisons into Lake Michigan, the city's water supply. The ironic consequence was that the stream responsible for the birth of Chicago also brought death in the form of waterborne diseases. To overcome this problem, the flow of the river was ultimately reversed, and it was interconnected with other area waterways through a system of navigation and drainage canals.

Because of this tragic aspect of its history, many are surprised to learn that the Chicago River and its branches are on the road to recovery. The water is cleaner due to the diversion of lake water, increasingly efficient water treatment procedures, and, most recently, the effects of the so-called Deep Tunnel, or Tunnel and Reservoir Project (TARP), which prevents much storm and sewer water from entering the river after heavy rains. As a result, wildlife is returning to the river, making it ever more attractive for recreation. Today as many as fifty species of fish are found in the combined channels and, as the water grows slowly cleaner, benthic microinvertebrates living on rocks on the stream bottom are increasing in number and variety. They further help to clean the stream. In addition, freshwater mollusks such as clams and mussels are present, as are freshwater sponges.

The improvement in water quality is reflected also in the wildlife populations adjacent to the stream. Although deer and even coyote are in evidence in forest preserves near the river, it came as something of a shock to the author when a pair of beavers was recently moved from the river forks downtown to a forest preserve on the edge of the city.

The growing attraction of the river is likewise mirrored by new residential and commercial construction along its banks. The Loop has expanded westward past the river, and the channel is now lined with high-rise office towers, many of which favor the river by their design. A broad esplanade runs along the river's west bank. Meanwhile, North Side conversions of old industrial lofts to residential uses have triggered a major struggle between industrial users and developers who wish to transform the character of the area to high-end residential.

The following guided tours of the area's waterways are intended for those who wish to explore them by foot, canoe, power boat, or automobile. But even the armchair traveler can enjoy a mental excursion along these wonderful streams.

THE CHICAGO RIVER

North Branch

The west and middle forks of the Chicago River North Branch arise from surface drainage and surface wetlands. Today, however, since the streams begin within an area of intense urban development, their tributaries include runoff from highways, industries, and golf courses, and from numerous outfalls and hardened surfaces that urban areas create. Indeed, it is not amiss to claim among the headwaters of these streams the rooftops of adjoining communities.

West Fork

The west fork of the Chicago River North Branch appears around Everett Road near the town of **Mettawa**. In this area only about one-half mile separates the west fork drainage from that of the Des Plaines River on the other side of the subcontinental divide. Along this stream are many places where one might portage across the low divide to the Mississippi drainage. But these many portage points are nonetheless inferior to the Chicago Portage since this stream is too shallow and inconsistent and so far from the rivermouth.

The west fork begins as an ephemeral stream that flows south for about two miles parallel to the divide. It then flows in a south–southeasterly direction through **Bannockburn**, west of **Trinity College**. The little stream contains darters, an endangered fish species, which speaks well for the water quality. It then continues south toward **Deerfield**, flows west of the WEEF Brickyard, and passes under the Tri-State Tollway. At about this point the west fork becomes more visible, with a considerable current in rainy weather. Property owners in the area tend to place fences across the five-to-fifteen-foot channel.

The growing stream passes under Lake Cook Road at the southern boundary of Deerfield and continues through parks, school grounds, and residential neighborhoods in **Northbrook**. South of Shermer Avenue near Church Street, it passes through the **Anets Golf Club**. The west fork then flows through two

CHICAGO RIVER FACT: THE CHICAGO RIVER'S NORTHERNMOST HEADWATERS ARE IN LAKE COUNTY, NEAR PARK CITY.

wetlands and passes near a large solid waste landfill. Development on this site includes an earthen dam and a sizable lake that is often filled with waterfowl. It is possible to reach this pond by driving north on Waukegan Road, turning left on Techny Road, parking immediately, and walking north to the top of the dam. However, such landfills are potential sources of stream pollution.

In Techny the west fork passes through agricultural land that is rapidly being converted to residential use, and a small tributary creek flows eastward through Northbrook to join the west fork north of Willow Road. This stream may well be the "north brook" after which the village is named. After the west fork passes under Willow Road, it enters another wetland area and receives water from a small tributary, "Navy Ditch," which comes in from the former **Glenview Naval Air Station** to the west.

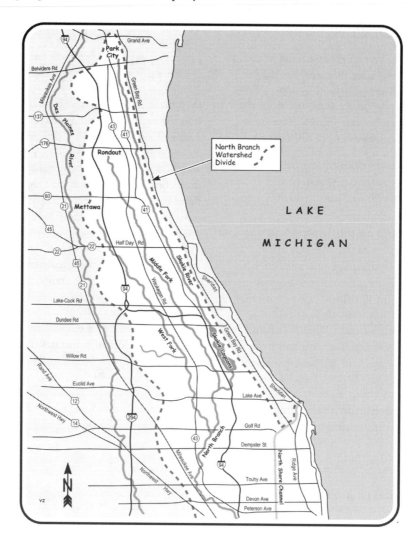

MAP 6.
The three tributaries and the watershed of the Chicago River North Branch. These tributaries draw water from a restricted watershed and join to form the North Branch. They reach far to the north and pull water from among the glacial moraine hills.

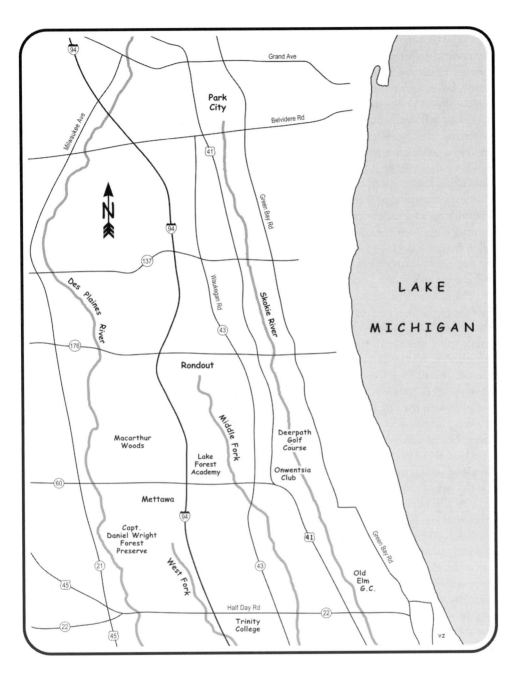

MAP 7.
The northern portion of the three tributaries of the Chicago River North Branch. The principal roads that give access to these streams are shown.

The channel of the west fork has been artificially deepened where it winds through **Glenview.** Here the entrenched stream flows eight to ten feet below the banks. After it passes through downtown Glenview, it flows through forest preserves and the **Glen View Club** on the way to its confluence with the combined middle and east forks at the **Chick Evans Golf Club,** just south of Golf Road. Canoe enthusiasts report that as the west fork approaches the confluence its channel is often clogged with branches fallen from the banks. In wet weather the current is so strong one must paddle furiously to stay in the same place.

Middle Fork

The middle fork of the North Branch is simply called the North Branch on many maps, following the lead of the U.S. Army Corps of Engineers. However, this relatively small stream is obviously inferior in flow to the much more dynamic east fork, usually known as the Skokie River. The middle fork arises near Rockland Road in the community of **Rondout,** near a major rail junction that was the site of a storied train robbery.

At this point the stream is ephemeral and flows intermittently southward along the tracks of the Soo Line Railroad, gaining strength through an area of farmland and wetlands. (This description will probably be rendered inaccurate by the pace of development in the area. In a very short time it seems likely that the entire drainage will be built up.) Happily, the stream builds rapidly and loses its ephemeral character, so the rest of the middle fork may be explored by canoe in wet weather. It is already about ten feet wide and one foot deep near Kennedy Road in **Lake Forest,** where it passes east of **Lake Forest Academy.**

The middle fork then flows through western Lake Forest between Waukegan Road and Route 41 and passes through a succession of forest preserves and affluent communities. Just south of Half-Day Road (Route 22) and east of Waukegan Road (Route 43) between Bannockburn and Highland Park is **Prairie Wolf Slough,** a tributary wetland that is the site of a major restoration project.

The stream continues through the western portion of **Highland Park,** flows beneath Deerfield Road and passes through the **Briarwood Country Club.** It then courses through eastern Deerfield and on to **Northfield,** where its canalized channel passes west of **Northbrook Court.** At I-94 and Dundee Road the middle fork passes through large culverts and continues through forest preserve land. From here the North Branch flows southward to join the Skokie River, west of Happ Road, and north of the **Wilmette Golf Club,** between Winnetka Road and Lake Avenue. At the confluence it is clear which stream is the principal tributary, for the flow of the middle fork is dwarfed by the exuberant waters of the Skokie River.

Skokie River (East Fork)

The east fork of the Chicago River North Branch, the Skokie River, seems to be its principal tributary. The little stream first appears near **Park City** from a somewhat hidden wetland southwest of the intersection of Washington Street and Route 41. Outflow from the wetland is carried some distance through a pipe under a trailer park, and the stream then appears somewhat ingloriously from the mouth of the pipe.

The Skokie River then flows southward through wetlands just east of and parallel to Route 41, through **North**

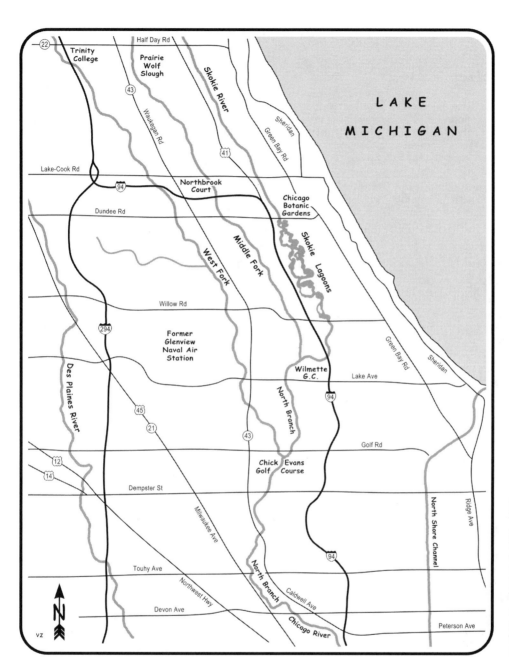

MAP 8.
The southern portion of the three tributaries of the Chicago River North Branch. The principal roads that give access to these streams are shown.

Prairie Wolf Slough Project

The Prairie Wolf Slough project combines efforts of the Lake County Forest Preserve District; the U.S. Fish and Wildlife Service; the Lake County Stormwater Management Commission; and the National Resource Conservation Service of the U. S. Department of Agriculture. David Ramsey of Friends of the Chicago River serves as project coordinator.

This remarkably successful wetlands restoration project drew $250,000 in funding from federal, state, and local agencies. In 1995 it received the National Wetlands Award from the Environmental Law Institute and the U.S. Environmental Protection Agency as an outstanding wetland development. More significantly, the project features the work of more than 700 volunteers, who planted 51,000 wetland and wet prairie plants. In addition, thirty specially trained volunteers work weekends as of this writing to maintain and enhance the area.

The project began in January 1994; its first phase was completed and the project dedicated on October 12, 1996. Phase 2 will see completion of the three-quarter-mile trail between the eight-acre wetland and thirty-four acres of woodland. This phase also involves construction of a bridge over the middle fork, which will connect the slough with Deerfield High School and Olson Park.

Chicago and **Lake Bluff.** This is an attractive section of the stream because it passes through the **Greenbelt Forest Preserve,** various park districts, and the **Officer's Golf Course of the Great Lakes Naval Training Center.** At this point the "river" is only about five feet wide and a scant few inches in depth.

The stream then meanders through many golf courses, forest preserves, and the affluent suburbs of **Lake Bluff, Lake Forest,** and **Highland Park.** In Lake Bluff it passes the **Lake Bluff Golf Course,** and then it bisects or borders the **Deerpath Park Golf Club,** the **Onwentsia Club,** and the **Old Elm Club** in Lake Forest. In Highland Park the stream borders the **Highland Park Country Club** and then passes through the **Sunset Valley Golf Club** and **Bob-O-Link Golf Course.**

South of Clavey Road in Highland Park the east fork flows past the **Clavey Road Sewage Treatment Plant** of the North Shore Sanitary District. Outflow from the plant greatly increases stream flow at this point, and the stream begins to look more like a river. It seems that the effluent is chlorinated only between Memorial Day and Labor Day, possibly from the mistaken view that canoeists use the stream only in the summer. In fact, a growing number of enthusiasts canoe this stretch almost year-round.

The ecosystem would benefit if this water were treated with ultraviolet light instead of chlorine. The benefits of using ultraviolet light are evident at the East Chicago, Indiana, Sewage Treatment Plant, where a stunning improvement in effluent quality has been observed. There the improving water quality has produced an upsurge in the number and variety of plants and animals in the stream. In fact, this effluent now supports a large population of freshwater sponges that seem to further clean the stream. As a result, the outflow from the plant leading to the Grand Calumet River is now home to growing populations of fish, including large and healthy rainbow trout.

Skokie Lagoons

Where the Skokie River flows under Lake-Cook Road and enters Cook County, its natural course was through the extensive wetlands known collectively as the Chewab Skokie, or great **Skokie Marsh.** In the 1850s farms bordered this large swamp. Farmers cut ice from the wetlands in the winter and peat in warm months. Efforts to drain the wetland and build roads proved largely unsuccessful, but lowering water levels opened the area to peat fires, which occurred intermittently until the 1930s.

Then, the Civilian Conservation Corps, acting under programs of the Roosevelt administration's New Deal, reconstructed the much-altered marsh into a series of lakes now called the **Skokie Lagoons.** Later, a Nike missile base was constructed here and subsequently removed.

The only remnant of the original marsh is a sedge meadow west of the south end of the lagoons, which is part of the **North Branch Prairie Project** of the Nature Conservancy. This meadow can be reached from a paved road on the north side of Willow Road, just east of the Edens Expressway (Route 94). Turn north at the first drive east of the Edens on the road marked by a large, red Cook County Forest Preserve sign. From the parking lot near the maintenance shed at the north end of the road, walk north about one-quarter mile. Further exploration is possible, but wet feet usually result.

In the wooded area west of the sedge meadow stands a giant burr oak

estimated to be 350 years old, dating it from the era of Marquette and Joliet. Unfortunately, borings made by the Forest Preserve District indicate that this tree is diseased and may soon be gone.

The northern section of the Skokie Marsh was altered to create the artificial lagoons and landscaped surrounds of the **Chicago Botanic Gardens.** In this area the Skokie River was diverted to the west so that its flow no longer discharges into the lagoons.

The Skokie River continues its diverted course southward, west of the lagoons that were its natural course. Then, immediately north of Willow Road, the lagoon water spills out from a dam into a sizable pond that links with the twenty-foot-wide river. A series of concrete steps in the dam provide canoe access for downriver voyages. Because of this access and the increasing stream depth, the Skokie River is a popular canoe route. Canoeists should take care, however, because a small dam at Winnetka Road must be negotiated without a convenient access. The little dam can be shot in periods of high water, but only experienced canoeists should consider this approach.

Now the greatly augmented and canalized stream heads almost straight west between levees on both sides of the channel. As it swings under I-94 it passes a square, concrete pumping station that drains the expressway and pours the runoff into the river. This has caused deep holes in the channel and islands of silt a short distance downstream that are visible from the frontage road. The river then passes under the Chicago and Northwestern Railroad bridge (now the Union Pacific Railroad) west of Happ Road, where the channel is frequently blocked by debris that accumulates against the pilings. A short distance west of the rail trestle, the west-flowing Skokie River is joined by the much-smaller middle fork coming in from the north (right).

From its junction with the middle fork, the river winds southward, first through the **Blue Star Memorial Woods,** then the **Glenview Woods,** and, finally, through **Harm's Woods,** one of the loveliest and most enchanting sections of the entire river. Here the thickest woods are on the east side of the stream, because persistent west winds often spread prairie fires toward the east, where the streams serve as a firebreak, protecting woods on their eastern banks.

From Harm's Woods south to **LaBagh Woods,** the river winds between small bluffs ten to fifteen feet high, adding interest to the generally flat landscape. The stream then passes under Golf Road and enters the **Chick Evans Golf Course,** where three footbridges cross the stream. Soon the river reaches its confluence with the west fork in the golf course just north of Beckwith Road. Here, the North Branch of the Chicago River is born.

North Branch

The North Branch flows south over a small dam, which canoeists must negotiate on the left over a rocky streambed. A short distance downstream, it passes through forest preserves in **Morton Grove**. These include the **Linne Woods,** where, at one point, the beauty of the landscape is marred by famously-ugly storm drains with twenty-foot-high concrete walls topped-off by a chain-link fence.

The North Branch then continues south of Dempster to Oakton, where the scenic **St. Paul and Miami Woods** lift the spirits. Lincoln Avenue ends at Dempster, just east of the river, where a pioneer named Miller built his sawmill (Hansen 1942, 198). In his honor, the last angling section of Lincoln Avenue is now called Miller Road. Lincoln Avenue itself was originally called Little Fort Road because, in the mid-nineteenth century, it was the main route north to the settlement then called Little Fort but now known as Waukegan.

A curious feature in the streambed in Morton Grove is a grouping of stones that the locals call the **Old Indian Fish Weir.** Some believe that this collection of stones dates from the time when the Potawatomi Indians lived in the area. It is a good story, and it could be true. However, no definite evidence has been established. The entire area, filled with game, was indeed a major hunting and camping ground for the native peoples who lived here.

South of Oakton the North Branch flows through the remains of the former championship **Tam-O-Shanter Golf Club** in **Niles.** The wooded areas near the river abound in wildlife, and deer populations in the area have become something of a nuisance to nearby homeowners. Be on the lookout—some very large snapping turtles have been sighted in this area. Attractive, well-marked hiking trails through the adjoining forest preserves give excellent access to the stream for canoeing.

South of **Howard Street** the river begins to wind more and is blocked by another small dam. Most canoeists should portage around this structure on the right bank. Only experts should shoot the dam and then only during high water. Industrial development on the west bank somewhat diminishes the charm of the stream.

Around **Touhy Avenue,** the North Branch turns dramatically southeastward, enters Chicago, and approaches very close to Milwaukee Avenue. Like most of the diagonal streets that interrupt the city's rectangular street system, Milwaukee follows an old Indian trail and was established in 1844 as the Northwestern Plank Road. Many travelers passed this section of the stream, prompting the construction of inns and other facilities in the 1870s. Highways are major catalysts for development so farms and small settlements also appeared along the road from the 1840s onward.

As it enters Chicago the river serves as the boundary between **Forest Glen** to the north and **Norwood Park** to the south. Settlement in Norwood Park began in 1833, when an English family founded a farm on well-drained glacial ridges above the marshy river floodplain. Despite fertile soil and some well-drained ridges, sizable residential development did not occur until the 1880s, when the marshes were drained. At that time, only about four hundred people lived in the area.

The North Branch continues southeastward through the **Clayton F. Smith Woods** and the **Bunker Hill Prairie.** The North Branch Prairie Project of which Bunker Hill is a part seeks to restore native habitats. This prairie may be a remnant of savannalike flatwoods,

MAP 9. Chicago River North Branch, city limits. Note the Chicago River Trail.

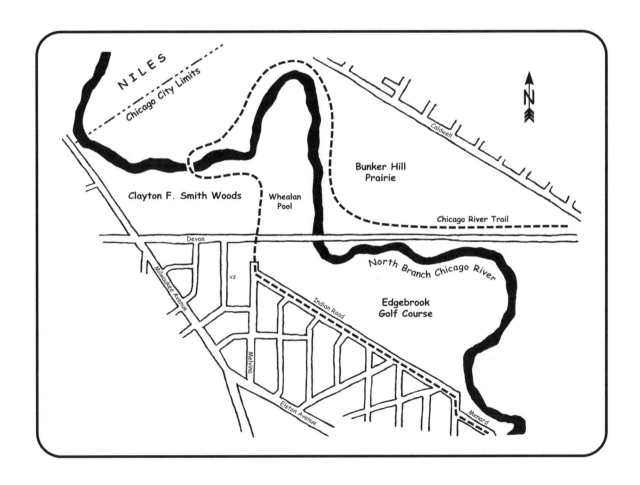

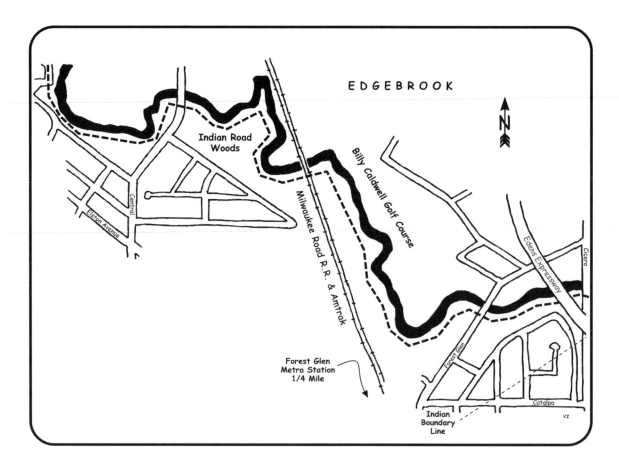

E D G E B R O O K

Indian Road
Woods

Central

Elston Avenue

Milwaukee Road R.R. & Amtrak

Billy Caldwell Golf Course

N

Edens Expressway

Cicero

Forest Glen

Forest Glen
Metra Station
1/4 Mile

Catalpa

Indian
Boundary
Line

vz

MAP 10.
Chicago River
North Branch,
Edgebrook.
The Chicago
River Trail
runs along
the south
bank. Note
the Indian
Boundary
Line.

and an effort has been made to reintroduce a wide variety of plants. These include stiff gentian, bottle gentian, rattlesnake master, smooth phlox, and prairie grasses. Native plants that were already present in the area include sedges, gayfeather, Virginia mountain mint, Canada bluegrass, prairie dock, slender gerardia, balsam ragwort, false dragonhead, ragged-fringed orchid, mountain blue-eyed grass, and wild strawberries.

The North Branch writhes its way southeastward, flows under Devon Avenue, and enters the **Edgebrook Golf Course,** west of the junction of Devon and Central Avenues. Here it forms the boundary between **Jefferson Park** and

Forest Glen. Nearby roads depart markedly from the rigorous grid pattern that characterizes most of Chicago's street system; in the neighborhoods south of the river, one is hard pressed to find a square corner. The river continues its serpentine wanderings as it wriggles in a generally southeastward direction across a broad floodplain.

As it passes under Central Avenue the North Branch enters the flower-dappled **Indian Road Woods,** summer campgrounds of the Miami and Potawatomi Indians. The river's north bank is covered with masses of Virginia bluebells in springtime. Here within a very short distance the stream flows southeast, east, northeast, south, and even slightly toward the west. In this section hikers could travel in a straight line and have to cross the river four times in a two-block distance.

The Forest Glen community to the north is a unique enclave isolated from the rest of the city by forest preserves, a golf course, and cemeteries. It contains the prestigious **Edgebrook** and **Sauganash** neighborhoods, where many high-ranking city administrators, police and fire department officials, lawyers, judges, and politicians live.

Between Central Avenue and the tracks of the Soo Line Railroad, the spring yields a huge field of wild hyacinth, and blue-flag iris may also be seen. When the stream passes under the Soo Line rail tracks (Metra and Amtrak), it enters the **Billy Caldwell Golf Course,** named after the man the Indians called Sauganash—their word for Englishman.

It is a joy to walk along the river trail in the spring and view the profusion of flowers. Every few days brings another variety of flower to the peak of its blooming. At the right time, one may see white and red trillium, butter-and-eggs, Dutchman's britches, clover, wild ginger, sunflowers, bloodroot, and violets. Later in the year wild orchids, daisies, thistles, Queen Anne's lace, sorrel and chicory appear.

Now the twisting channel of the North Branch moves in a more easterly direction as it flows beneath Forest Glen Road and the Edens Expressway (I-94). It then passes beneath Cicero Avenue and crosses the **old Indian Boundary.** The west section of LaBagh Woods follows the southern bank of the river; and the **Sauganash Prairie,** part of the North Branch Prairie Project managed by the

Billy Caldwell

Caldwell's mother was Potawatomi and his father Irish, so his life was lived between these two worlds. He played an important part in getting the Potawatomi to sign treaties ceding much of their territory to the expanding United States.

The federal government rewarded Caldwell for his help by granting him a sixteen-hundred-acre tract immediately north of the so-called Indian Boundary. This line marked the north edge of a strip of land that lay in a northeast to southwest direction about ten miles on each side of the Chicago River mouth and included the famed portage to the southwest. Caldwell's land occupied both sides of the North Branch in this vicinity, and the **Chicago River Trail** passes through it. The northern Indian boundary is marked today by Rogers Avenue in the east and Forest Preserve Drive farther west.

Early Jefferson Park

Jefferson Park, the so-called Gateway to Chicago, lies south of the river. In 1830 John Kinzie Clark built a log cabin on the prairie; and by 1844 farmers began to move in, attracted by rich local soils. The **Northwest Plank Road** was built in 1844 following an ancient Indian trail. It provided much-improved access to the growing city and its markets to the south. But the plank road was a toll road, and it was extremely uncomfortable. Hot summer sun caused the planks to warp, and the resulting wagon rides were so full of bumps and bounces that they rearranged even the priorities of those who rode along them. Local legend has it that farmers, starved for wood and in rebellion against high tolls, dressed up as Indians, ripped away the planks for fuel and chopped down the toll gates, burning them on the spot.

In the 1870s Jefferson Park served as a market town for farmers in the area, and the Chicago and North Western Railroad made it accessible for workers commuting to the city.

Nonetheless, despite the improved access given by the plank road and the railroad, the community was still primarily agricultural when it was annexed to Chicago in 1889.

Nature Conservancy, lies along the north bank. **LaBagh Woods** here includes a small wetland in a former river channel. A surprising variety of wildlife inhabits these woods: bats, deer, and woodcock are often seen in addition to raccoons, squirrels, and a wide variety of waterfowl.

The Sauganash Prairie features one of the few remaining wet savanna communities in Illinois. Here one sees swamp white oak along with many types of grasses, including cordgrass, switchgrass, and bluejoint and blue-eyed grass. Sedges, swamp saxifrage, turtle head, sundrops, Michigan lily, marsh gayfeather, and tuberous Indian plantain are among the plants and flowers. Be prepared to be pleasantly surprised at the richness of the plants along the stream.

Friends of the Chicago River cautions that such prairies are "living laboratories which must be treated with respect. . . . Never pick prairie flowers or seed heads, . . . walk on the footpaths in single file . . . and stay on the footpaths while taking photographs." Friends also cautions hikers to exercise caution where the river trail crosses railroad tracks. One final warning: Poison ivy grows in abundance throughout the Chicago region, both as a low shrub and as a climbing vine. It is very plentiful in the woods and prairies near the river. Learn to recognize and avoid this hazardous plant.

The North Branch continues its eastern flow and passes under the tracks of the Chicago and Northwestern Railroad (now the Union Pacific Railroad). The stream drifts between the eastern section of LaBagh Woods and **Saint Lucas Cemetery** to the north and forms the boundary between **North Park** and **Albany Park**.

Recent construction of an apartment complex at the south edge of the cemetery underscores the importance of citizen involvement in river issues. The apartments are located in the greenbelt that lies along the river. Without citizen attention, it is highly likely that much of the remaining greenbelt along the North Branch will be lost.

On the south side of Foster Avenue adjacent to the river is forty-acre **Gompers Park,** in the area where German and Swedish farmers raised cucumbers, onions, and cabbages in the 1850s. This park, first called Matson Park, was initially built on land purchased from Saint Lucas Cemetery. Friends of the Chicago River recently organized and directed a project to redevelop a one-acre wetland along the river that previous urban development had destroyed. Scores of children and adults worked over a period of three years to replant wetland vegetation. Now this marshy ground is beginning to assume its original character. Recent floods on the Mississippi River and elsewhere underscore the importance of such wetlands. They not only provide a habitat for many species of plants and animals but also serve as spongy reservoirs that help to control flooding.

The river next weaves from one side of Foster Avenue to the other. Here, on the north bank, is a collection of cemeteries. The Saint Lucas and **Bohemian National** cemeteries are adjacent to the stream, while the **Montrose Cemetery** adjoins the Saint Lucas Cemetery on the north. Montrose Cemetery contains a memorial to those who perished in one of Chicago's major disasters, the **Iroquois Theater fire,** and the nearby Bohemian National Cemetery,

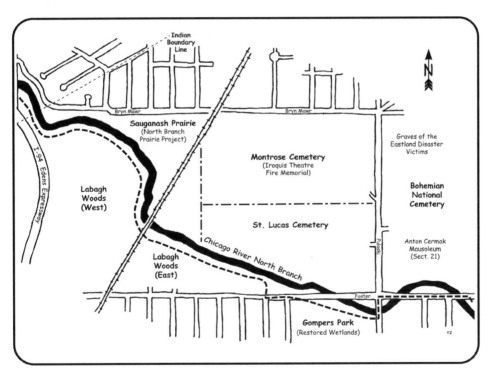

MAP 11.
Chicago River North Branch, Saint Lucas Cemetery.

MAP 12.
Chicago River
North Branch,
Albany Park.
Note the wa-
terfall at the
confluence of
the North
Branch with
the North
Shore
Channel.

established in 1877, includes the graves of many victims of the *Eastland* disaster. Here also is the mausoleum of **Anton Cermak,** the former mayor of Chicago who was killed in Miami, Florida, by a sniper's bullet while he stood next to President-elect Franklin Roosevelt.

As the river passes under Foster Avenue for the third time, it flows through **Eugene Field Park** and enters a residential area in the northern section of the Albany Park community. Here the North Branch picks up speed where it has been contained in a concrete channel to retard erosion. In this area it flows behind buildings so that the view from the

street is all but lost. Residents of the neighborhood's old three-flats have the river as a hidden treasure. Their back windows look out over the murmuring beauty of the stream.

Now the slowly winding North Branch skirts south of **Von Steuben High School,** crawls diagonally under a footbridge where Carmen Street and Spaulding Avenue meet, and continues beneath the overhanging buildings on the south edge of **North Park University** (formerly North Park College). German and Swedish farmers were the earliest settlers here. In 1893 the Swedish Evangelical Mission Covenant purchased

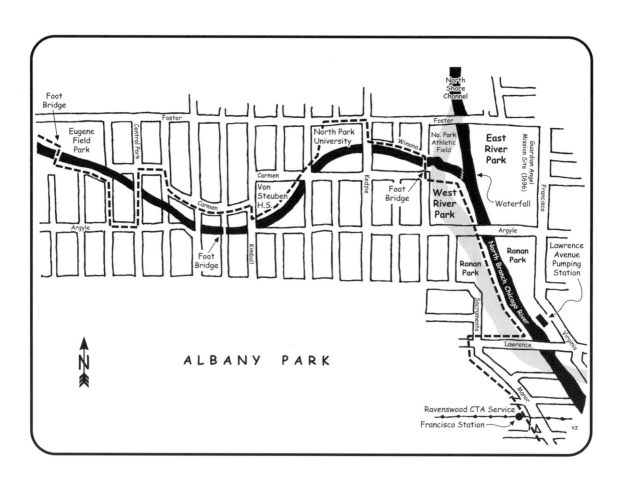

a tract of land in the area for the construction of a college and seminary. The first buildings opened the following year.

After passing under Kedzie and the footbridge at Albany Avenue, the North Branch flows between the university's Hedstrand athletic field, and the **West River Park** to the south. When North Park was established as a college in 1910, there were fewer than five hundred people in the community, which was mostly undeveloped and still covered by woodland and prairie.

Note that the Albany Street footbridge is the best place to take canoes out of the stream after a day trip from the Skokie Lagoons. People who canoe on the northern reaches of the North Branch should beware of the dangerous confluence with the North Shore Channel, where the North Branch plunges over a four-foot waterfall. Canoeists seeking to follow the river south may portage around the falls on the right side of the stream. A sandy beach at the confluence just past the falls provides excellent reentry access.

Confluence with the North Shore Channel

The North Branch grows suddenly larger as it falls four feet over Chicago's only waterfall and tumbles into the North Shore Channel. The channel brings lake water from the Wilmette Lock and effluent from the Metropolitan Water Reclamation District North Shore Plant into the North Branch in order to increase its flow, to help the stream clean itself as it moves southward.

Near Foster the newly enlarged and canalized stream turns southward next to **East River Park** and forms the boundary between **Albany Park** and the **Lincoln Square** community. The eastern portion of River Park includes the site of the former **Guardian Angel Mission**, which was built and occupied from 1696 to 1699 by **Father Pierre François Pinet**, a Jesuit missionary. He thus became the first outside settler in the entire Chicago region. At the time Father Pinet set up his mission, the area was apparently home to a major Miami Indian encampment. A plaque on the California Avenue side of Swedish Covenant Hospital commemorates the mission.

As the stream flows southward it passes through progressively older communities that were annexed to Chicago in the mid-1800s or earlier. While many of the northern community areas were

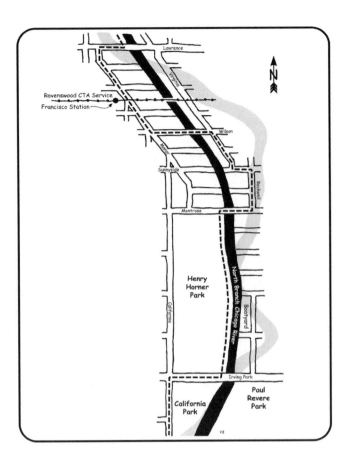

MAP 13.
Chicago River North Branch, Horner Park. The Chicago River Trail is shown as a dashed line. The original river channel is indicated by a gray tone.

The Lawrence Avenue Pumping Station of the Metropolitan Water Reclamation District. This station distributes wastewater during storms and shunts waste to sewage treatment plants.

annexed to the city in 1889, the older and more southern communities became part of Chicago in the 1860s or 1850s, or they were part of the original town in 1833.

In the 1890s the northwest section of the Lincoln Square community was part of a large truck farm operated by **Lyman A. Budlong.** In addition to the farm, he owned a pickle factory. With his brothers Budlong eventually expanded into the flower business and operated eighteen greenhouses. This mature residential area with beautiful brick homes along the river is still known as **Budlong Woods.**

The river trail indicated on the accompanying maps shows a safe, legal route along and near the river. It follows streets and public lands and skirts private property. Alternate trail sections are also shown to enable walkers to cross railroad tracks along public streets. A new trail section now follows the west bank from Argyle to Lawrence. At this point, the trail is forced to the west along Manor Drive because property owners in the **Ravenswood Manor** neighborhood along the river's west bank have closed the publicly owned riverbank to public access. This unfortunate situation also occurs along the river's east bank in the area. Friends of the River is working with the Metropolitan Water Reclamation District to resolve the situation.

Many changes have been made in the channel of the Chicago River North Branch by the Sanitary District (now the Water Reclamation District). The original channel meandered through the area between Foster and Belmont Avenues, and a small tributary entered the stream from the east near Wilson Avenue. The Sanitary District deepened and straightened the stream channel to help it carry the additional flow when the North Shore Channel was completed in 1909.

At Argyle Street the river explorer reaches the first major bridge on this route. It is a fixed bridge constructed in 1975 in the modern efficient style. **Ronan Park** straddles the river south of Argyle. On the west bank the park extends to Lawrence, but the Water Reclamation District's **Lawrence Avenue Pumping Station** occupies a section of the east bank north of Lawrence. The southern section of the park on the west bank was opened to the public in 1996 after equipment used in the Deep Tunnel Project was removed from the site. This section of the park was formerly the location of a community garden established by the Hmong people from Southeast Asia who migrated here after the Vietnam War.

As part of the effort to protect the city's water supply from pollution, a series of enormous interceptor sewers was built along the lakeshore beginning in 1900 and completed in 1907. The interceptors on the city's North Side conduct water to the Lawrence Avenue Pumping Station, which, like the Racine Avenue Pumping Station on the South Side, acts to distribute runoff during storms and to shunt wastewater to sewage treatment facilities. This station is quite attractive and speaks of a time when such engineering works were designed to enhance the appearance of the neighborhoods in which they were built.

The Lawrence Avenue Bridge is a fixed span in the **Chicago Beautiful style,** which features twenty-five-foot light posts. Charming water's-edge neighborhoods continue south from Lawrence to Montrose on the west bank and Berteau on the east. They benefit from the river's increasing value as a scenic amenity. Between Leland and Eastwood is the 1981 sleek steel bridge structure that carries the Ravenswood rapid transit line across the river. Bridges at Wilson and

Houseboats

During the Great Depression, many people who lost their homes moved onto houseboats and lived along this part of the river as floating squatters until they could afford better housing. The houseboats were found along the North Branch from Lawrence Avenue to Berteau, with some vessels lingering on into the 1960s. Harry Hansen, writing in the early 1940s, described these boats, which were often built on old barges: "From the bridge they seemed shabby and unkempt, with their tar paper sides, flat roofs and tiny stovepipes, but artists who came to paint them found them picturesque. . . . Close at hand . . . the pituresqueness increased. . . . Several boats had flower boxes and window curtains and their 'front yards' were swept clean" (Hansen 1942, 203).

Montrose provide two more examples of the Chicago Beautiful style, dating from 1914 and 1917, respectively.

Montrose Avenue

Henry Horner Park occupies the west bank of the river from Montrose Avenue to Irving Park Road. This large, well-equipped park has a fieldhouse at its northern end. **Irving Park Road**, a major thoroughfare in the area, follows the route of an ancient Indian trail. The fixed bridge at Irving Park Road is a widened three-span structure.

Between Montrose and Irving Park lie the communities of **Irving Park** to the west and **North Center** along the river's eastern bank. Before 1871 this area was sparsely settled farmland, with primary access via Little Fort Road (Lincoln Avenue) and the river. People who were displaced after the Great Fire of 1871 moved northward along the river, and, until the 1890s, truck farms were the economic mainstay of the area. During this time the community became part of the largest celery-growing area in the United States, and local farmers were the first to develop the technology of greenhouse agriculture.

Today the residential character of the riverbank changes south of Montrose, where the stream begins to exhibit a more industrial face. This change begins gradually with **Bonds Boatyard** and a small industrial site on the east bank just north of Irving Park Road. The north end of the boatyard is one of the finest canoe access sites on the river.

The west bank remains nonindustrial to Addison Street and includes **California Park** in its northern section. The fenced campus of **Gordon Technical High School** fills the west bank from California Park south to Addison, where the fixed span of the 1920 Chicago Beautiful–style bridge is graced by twenty-foot light posts.

Wildlife abounds in this area. Here, one finds red and gray foxes, deer, and signs of beaver. Some knowledgable folks say that the "River Rats" Club at Bonds Boatyard has the wildest wildlife in the area.

Black squirrel

A **Commonwealth Edison Company** substation occupies the west bank south from Addison to Roscoe Street in the Avondale community, and the section between Roscoe and Belmont is the site of the former **Grebe Boat Yard.** Grebe developed a reputation for building fine, handsomely outfitted wooden cruising yachts, many with unique designs. During World War II this yard built scores of steel tankers, oceangoing tugs, wooden minesweepers, and other vessels, including the famed PT boats, turning out about one boat each day. To protect them from enemy U-boat attack, these boats were floated down the Chicago River, through the Sanitary Canal into the Illinois lakes to Gulf waterway, via the Mississippi River, to the Gulf of Mexico. In 1995, after seventy-four years of operation, the boatyard closed. The site awaits redevelopment as upscale condominium residences.

One interesting historical note of the **Avondale** community was the presence of about twenty African-American families around 1880. After World War I, most African Americans in Chicago were restricted to the so-called Black Belt that stretched south along State Street. Prior to that time, the small black population, although somewhat segregated, settled more or less at will throughout the city. The African-American settlers were among Avondale's earliest residents, and they built Allen Church, the first church in that community.

Paul Revere Park fills a small section of the east bank south of Irving Park, and the old Victor Comptometer Company and a small industrial park occupy the riverbank south to the studios of **WGN.** This television "superstation" is a subsidiary of the Chicago Tribune Company. It is known nationwide for its

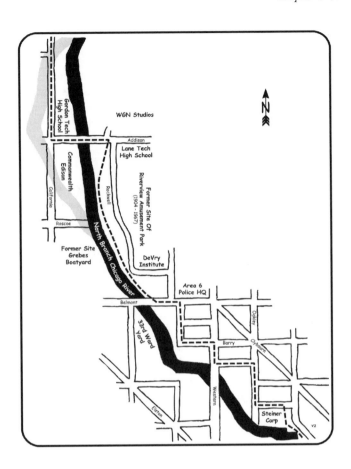

sports programming—especially the telecasts of Chicago Cubs baseball, which is yet another Tribune property.

After the Great Chicago Fire, the riverbanks north of Diversey were the location of many clay pits for brick making. The laws enacted after the fire stipulated that nonflammable construction materials be used in the central part of the city. A huge demand for brick resulted, and the North Branch was the center of intense brick-making activity. Clay pits lined the river channel until they began to be phased out around 1910. The pits were then used as garbage dumps, and their terrible stench

MAP 14.
Chicago River North Branch, Riverview. The Chicago River Trail is shown as a dashed line. The original river channel is indicated by a gray tone.

prompted outcries from the growing residential communities nearby. Finally, the old clay pits were filled in, and the landfills eventually became sites for industrial, warehousing, educational, residential, recreational, and communications activities.

Belmont Avenue

Bricktown was the name of the area near the river at Belmont Avenue where clay pit workers and brick makers lived until the end of the nineteenth century. In the late 1800s, a tract of swampy land on the east bank of the river just north of Belmont was operated as a private skeet-shooting club by the William Schmidt family. Eventually, the family added various diversions for the sportsmen's families. From this simple beginning rose an attraction that captured the city's imagination for sixty-three years. On July 2,

1904, the great **Riverview Amusement Park** opened on a seventy-acre site along the Chicago River's North Branch. With characteristic overstatement, it was billed as the world's largest amusement park. The park was to eventually include more than one hundred rides and three midways. Perhaps it was best known for its 212-foot-high parachute drop, its huge funhouse, and its many roller coasters.

Riverview's most famous ride was a sensational roller coaster called the Bobs. While the Bobs pales in comparison with the high-tech, upside-down, twisting tubular steel coasters of today, it thrilled generations of Chicagoans, and it furnished this author with his first (and immediate second) and still most unforgettable roller coaster ride.

Riverview bore no special relation to the river except for its location. However, one of the park's most disastrous episodes did involve it. In the mid-1920s one of the airplanes from the Strat-O-Planes ride broke free from its cables, hurtled across the midway and into the North Branch, where its two hapless riders drowned (Sawyers 1995, 231–33).

At the end of its 1967 season, Riverview was sold to a developer who razed the park. In doing so, he brought to an end an era still viewed with nostalgia by many Chicagoans. Today this site is home to much less romantic uses: the **Area 6 Police Headquarters**, the **DeVry Institute of Technology**, and the 136,000-square-foot **Riverview Plaza shopping center**. The fixed bridge at Belmont was built in 1978. It replaced what previously had been the northernmost of the city's drawbridges.

Industrial uses predominate south of Belmont. A true eyesore, the 33rd Ward Yard sits in ugly disarray on the

Planned Manufacturing Districts

The land-use conflicts that attend industrial loss and gentrification are classic examples of the stress on the U.S. economy as it moves into the postindustrial age. They also illustrate the dislocation and despair that such change creates in industrial cities. Because nearly the entire river edge from Belmont to the Loop is under threat of redevelopment, the city has designated some of the land as Planned Manufacturing Districts.

Some areas have also been included in Tax Increment Financing districts (TIFs). This designation facilitates financing and infrastructure assistance either to keep older industries in the city or to attract new ones. So far, the city has established a group of planned manufacturing districts along the North Branch, but only time will tell if such efforts can help to stem the loss of industrial jobs.

west bank. Across the river an old Material Service Company yard is now cleared and awaiting redevelopment. From this point south to Diversey a variety of heavy industries lines the banks. These include many metal specialty and supply firms in addition to engineering, enamelling, electrical, design, and display companies. On the west bank southeast of Western Avenue, the **Chicago Riverfront Antique Market** occupies old industrial buildings.

Even with these industrial and commercial activities, great blue herons occasionally wade in the river shallows near Western Avenue, which crosses the river on a three–span fixed bridge built in 1973. More waterbirds can usually be seen south of Diversey where the river widens into a turning basin. Unfortunately, the turning basin also slows the stream, so it tends to be a catchall for any debris coming down the river.

On the west bank of the river, Diversey Avenue marks the boundary between the **Avondale** and **Logan Square** communities, while on the east bank it divides North Center from Lincoln Park. The fixed bridge that carries Diversey across the river replaced an earlier swing bridge that had a tiny nineteen-foot roadway.

Diversey also forms a divide in the land uses along the riverbanks. Gentrification and adaptive reuse of old industrial structures is occurring farther north along the river, but from Diversey south, the process moves into high gear. On the west bank just north of Diversey is the **River Park development**, which features an industrial building converted to condominiums. Then, on the west bank south of Diversey, the **Diversey River Bowl**, a bowling alley, separates

Diversey from the **Riverfront Plaza,** a large shopping center that illustrates another type of industrial conversion.

These conversions are welcomed by many, and they most assuredly proclaim the improving vitality and utility of the river. On the other hand, they also mean a loss of manufacturing jobs in a city where industrial activity has long played a major role in the economy. At the local

Urban Land Institute

Recently, the Urban Land Institute, a nonprofit organization of realtors, planners, and developers based in Washington, D.C., examined a five-mile corridor centered on the North Branch of the river. It concluded that the city should apply its best efforts to keep its existing industry. The institute also points out, however, that many of these firms are in declining industries. The mix of declining older industries with a strong residential conversion market produces a conflicted land use pattern.

The institute researchers suggest that while the city tries to help the old industries, it should focus chiefly on area improvements that will retain the economically and ethnically diverse population as the area attracts higher income groups and the high-tech information and distribution industries

that characterize the postindustrial age. Such modern industries can coexist more easily with residential development than could their predecessors.

Many of the improvements suggested by the institute involve affordable housing, street improvements, zoning changes, and areawide planning. Yet one of its chief recommendations is the cleanup and improvement of the banks of the Chicago River. The research group sees the river as the unifying feature and chief amenity for this section of the city. It urges that the river become the area's "front door" instead of its "backyard." To this end the institute recommends the creation of a continuous river walk so that public access to the river will be assured.

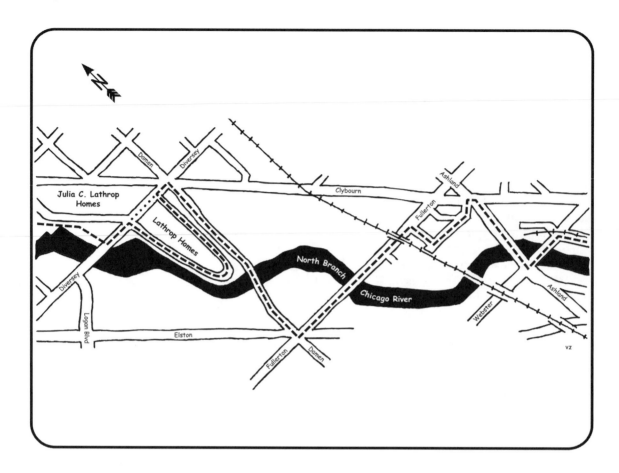

MAP 15. Chicago River North Branch, Lathrop Homes. The Chicago River Trail is shown as a dashed line.

level, neighboring communities are very hard hit by such conversions, since their blue-collar populations are much in need of the industrial jobs that are lost.

Diversey Avenue

The east bank of the river south of Diversey Avenue is the site of the **Julia C. Lathrop Homes,** a public housing project built in the 1930s and named for a Chicago social worker. Lathrop comprises one high-rise building for the elderly and sixty-three low-rise buildings that house almost one thousand families. It is a racially mixed development, with about 50 percent of its population

Hispanic and about one-quarter African American.

Young people from the Lathrop community are working with volunteers from Friends of the Chicago River to clean and improve the nearby riverbanks. Friends is currently using grant funds to study possibilities for developing canoe launches and other water-based amenities for the residents.

Immediately south of the Lathrop Homes, the river turns southeasterly, passing under the **Damen Avenue Bridge** and then the **Fullerton Avenue Bridge.** The span at Damen dates from 1930. It is of the single-leaf bascule type, with so-called pony trusses. Although the bridge is movable, it is inactive, and plans are currently under way to lower the bridge structure and fix the bridge in place. The nearby Fullerton Avenue Bridge is already a fixed span. In 1961 it became the first drawbridge removed in Chicago.

In the nineteenth century a great many industries felt the need to locate their manufacturing facilities on water. Factories used the water for industrial processes and, most importantly, for transportation. This was certainly the case for manufacturers of agricultural equipment.

The growth of the agricultural equipment industry is strongly associated with the growth of Chicago. Cyrus McCormick's reaper and the huge riverside factory that produced it are hallmarks of the city's economic history. But Chicago was also the home of the other leading manufacturer of harvesting equipment: the **Deering Harvester Company**. Founded in 1869 by William Deering, the firm and its production facilities eventually occupied eighty-five acres along the east bank of the North Branch, from Fullerton all the way north to Wellington Avenue. This enormous industrial enterprise occupied land formed by filling in clay pits between the river and Clybourn Avenue.

In 1902 Deering merged with the McCormick Harvesting Machine Company to form the giant International Harvester Company. Deering owned the **Wisconsin Steel Works** on the Calumet River, and, by 1924, International Harvester operated at nine different sites throughout Chicago. After company operations were consolidated, the Deering works were razed. The land then became

Movable Bridges

Chicago has long boasted the world's largest collection of movable bridges. But today more and more of these famed structures are being converted to fixed spans to relieve the high costs associated with movable bridges.

The movable bridge has lost its importance because large lake vessels no longer ply these waters, and because nearly all river towboats are fitted with movable pilothouses. The pilothouses are built atop pneumatic pistons that allow them to be raised for ease in steering or lowered to fit under fixed bridges.

available for construction of the Lathrop Homes and a variety of industrial and commercial enterprises.

For many years Cotter and Company, a wholesale hardware business, operated on the river's east bank just east of the Damen Avenue Bridge. The **Vienna Meat Products Company** sits across the river from Cotter on a triangular plot formed between the Damen and Fullerton bridges and the river. Vienna was founded in 1893 and has occupied its present plant for more than twenty-five years. It produces about $100 million worth of sausages, hot dogs, and other meat products annually for a national market.

Recently, Cotter closed its facility, making its twenty-acre site available for redevelopment. Should Cotter sell the property for industrial use, its estimated worth would be $4 million. On the other hand, if the land is rezoned and sold for residences, it probably would bring around $17 million. Ensuing events well illustrate the conflict between competing industrial and residential land use.

Within a few months of the Cotter decision to vacate its site, an interesting plan was presented for a $125-million, 525-unit residential development. This plan was attractive and in general compliance with guidelines for riverbank development. Construction was to be sufficiently set back from the river, and there was room for extension of a river trail long advocated by civic organizations.

However, the plan ran counter to the views of the Vienna Company, which maintained that upscale residents would soon object to the noise, traffic, and occasional odors associated with its meat processing operations. Vienna stated categorically that it would be forced to move its operations out of the city if the proposed residential development was allowed to proceed. The prospect of the loss of five hundred industrial jobs with an annual payroll of $18 million at a time when such jobs were already in short supply killed the residential project. Whether this decision will ultimately lead to victory for industrial land-use interests, or whether it is just a momentary delay in the eventual redevelopment of the river edge for residences, is still unclear.

Fullerton Avenue

Even though residential development at this spot has been stymied for the moment, commercial redevelopment of the riverbanks proceeds apace. The **Mid-Town Tennis Club** adjacent to the Vienna plant and the new **Riverpoint Mall** on the river's east bank, north of Fullerton Avenue, are good examples. Both are large operations, and both serve the increasingly affluent populations moving into gentrified areas near the river. The 201,000-square-foot shopping center is but one of a number of malls that have been developed recently in the old industrial corridor centered on the river.

South of the Riverpoint Mall across Fullerton between the river and the tracks of the Chicago and North Western Railroad (now part of the Union Pacific Rail empire) is a large property that is also scheduled for commercial development. As of this writing, its developers have been working closely with Friends of the Chicago River so that the project will comply with river guidelines.

Elston Avenue follows an old Indian trail and runs close to the river between Fullerton and Webster Avenue. The narrow strip of land between Elston and the river has long been associated with industry. Today it is mainly in commercial and light-industrial use, with the largest area given over to a *Chicago Sun-Times* newspaper distribution center.

As the river makes a short bend east before resuming its southeast flow it passes under the 1908 bridge of the Chicago and North Western Railroad (Union Pacific Railroad). Like the majority of Chicago's movable bridges, this structure is a trunnion bascule design. But it is a bascule bridge without its "makeup." Instead of having its the trunnion bearings and counterweight hidden in a pit below ground, everything is aboveground and on display.

The **Green Dolphin Street,** a restaurant and jazz club sits on the west bank, shoehorned between the railroad bridge and the Ashland Avenue Bridge. A large public utility structure on the east bank across from the restaurant replaces the Medill Avenue Incinerator. The present facility is operated by Waste Management Corporation as a collection center for the city's "blue bag" recycling program.

Built in 1936, the **Ashland Avenue Bridge** is another of the city's bascule structures. It is a single-leaf span decorated with bas-relief in the style of the Works Progress Administration. Its trunnions, machinery, and counterweight are out of sight, below ground. Although not a fixed bridge, it has been inactive as a drawbridge for many years.

Webster Avenue

The river here turns southward and the Ashland Avenue and Webster Avenue Bridges meet at a right angle, creating another small triangular area next to the river. On the east bank, the Metropolitan Water Reclamation District (MWRD) operates an experimental aeration station designed to increase dissolved oxygen in the stream and so promote aerobic decomposition of organic wastes in the river. Canoeists should steer well clear of the dangerous waters near the east bank by going to the far side of the stream. A canoe may lose buoyancy if it gets into the rush of aerated water coming to the surface.

Landward from the MWRD facility is a collection warehouse operated by the Salvation Army, and a row of small stores faces Webster Avenue from the north. The **Webster Place shopping center** sits on the south side of the street leading to the **Webster Avenue Bridge.** This 1916 bascule structure, an inactive drawbridge, features copper-topped bridge tender's houses.

In 1895 the west bank just south of the Webster Bridge contained a large hemp-drying field—a land use that is inconceivable from today's viewpoint. Hemp was widely used for making ropes and lines for ships and baskets and other packaging needs.

Industries along the river once included meatpacking, metalworking, soap and glue manufacturing, and more than forty tanneries. Many of these factories were established to use the animal byproducts from the meatpackers. Vestiges of these old linked industries may still be seen along the river between Webster and Armitage Avenues. Of all the tanneries that once operated in this area, only two remain, the **Horween Leather Company** and the **Gutmann Leather Company.** They continue to operate across from each other on opposite banks of the river.

Gutmann has operated on this site for nearly 120 years since its founding in 1878, and this plant is one of only three vertically integrated tanning operations in the United States. Today more than

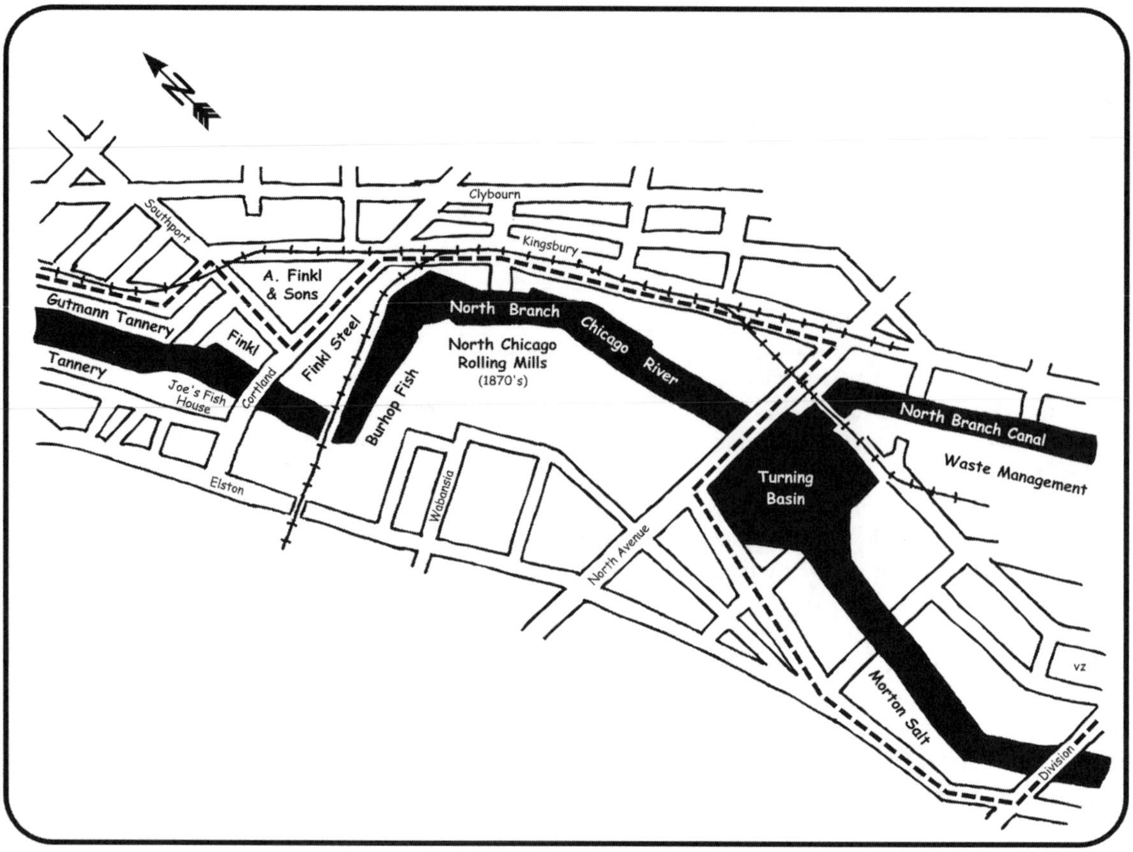
N
Clybourn
Southport
Kingsbury
A. Finkl & Sons
Gutmann Tannery
Finkl
Tannery
Finkl Steel
North Branch
Chicago River
North Chicago Rolling Mills (1870's)
Joe's Fish House
Cortland
Burhop Fish
North Branch Canal
Waste Management
Turning Basin
Elston
Wabansia
North Avenue
Morton Salt
Division
vz

MAP 16. Chicago River North Branch, North Chicago Rolling Mills. The Chicago River Trail is shown by a dashed line.

one hundred employees work at Gutmann making high-grade shoe and belting leathers, mostly for export to high-fashion manufacturers in Europe.

Ozinga Cement Company sits on the west bank of the river, south of the Horween tannery. Immediately south of Ozinga is **Ashland Aluminum.** Ashland has operated on this site for thirty-five years, manufacturing aluminum coils in its rolling mill. Still farther south, a wide variety of commercial and manufacturing operations line the west bank.

Inland from these industries, neighboring industrial lofts now house art galleries and picture-framing operations. Then **Joe's Fish House** appears between Armitage Avenue and Cortland Street on the west bank, recalling the days when Lake Michigan was a major commercial fishery. Although Joe's catches up to seventy thousand pounds of yellow perch and chubs each year in Lake Michigan, today only three commercial fisheries still operate in Illinois. The state has placed severe restrictions on such operations because of the impact commercial fishing has on fish populations.

The heavy industry and commercial operations along the river contrast sharply with the expensive residences in other sections of the Lincoln Park community. Recent years have seen a spurt of new development and gentrification of the old neighborhoods near Lincoln Park and the north campus of **De Paul University.** This urban revitalization has spread westward, engulfing former working-class and industrial areas along Clybourn Avenue. The so-called **Clybourn Corridor** has been one of the hottest development areas in the city in the last decade. As a result, the industrial belt along the river has thinned, with heavy industrial firms and scrap yards often backing up against new shopping malls and upscale shops and restaurants.

Even so, the land immediately adjacent to this area of the river has maintained a strong industrial character. The 1870s marked the beginnings of Chicago's vast iron and steel industry, and most of the original activity took place here. Today only one of the old firms survives: **A. Finkl and Sons Company.** This firm, located on the east bank on both sides of Cortland Street, was part of a large metal-casting and mold steel industry that grew up on the North Branch of the Chicago River after the Great Fire.

Anton Finkl founded the company in 1879 as a blacksmith shop and moved the plant to its current site in the 1890s. Now more than one hundred years later, the company, again under family management, is a leader in the production of high-quality mold steels. Finkl's more than four hundred workers produce molds that are used in automotive manufacturing, in the production of aircraft components, and in the electronics and appliance industries. Huge glowing cherry-red molds, fresh from the forge, are transported across Cortland Street by specially-designed haulers for further processing.

Adolf Luetgert

A curious event related to the meat industry occurred in this area in the spring of 1892. It involved the disappearance of the wife of Adolf Luetgert, a local sausage maker, after a family quarrel. A rumor circulated that, on the day she disappeared, Luetgert had ordered the watchman at the factory to fire up the furnaces, although the factory was no longer active. It was also whispered that Luetgert had purchased corrosive materials not used in regular operations.

Later, when police examined the factory, they discovered pieces of bone, blond hair, part of a gold tooth, and Mrs. Luetgert's two golden rings—at the bottom of a sausage vat! Mr. Luetgert was sent to the penitentiary in Joliet, where he died in 1908, without confessing to the murder. It is said that for quite some time after the crime, sausage consumption fell to record low levels everywhere in the city.

Finkl has survived and thrived by pioneering new techniques. The firm holds one hundred worldwide patents in steel production, and Finkl die steel is the first and only die steel in the world to be protected by a warranty against breakage. To produce this extraordinary quality, Finkl pioneered the use of vacuum arc degassing, which creates very clean, low-hydrogen steels. Finkl's commitment to environmental quality is evidenced by the millions of trees the company plants each year and also by the orderliness and cleanliness of its plant facilities.

Two interesting bridges are near the Finkl plant. The first is the bascule bridge at **Cortland Street**. This historic bridge, built in 1902, has the distinction of being the very first trunnion bascule bridge built in the United States. It has been placed on the list of National Historic Civil Engineering Landmarks.

The Cortland bridge features intriguing ornamentation, including a curious navigational "daymarker" and a picturesque bridge house. This formerly movable span is currently undergoing renovation as part of a massive citywide program to repair, replace, and renew Chicago's wealth of bridges. A number of formerly movable bridges will become stationary under this program.

The second bridge is a 1906 swing bridge owned by the Soo Line (now part of Canadian Pacific). It is the only operating swing bridge on the North Branch of the river. A number of the early bridges in Chicago were center-pier swing bridges, meaning that they turned upon a center pier in the river channel. Today four bridges of this general type, although fixed in position, still exist on the Sanitary and Ship Canal. The rail swing bridge south of Cortland, however, pivots not on a pier in the channel but

on a bearing set on the east riverbank. Because of this unique design, it leaves the channel unrestricted.

Although shipment by water is generally the cheapest form of transportation, it is relatively slow compared with shipment by truck, rail, or air. For these reasons, water transportation is favored for the shipment of heavy, bulky materials that do not require rapid delivery. Sand and gravel, coal, iron ore, stone, salt, grain, cement, chemicals, petroleum, and scrap are among the commodities commonly carried by water. Consequently, facilities handling these and similar products can be found on the banks of the Chicago River and other area streams.

Scrap yards appear on every waterway in the Chicago area and occupy the riverbanks opposite to and south of A. Finkl and Sons. These yards and similar metal recycling facilities serve the needs of the Chicago District steel mills at the south end of Lake Michigan. Recycling has long been practiced in the iron and steel industry—scrap is a major input for steel production. Its high bulk and low value make water transportation highly desirable.

Immediately south of the Finkl plant, the river jogs due east for about one block. Huge blocks of concrete that line the south bank are collapsing into the stream here, threatening to impede transportation. Industrial buildings and scrap yards dominate both banks, and scrap yards continue along the east bank all the way to North Avenue.

A **Procter and Gamble** soap-making plant formerly occupied a fifteen-acre site on both sides of North Avenue along the west banch of the North Branch. It was originally a plant of the Kirk's Soap Company, which, like the

tanneries, was an offshoot of the meat-packing industry. The firm's first factories were located near what is now Michigan Avenue and the main stem of the river. It moved its operations to the North Branch from the Michigan Avenue (Pine Street) plant when nearby commercial developers objected to the foul smell. In later years, when the wind was from the west, the old scenario repeated itself. Then Procter and Gamble, the successor firm, perfumed nearby fashionable neighborhoods with the heady fragrance of laundry detergents.

The large workforce at the plant also helped generate a highly specialized business across from the plant entrance that served both the workers and the

traffic on North Avenue. For many years, in even the coldest weather, ladies of the night in hot pants could be seen strolling the avenue selling their favors to plant workers and other passersby.

Today, the ladies and the soap plant are gone, and on the site has risen the huge City of Chicago Automotive Fleet Maintenance Facility and a large operation selling building products. The old rough-and-tumble industrial atmosphere of the plant and its workers has been replaced by the much more citified, gentrified clientele who frequent the store. This business demonstrates not only the changing character of the area but also how developers reneged on agreements to open the riverbank to

Cortland Street Bridge, the first of the city's large number of trunnion bascule bridges. The Cortland bridge has been completely refurbished and the machinery removed. The historic bridge is now a fixed structure.

Chicago's Steel Industry

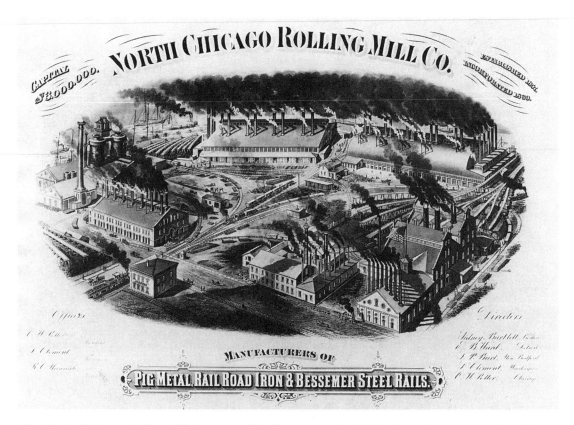

The North Chicago Rolling Mill Company. The first steel rail rolled in America were produced here in 1865. (Courtesy, Chicago Historical Society.)

The west bank of the river was once home to the **Illinois Steel Company North Works.** This steel mill at 1319 Waubansia, which eventually became part of **United States Steel Company,** was the successor to the **North Chicago Rolling Mills** and stretched all the way from the river's south bank in the "elbow" to the **Kirk's Soap plant** that fronted North Avenue. It was here that the first steel rails in the United States were rolled on May 24, 1865.

Steel rails had an immediate impact on the size and weight of steam locomotives, the trains they hauled, and the cargoes they carried. With the introduction of high-strength steel rails, the railroads came into their own and became the principal heavy freight hauler for the nation.

But steel also had a revolutionary impact on construction technology as steel skeletons were employed to take the weight of buildings off of their walls. This improvement thus made taller buildings possible, and it also allowed architects to design larger windows.

The old North Chicago Rolling Mills was founded by Eber B. Ward in 1857. By 1860 the firm employed two hundred men and made one hundred tons of iron rails each day. Ward was known for his generous and fair salaries, and he and his workers prospered. An additional mill built in 1864 doubled plant capacity. The mill burned down in 1866 but was rebuilt, and in 1870 two blast furnaces were added. In 1872 a Bessemer steel plant was introduced.

In 1889 the North Chicago Rolling Mill Company merged with Union Steel at Archer and Ashland Avenues; Milwaukee Iron Company's plant at Bay View, Wisconsin; and a Joliet mill to form the **Illinois Steel Company.** This in turn became **Carnegie Illinois Steel** and finally became part of **United States Steel Company.**

For a time, iron and steel production in the Chicago area was concentrated along the Chicago River, and industries related to steel manufacture clustered near the mills. Then, beginning around 1880, the mills began to move to large, inexpensive waterfronts in the Calumet River area to the south. In 1882, Illinois Steel, attracted by cheap and plentiful waterfront land near the mouth of the Calumet River, added a new plant in South Chicago with four blast furnaces, three Bessemer converters, and a steel rail mill. This plant became known as the South Works. The North Chicago mills were then called the North Works and were dismantled in 1901.

Despite the departure of the mills southward, a concentration of metalworking industries still persists on the Chicago River North Branch. The A. Finkl and Sons plant, described in this chapter, is just such a remnant.

public access. The earlier call for citizen oversight of new development gains intensity after such setbacks.

The double-leaf bascule bridge at North Avenue dates from 1907, and was designed with portal or through trusses. Although a historic bridge, it unfortunately creates a two-lane bottleneck and thus is scheduled to be rebuilt as a fixed four-lane span.

A scenic overlook west of the bridge was constructed on the south side of the road by the MWRD. The view south from the overlook is impressive. Nearby, the turning basin is often visited by wild ducks and seagulls, with herons and other waterbirds stopping by occasionally. In the middle distance rise industrial lofts, piles of scrap, and the heavy machinery used in scrap recycling, salt shifting, and cement mixing. The giant skyscrapers of the Loop form an imposing background. The view is remarkable because it encompasses public housing, railroads, industrial areas, roads and bridges, boatyards, churches, wildlife, gentrified residences, and the majesty of the city's commercial core. It is like a snapshot of the whole city in miniature.

North Avenue

Immediately south of the North Avenue Bridge, the river suddenly broadens out into a large turning basin that marks the north end of mile-long **Goose Island.** The turning basin, eight hundred feet across, is the widest point on the Chicago River. It is also just about the dirtiest point in the river. But help is at hand. A nearby circular shape on the sidewalk marks a Deep Tunnel drop shaft, which carries excess stormwater three hundred feet belowground to be stored, treated, and eventually released into area waterways after the storm has abated.

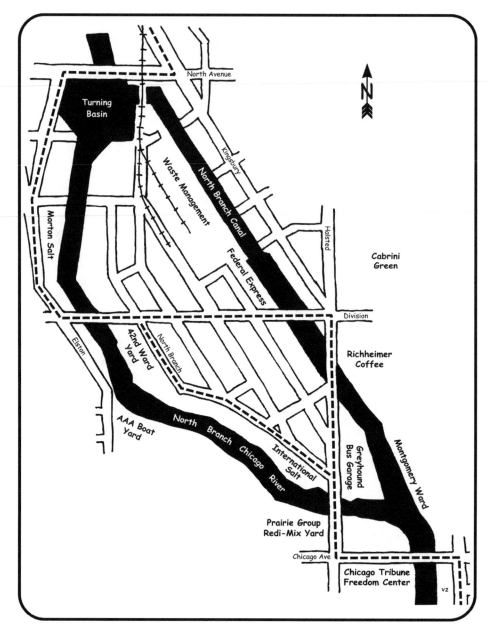

MAP 17.
Chicago River
North Branch,
Goose Island.
The Chicago
River Trail is
shown as a
dashed line.

One-hundred-sixty acre Goose Island is artificial. It was first called Ogden Island because it was created by the operations of one of William Ogden's many businesses. In this case, clay for brickmaking was dug from a low, swampy area east of the Chicago River's North Branch. The resulting channel formed the island. Here again, Ogden's commercial genius is demonstrated. For, by digging clay for brick making, he simultaneously created new and very valuable waterfront land for the rapidly expanding industries of nineteenth-century Chicago. Apparently, the island took some years to appear, but it is clearly shown on maps dated in the late 1850s. There is some evidence that it was partially filled-in later, but by 1871 it was an island once more and remains so today.

The eastern channel dug by Ogden's firm is now known as the North Branch Canal. In the past it was navigable by large vessels, but it has been allowed to shoal, and so is less than three feet deep in many places. Lumberyards and related industries filled the east bank facing Goose Island as late as 1895; in fact, lumberyards were found almost everywhere along navigable water in the Chicago area.

Yards were plentiful on the North Branch from north of Belmont and continued all the way to the main stem. The South Branch was, however, the main lumber district and, up to the end of the nineteenth century, its banks were flooded with lumber.

The west bank was home to at least three major tanneries that, like soap-making, were related to byproducts from meatpacking operations. Tanneries were also present on the island itself.

Early in Goose Island's history, it became home to poor Irish immigrants, who named the area **Kilgubbin** after the village they had fled during Ireland's potato famine. They farmed on the island and kept flocks of geese that were often seen swimming in the river. Presumably, this was the origin of the name. It is said that the Irish "patch" on the island produced more policemen, firemen, streetcar conductors, and ward bosses than any comparable area of the

city. It was also the birthplace of Chicago mayor **William E. Dever,** who worked in the local Griess-Pfleger tannery while a young man (Hansen 1942, 214).

Goose Island was later the site where **Philip Armour** headed off a plot by rival grain traders to ruin him. These traders bought wheat and filled all of Chicago's grain elevators so they could force Armour to buy their wheat "at extortionist prices in order to fulfill his heavy futures contracts." He learned of the "corner" just four weeks before his contracts were due, and his response was the stuff of legend. He bought land on Goose Island and set crews working there day and night to build what were then the world's largest grain elevators, into which he poured grain from huge lake vessels just in time to fulfill his contracts (Miller 1996, 213). Armour's elevators brought the total number of grain elevators on the northeast edge of Goose Island to five, helping to attract other industries that either shipped or used grain.

Flames from nearby blast furnaces of the North Chicago Rolling Mills created such a continuous fiery glow about the island that the whole area soon became known as **"Little Hell."** And hell was busy, because a steady parade of immigrants settled there and then moved on, only to be replaced by yet another group. The parade picked up speed when the island became a temporary refuge for people displaced by the Great Fire of 1871. Later, Swedes lived on the island, eventually replaced by more Irish immigrants and still later by Sicilians. Eventually, railroads, grain elevators, tanneries, metalworking, and other industrial activities pushed island settlers northward until by the 1930s only a handful of people lived on the island.

Today Goose Island is a Planned Manufacturing District, with more than forty-eight industries and distribution facilities employing more than twelve hundred people. **Budweiser** operates a major distribution center, as does the **Charles Levy Circulating Company,** which employs three hundred workers and distributes periodicals and books throughout metropolitan Chicago. A large waste collection facility owned by Waste Management Corporation and operated as Ace Disposal is where the old grain elevators once stood, and the south tip of the island is used for a local garage by **Greyhound Bus Company.**

In addition to these firms, salt, lumber, cement, paper recycling, and metal fabrication facilities make the island their home. The island is served by the Canadian Pacific/Soo Line Railroad, and there are half a dozen operations with rail service.

Two very large new industrial and distribution facilities are currently under construction. **Federal Express Corporation** is building a $14 million package transfer and distribution center that will employ 330 workers to staff its round-the-clock operations. Also under construction is the $20-million, 15 1/2-acre, 350,000-square-foot factory of the **Republic Window and Door Company.** This plant is being built on former rail yards and will employ about 750 workers. When completed it will become the largest employer on the island.

View eastward over Goose Island. A large saltyard sits on the island's west bank, and the towers of the John Hancock Center and other skyscrapers of the Magnificent Mile rise in the distance.

Plans are also being finalized to create three hundred thousand square feet of additional speculative industrial space on the remaining eleven acres of the former rail yard. When these facilities are completed and in operation, the workforce on the island is expected to top two thousand five hundred.

Perhaps the most charming of the current operations on Goose Island is the distribution center for **Christopher Farms.** This company produces and distributes garlic products in a city named for a river that was named for the wild onion or garlic that grew along its banks.

Goose Island has an outstanding location connected by major streets and the Kennedy Expressway with the rest of the metropolitan area. It also has, of necessity, quite a collection of bridges: Division Street, with two bridges, bisects the island east and west; Halsted Street, also with two bridges, cuts across the island's southern tip. An unusual swing rail bridge reaches the island from the north.

Division Street

The **Division Street Bridge** over the North Branch Canal is a bascule design featuring the Chicago "Y" symbol in its decoration. This symbol represents the main stem of the Chicago River and its two branches. The bridge, completed in 1903, was the second trunnion bascule bridge built by the City of Chicago.

The double-leaf bascule bridge where Division crosses the North Branch was built in 1904 and is now the northernmost of all the working drawbridges in the city. It also carries the honorary title of **Studs Terkel Bridge.** Studs is the famed author, interviewer, social critic, and radio personality who for forty-five years has conducted a radio interview show known nationally for its compassionate, artistic,

literate, and intelligent character. His best-selling series of oral histories, including *Division Street America,* has won wide acclaim. Like the bridges, Studs is a Chicago original.

The **Halsted Street Bridge** over the canal is a 1908 bascule design, with wooden houses for the bridge tenders. This bridge is being permanently fixed, since navigation is no longer possible on the canal. Halsted crosses the Chicago River on a modern, double-leaf bascule bridge with deck trusses and Beaux Arts bridge houses, built in 1955.

A unique bobtail swing railroad bridge built in 1906 carries the Canadian-Pacific/Soo Line Railroad to Goose Island from the north, and six active rail spurs serve island industries. There has been talk recently of converting this **Cherry Street Bridge**, as it is known, to pedestrian use to link North Avenue with a hoped-for park at the north end of the island.

Because of its excellent location near the Loop, this area has become another battleground between residential developers and government agencies favoring industry. Since Goose Island is a Planned Manufacturing District, the Local Economic and Employment Development Council (LEED) of the New City YMCA is working to promote industrial retention and development, foster jobs for local residents, and balance competing land uses.

The distribution facilities already on the island are soon to be joined by others as this remarkable part of the city prepares for the twenty-first century. The whole area is rebounding, with motion picture postproduction facilities (including the famed **Essanay Studios**) joining the warehouses, salt yards, and fabricated metals industry. In addition, a new public high school is scheduled for construction just off the island at the corner of Halsted and Division Streets. As of this writing it seems that the commercial and industrial forces have the upper hand, but residential developers are waiting in the wings should the current industrial impetus be lost.

South of North Avenue, the west bank of the Chicago River is filled with heavy industry. Between Le Moyne and Blackhawk Streets is a large metal recycling operation; between Blackhawk and Division Streets is the distribution center for the **Morton Salt Company.** The Morton facility receives up to one hundred barge loads of salt each year; about 150,000 tons of product.

The west bank in this area is part of the **West Town** community, which dates to the time of Chicago's origin. West Town's growth was spurred by the completion of both the Southwest (Ogden Avenue) and Northwest (Milwaukee Avenue) plank roads in the 1840s. Today new housing is appearing amid some of the oldest residences in Chicago, creating a hidden community between converging rail tracks and the industry along the North Branch of the river.

West Town also was home to the city's first railroad, the **Galena and Chicago Union,** which William Ogden developed and promoted. This rail line was eventually absorbed by the Chicago North Western, which now is part of the Union Pacific.

For one hundred years, the Chicago North Western Railroad and the Union Pacific Railroad have been circling each other in a complicated corporate waltz. In the 1890s, when the Union Pacific Railroad was in financial crisis and the North Western was highly profitable, the North Western considered buying out

the UP. Later, the railroads sparred with each other as they fought over acquisitions. Finally, in 1995, the Union Pacific took over the Chicago North Western during the great wave of rail consolidations that accompanied deregulation.

The **Near North Side** community includes Goose Island and the land east all the way to Lake Michigan. It is a community of stark, extraordinary contrasts already described in the 1920s as "an area of highlight and shadow, of vivid contrasts—contrasts not only between the old and the new, . . . but between wealth and poverty, vice and respectability, . . . luxury and toil" (Zorbaugh 1929, 4).

The contrasts described so vividly in the 1920s still remain very much in evidence. A trip eastward from the river along Division Street takes one up a socioeconomic slope of almost unbelievable steepness. On the west near the river is the **Cabrini-Green public housing complex,** while just past the elevated tracks immediately to the east rise fashionable buildings, the upscale apartment towers of **Carl Sandburg Village,** and the historic brownstones and cooperative apartments of Chicago's **Gold Coast.**

Plans are now being created to demolish 1,324 units at Cabrini and to redevelop a sixty-five-acre area for 2,200 units of mixed-income housing with parks and shopping malls. But, like many urban projects, this effort faces obstacles from both the inside and the outside. Even so, Cabrini-Green is an island of dire poverty in an increasing sea of affluence that is steadily rolling toward the river. There seems little doubt that, in its present form, Cabrini-Green's days are numbered.

Ogden Avenue is the modern successor to the old Southwest Plank Road,

which was built in the 1840s to allow some ease of movement through the swampy country around Chicago. Eventually, Ogden was placed on a viaduct that leaped over Goose Island, soared above the intersection of Halsted and Division, and returned to earth near Clybourn Avenue. When this viaduct was removed in the 1990s, it allowed the sun to shine once more on the southwestern and western portions of Cabrini-Green and on Halsted Street. The removal of the viaduct also produced some peculiarities in the numbering system. So today, on the middle of Goose Island, one may find a Pickens-Kane moving and storage building with the address 1000 Ogden

although the street on which it is presumably located has departed. This building also features doors that now open onto empty air thirty feet above the present street level.

The **Richheimer Coffee Company** sits on the east bank of the canal at the southeast corner of Halsted and Division, and the great Catalog Building of **Montgomery Ward and Company** stretches southward along the east bank of the river all the way to Chicago Avenue. This giant structure was built in 1908 and other sections were added until as late as 1963. The architects for the first sections of the building were Schmidt, Garden, and Martin. Richard

The 1908 Catalog Building of Montgomery Ward and Company was designed by Schmidt, Garden, and Martin in the prairie style.

Schmidt was a colleague of Frank Lloyd Wright, and the building is in the prairie style with long horizontal lines. It covers 3 1/2 acres and contains 2,371,000 square feet of usable space.

Across Chicago Avenue to the south is the Art Deco–style **Montgomery Ward Merchandise Building.** The architects of this eight-story, 352,230-square-foot building are unknown. Its continuous vertical lines contrast sharply with the long horizontal lines of the Catalog Building to the north.

A statue, *The Spirit of Progress,* adorns the tower on the northeast corner of the building. This statue is the third associated with Montgomery Ward. The first stood at the World's Columbian Exposition in 1893, although the fate of the sculpture is in dispute. The second statue graced the tower of the Montgomery Ward Building built in 1899 at the northwest corner of Michigan Avenue and Madison Street. With the statue and the tower on which it stood, this building was, for a time, the tallest skyscraper in America west of New York. The Catalog and Merchandise Buildings were designated National Historic Landmarks in 1978, honoring Montgomery Ward as the first true mail order merchandiser in the United States.

Minoru Yamasaki designed the twenty-six-floor corporate tower added to the Montgomery Ward complex in 1974. This office tower contains six hundred thousand square feet of space and features an open "office landscaping" interior and a penthouse atop the building. It is linked with the two buildings along the river by a complex network of underground tunnels. A fourth building in the complex, the former Sprague-Warner Building south of the Merchandise Building, was demolished in 1983 and replaced by a private park along the river for Montgomery Ward associates.

As one of Chicago's unique firms, Montgomery Ward was the first that took full advantage of the city's unsurpassed transportation connections to establish its mail-order empire. In truth, other companies had made mail-order sales, but Ward was the first to offer a broad range of goods and sell only through the mail (Miller 1996, 244–50).

Montgomery Ward himself hit upon many of the merchandising innovations that propelled his company to become one of the giants of American merchandising. His first great warehouse—"the Busy Hive"—was located on Michigan Avenue, but in 1908 he moved warehouse operations to the banks of the Chicago River. Today, competitive pressures from Wal-Mart and other giants has driven this old firm to seek protection from its creditors under Chapter 11. Rumors concerning conversion of these giant warehouses to expensive condominiums may eventually become reality.

The **AAA Boat Yard** appears on the west side of the river south of Division Street, following the bank south to the area where the old Ogden Avenue viaduct spanned not only the river but also the south end of Goose Island and the North Branch Canal. Paper recycling activity comes next along the west bank, and then huge, bright-orange machines sit at an asphalt plant. A large and picturesque Redi-Mix concrete yard owned by Prairie Materials Company was recently purchased from the Material Service Corporation. The storage yard extends southward along the west bank all the way to Halsted Street and Chicago Avenue, and continues to use Material

Opposite: *The Spirit of Progress* adorns the northeast corner tower of the Montgomery Ward Merchandise Building on Division Street east of the river.

Service Company barges to transport the building materials it supplies. These barges are often seen tied up alongside the yard.

Chicago Avenue

Chicago Avenue runs between Montgomery Ward warehouses and leads east to the company office building on the south side of the street. It crosses the North Branch on a double-leaf bascule bridge built in 1914.

South of Chicago Avenue on the west bank is the twenty-one-acre site of the **Chicago Tribune Freedom Center,** one of the world's largest and most technologically advanced newspaper printing, paper storage, and distribution facilities. Here, ten giant offset presses print seventy thousand newspapers per hour and use five thousand rolls of newsprint every week. The *Tribune* built this modern structure along the river because it intended to continue using lake bulk carrier vessels to bring fifteen-hundred-pound rolls of newsprint from Three Rivers, Canada. The huge vessels would then offload directly into the new facility as they had done previously at the old *Tribune* docks east of Michigan Avenue.

This plan proved useless because the Environmental Protection Agency determined that river bottom sediments in the area were too toxic to allow them to be removed. For this reason, no dredging has occurred since 1977, and the river is now only about nine feet deep alongside the *Tribune* plant. Since the sediments have been upgraded from toxic to very polluted, it is conceivable that dredging will one day be resumed, enabling lake bulk carriers once again to ply these waters.

The riverbank opposite the *Tribune* printing plant is filled with in-dustrial loft buildings that have been converted to expensive apartments. **SuHu** is the name for this area immediately east of the river, taken from Superior-Huron, the streets in the center of an old warehousing and industrial district. The area has been reborn as Chicago's gallery district, our version of New York's famed SoHo.

Commercial operations mix with warehouses, restaurants, galleries, a private park, and residential conversions near the Ohio feeder bridge, a double-leaf bascule structure that crosses the North Branch on its way to join the Kennedy Expressway just west of the river. Mixed land uses continue south along the east bank all the way to Grand Avenue, which has a recently rebuilt double-leaf bascule bridge.

The East Bank Club occupies the east bank of the river from Grand Avenue south to Kinzie Street. This ostentatious health club is perhaps the ultimate expression of the yuppie lifestyle that has invaded the river corridor. East Bank presents a blank wall to the river and provides no public access or landscaping. Such development is exactly counter to that urged by the city, the Urban Land Institute, and civic organizations; instead it represents the kind of situation that the urban river guidelines seek to prevent.

The west bank of the river between Grand Avenue and Kinzie Street holds a parking lot and the yard of the City of Chicago Department of Transportation. However, this area too is set for radical change. The creation of **"Kinzie Park,"** a $120-million development of more than 500 homes, was announced in late 1996 for the site. The project is just north of the **Fulton River District,** a rapidly developing area of residential loft conversions and new townhouses, which has brought hundreds of residents to a formerly forbidding tract of dilapidated factories.

The neighboring **Kinzie Street Bridge** is a storied span with a checkered past. The wooden bridge that preceded it in 1900 caught fire and burned and, more recently, the current bridge crushed a taxicab between the leaves as it opened, killing the driver.

The latest and most curious event involving the Kinzie Street Bridge occurred in 1992 when workers driving piles to strengthen the bridge accidentally penetrated the system of freight tunnels that run under the river and throughout the Loop. The resulting underground flood—the Great Chicago Flood—was legendary and caused widespread difficulty and damage in the tens of millions of dollars. It took more than a week before the leak was plugged and several more weeks before all the water was finally pumped from the basements of Loop buildings. Litigation is still pending and damages may exceed $150 million.

The river's west bank south of Kinzie holds two projects of the noted architect **Harry Weese.** Next to Kinzie Street are Weese's famed **River Cottages,** multilevel, single-family residences designed to take full advantage of their riverbank location. Porthole windows and decks offer playful touches with a nautical theme. "Water is a magnet," says Weese. "It draws people to it" (Cassidy 1979, 100).

It was not far from this site where **Archibald Clybourn,** Chicago's first constable, built and operated the city's first slaughterhouse in 1827. In so doing he sparked the creation of many meatpacking operations as well as tanneries and

Kinzie Street Bridge

The **Kinzie Street Bridge** is opened more than any other bridge on the Chicago River—about thirty-one hundred times in 1989 alone—because the bridge clears the water by only fifteen-feet. As a result, it must be opened even for barges and so requires bridge tenders around the clock. The city plans to remedy this expensive traffic–snarling problem by replacing the present span with a new bridge built five to six feet higher over the channel.

View southward over the forks of the Chicago River toward the AT & T Corporate Center and other buildings of the west Loop.

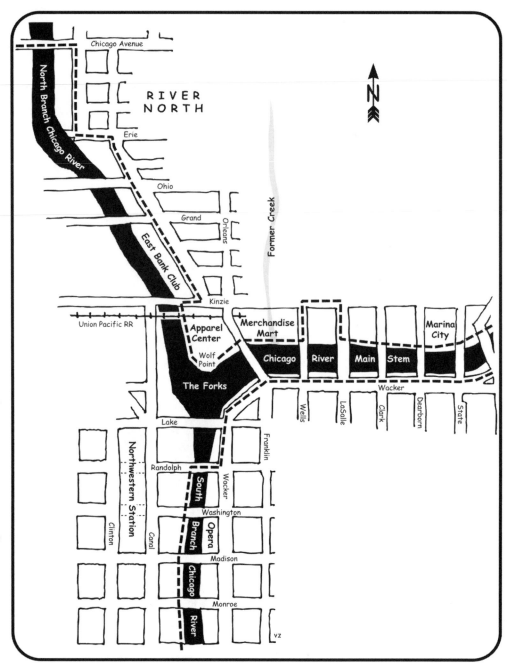

MAP 18. Chicago River North Branch, the Forks. Includes the forks where the North and South Branches join to form the Main Stem. The gray tone shows where a tributary creek originally flowed into the river. The Chicago River Trail is shown as a dashed line.

soap, candle, and glue plants, that used the byproducts left over from the meat-packing operations. Clybourn also operated the city's first ferry from the foot of Lake Street to the west bank of the river's South Branch.

Fulton House sits just south of the River Cottages. Here Weese recast an old cold-storage building for office and residential use. It is said that penetrating the three-foot-thick walls to add windows cost a fortune and severely discomfited the architect. In this design Weese is again preoccupied with the river location, so docks along the water allow some of the tenants to moor their boats.

Between the River Cottages and Fulton House runs a Union Pacific Railroad spur that allows trains to enter the **Apparel Center** and the **Merchandise Mart** on their lower levels. This line follows the route of Chicago's first railroad, the **Galena and Chicago Union,** and it crosses the North Branch on a bascule bridge that usually closes only twice a day: once in the morning and once in the evening. Residents of Fulton House on the west bank say they enjoy the sight of the raised bridge as a piece of urban sculpture, but that the occasional sight of the bridge closing arouses the strange feeling that the bridge is falling on their building.

The Forks

On the east side of the stream, the Apparel Center commands the site at the river forks now known as **Wolf Point.** Originally the name applied to a small peninsula that jutted out from the river's west bank at the forks. But years later, after this small impediment to navigation had been removed, the name shifted to the site on the north bank, where the North Branch and main stem of the river join.

The Apparel Center holds a Holiday Inn on its upper floors and has showrooms and offices for many clothing manufacturers and distributors as well as meeting facilities. Before Chicago was a town, the Apparel Center site was the location of **Miller House,** possibly built as early as 1827. It became one of three taverns that graced the river forks at the original center of settlement nearly one mile west of Fort Dearborn.

Archibald Clybourn was a partner of Samuel and John Miller in their Miller House tavern. In 1829 Sam Miller and Clybourn were authorized to run a ferry "across the Chicago River at the lower forks, near Wolf Point, crossing the river below the northeast branch, and to land on either side of both branches to suit the convenience of persons wishing to cross" ("Wolf Point," Commission on Chicago Historical and Architectural Landmarks 1975c, 7).

In 1828 James Kinzie and his half-brother David Hall built a log house, the first of Chicago's taverns, on Wolf Point, renting it to Archibald Caldwell who obtained Chicago's first tavern license. However, Caldwell decided to move to Wisconsin, so Elijah Wentworth rented the cabin from Kinzie and became the tavern's second manager. The **Wolf Point Tavern** was considered the best in the settlement, but this did not stop the settlers from justly labelling it "Rat Castle" in honor of its most numerous inhabitants (Ibid., 10). It passed through a succession of managers, none of whom lasted long, before it was closed in 1834. By this time James Kinzie had built a new hotel, the **Green Tree Tavern,** near the forks where it stood until 1880, when it was moved to Milwaukee Avenue.

View southeastward over Wolf Point and the forks of the Chicago River around 1900. In the foreground are the remains of the yards of the city's first railroad, the Galena and Chicago Union. Commercial buildings line the river's south bank before the completion of Wacker Drive created a totally new look. (Courtesy, Chicago Historical Society.)

Beginning in 1829, Mark Beaubien operated the **Eagle Exchange** tavern on the south bank. After the building was enlarged it became known as the **Sauganash Hotel.** It was in that hotel in 1833 that thirteen settlers voted on the question of the city's incorporation. The favorable vote that created the town of Chicago was twelve to one. By 1829 Chicago had three taverns and from that day a shortage of taverns has been one problem that Chicago has not had to face.

In 1831, when Beaubien built his hotel addition, Chicago consisted of three taverns at the fork in the river, a few cabins scattered along the north and south banks of the main channel, Fort Dearborn, and a few cabins along the North and South Branches of the River. Otherwise, there was nothing but mud and prairie ("Sauganash Hotel," Commission on Chicago Historical and Architectural Landmarks 1975a, 4).

In those early days a quarter could buy "a half pint of wine, rum or brandy or a full pint of whiskey; breakfast, dinner or supper." Nearly all the activities in the emerging town occurred either at Fort Dearborn or at Wolf Point. The lusty, carousing character of the settlement, populated by traders, farmers, hustlers, and Indians, is glowingly described by many historians and, in particular, by Nelson Algren in *Chicago, City*

on the Make: "Whiskey-and-vermillion hustlers, painting the night vermillion." But the hell-for-leather frontier life was tempered slightly by a number of church congregations organized in the 1830s. The Methodists were led by the Reverend Jesse Walker, a circuit rider, who established his congregation in a cabin at Wolf Point and later held services in Billy Caldwell's log council house and Chester Ingersoll's tavern.

In 1851 the old Sauganash Hotel burned to the ground. Nine years later, in 1860, its place was taken by a temporary building, the **Wigwam,** which was built to house the 1860 Republican National Convention. This structure was built in five weeks at a cost of six thousand dol-

lars, and accommodated ten thousand conventioneers. Its architect was W. W. Boyington, who also designed the city's famous Water Tower. After Abraham Lincoln was nominated in Chicago's first national political convention, many other political meetings were held in the hall, including Stephen A. Douglas's last public speech in 1861. In 1862 the Wigwam was remodeled into stores, and it was destroyed by fire in 1869. Today, the **333 West Lake Street Building,** rises on the old site of the Wigwam.

At this point the long, fascinating journey on the unreversed North Branch of the Chicago River comes to an end at the forks, where the North and the South Branches join to form the river's main

The forks of the Chicago River in 1833 when the town was incorporated. (From a painting by Justin Herriott. Courtesy, Chicago Historical Society.)

stem. The journey has taken the river explorer from the bucolic upper tributaries to the heart of the commercial district near the city center. It has led through forest preserves and parks, rich and poor neighborhoods, industrial districts, and areas where industrial spaces are being converted to fashionable residences. From this point onward, the waters of the North Branch mingle with lake water and flow southwestward toward the Mississippi River and the Gulf of Mexico.

THE NORTH SHORE CHANNEL

Wilmette to Green Bay Road

The daunting problem of protecting Chicago's water supply was ultimately solved in 1900 by a massive engineering effort that reversed the flow of the Chicago River. The purpose of the reversal was to sweep the city's waste away from the lake and into the drainage of the Illinois River. Actually, only the main stem and South Branch of the river were reversed, since the flow of the North Branch remained essentially unaffected.

However, the movement of water toward the southwest was insufficient to scour the channel wastes from the river's North Branch, which was heavily polluted from steel mills, brickyards, tanneries, soap plants, and other industries. To supply the additional flow, the eight-mile North Shore Channel was dug from Wilmette to the North Branch at Lawrence Avenue.

Large interceptor sewers were installed along the Chicago lakefront to seal off the lake from the city sewer system, collecting wastewater from a wide variety of sources and channeled it to the Lawrence Avenue Pumping Station on the North Branch and the Racine Pumping Station on Bubbly Creek. These sewers were begun in 1900 and completed in 1907 just as North Shore Channel construction began.

The principal task of the North Shore Channel was to supply additional flow to the Chicago River North Branch, but it also helped to drain wet areas in Wilmette, Evanston, and neighboring communities. Today the channel also carries treated effluent from the North Shore Treatment Plant to the Chicago River system.

CHICAGO RIVER FACT: THE NORTH AND MAIN BRANCHES JOIN AND FLOW SOUTH UNTIL THEY MEET THE SANITARY AND SHIP CANAL AT DAMEN AVENUE. THE CANAL FLOWS IN A SOUTHWESTERLY DIRECTION TOWARD ITS RENDEZVOUS WITH THE DES PLAINES RIVER IN LOCKPORT.

The areas through which the channel was cut had always been marshy, and most settlement was concentrated along high ground on the north–south ridge that today carries Ridge Avenue. In the 1840s Edward Mulford and Edward Murphy built a wooden box drain between Chicago and Ridge Avenues that ran north to the Northwestern University campus and emptied into a ravine that flowed to Lake Michigan. Northwestern students celebrated its foul character and the occasional difficulty of crossing when rain swollen by calling it the Rubicon.

After "Mulford's ditch" fell into disrepair, a drainage plan used the long ridge parallel to the lakeshore as a divide. The new effort channeled waters east of the ridge into the lake and carried runoff west of the ridge into a ditch that ran on the line followed later by the North Shore Channel. By this means, water on the western slope of the ridge was brought into the North Branch of the Chicago River.

The construction of the North Shore Channel was difficult. The much larger Sanitary and Ship Canal was dug mostly through limestone and mixtures of earth and rock. Only occasionally did workers have to contend with large sections of clay. By contrast, the North Shore Channel was dug almost entirely through difficult clay bodies. This meant, in addition to the difficulty of digging, that the slippery material tended to slide back into the ditch when heavy rains occurred. Special treatment of the banks

The sluice gate that regulates the flow of lakewater into the North Shore Channel near Sheridan Road in Wilmette.

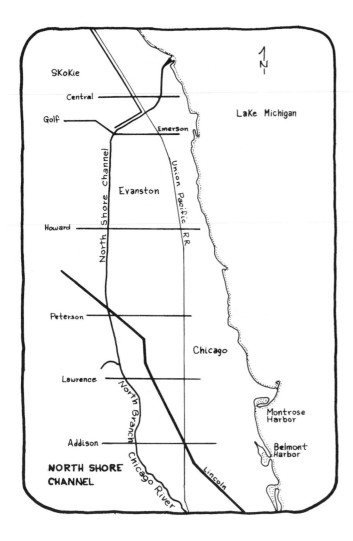

SKokie
Central
Golf
Emerson
Lake Michigan
North Shore channel
Union Pacific RR
Evanston
Howard
Peterson
Chicago
Lawrence
North Branch
Montrose Harbor
Addison
Belmont Harbor
NORTH SHORE CHANNEL
Chicago River
Lincoln
N

MAP 19.
The North
Shore
Channel.

became necessary to stabilize them against repeated slides.

The Sanitary District, precursor to the Metropolitan Water Reclamation District, did most of the stabilizing work itself. It also entered into agreements with neighboring communities to dump clay excavated east of the North Western tracks into Lake Michigan to create a breakwater and thirty-acre park in Wilmette. Material excavated west of the tracks was sold to brick manufacturers.

The channel was about one hundred feet wide and nine feet deep. Originally it was designed to add one thousand cubic feet of water per second to the flow of the North Branch of the Chicago River. In addition, it was large enough for barge navigation, although it has now been many years since it was used for that purpose.

The North Shore Channel originates in Wilmette at the south end of **Gilson Park,** which was made from material dug from the channel during its construction. The channel broadens out into a harbor where it reaches the lake. **Wilmette Harbor Association** and **Sheridan Shore Yacht Club** have their facilities there, and the varied pleasure craft give the little harbor a quaint, picturesque character. It is noteworthy that members of the Sheridan Shore Yacht Club, finding the harbor too shallow, built a coffer dam, dewatered the channel, and dug out the harbor by hand.

As the channel passes under Sheridan Road, it is blocked by a lock (now closed to navigation) and by a sluice gate that regulates the amount of water that enters from the lake. This sluice is directly below the elevated gardens of the uniquely beautiful **Baha'i Temple** that rises above the south bank. The **Peter N. Jans Community Golf Course** lies along the channel's north bank from Sheridan Road to Central, and the channel passes under fixed bridges at Linden and Maple Avenues and Isabella and Central Streets.

Between Isabella and Central, the channel passes just west of **Evanston Hospital,** and about two blocks east of the recently renamed **Ryan Field** (formerly **Dyche Stadium**), where Northwestern University's football team

The Bahai Temple rises majestically above the North Shore Channel in Wilmette. This beautiful structure was designed by Louis Bourgeois and built over a 40-year period from 1913 to 1953. Its actual name is the Bahai House of Worship, and it serves as the center for the Bahai faith in the United States.

recently found a winning formula after decades of frustration.

As the channel passes Central, it begins to curve to the west and passes under the **Lincoln Street Bridge.** Broad grassy areas front the channel on the east bank, and attractive residential neighborhoods follow the stream south. Then it passes under the Chicago North Western Rail Bridge (now Union Pacific) and the parallel bridge of Green Bay Road immediately to the south.

Green Bay Road

At this point McCormick Boulevard meets Green Bay Road and continues southwest parallel to the North Shore Channel. The **Ladd Arboretum** follows the channel along its west bank and features the **Evanston Parks Ecology Center** immediately north of Bridge Street, on land leased by Evanston from the Metropolitan Water Reclamation District. The Ecology Center is being enlarged to make the operation more of a nature center with exhibits.

A canoe program operates out of the center, and plans are under way to expand the program and to include water studies. The center actively supports the use of people-powered water craft so that greater numbers can enjoy the natural surroundings of the North Shore Channel. The City of Evanston is also planning a canal overlook in the Twiggs Park area, north and east of the Ecology Center. South of the center, a lovely **Peace Park** has been developed within Ladd Arboretum.

South of Bridge Street, the channel passes the **Community Hospital of Evanston.** Then, at about the Emerson Street Bridge (Golf Road), it passes **McCormick Park,** turns straight south, and flows under the bridge at Church Street.

A Cleaner Channel

Since the opening of the Deep Tunnel project, the North Shore Channel's water quality has improved markedly. It received a further boost when the Metropolitan Water Reclamation District stopped sending chlorinated water into the channel from the North Side Treatment Plant at Devon Avenue. Improved stream quality is indicated by rising fish populations, which include largemouth bass, bluegill, and crappie along with red-eared and snapping turtles. And as the numbers and varieties of fish increase, the bird population also rises. It is common to see great blue herons, green herons, and black-crowned night herons along with gulls and a variety of ducks.

Ecologist and planner Richard E. Carter emphasizes the significance of the channel as "an important, although little recognized corridor for wildlife." Carter describes the open space along the channel corridor in his management

plan report, but he focuses his primary attention on the "Wild Zone" along the channel banks (Carter 1992).

Carter points out that the banks are formed of heavy glacial clays from the dredging of the canal. These are not normal soils, so they have proved a difficult environment for plant growth. He characterizes the waterway corridor as "a highly disturbed area which has had some heavy-handed engineering followed by a combination of succession and man-made landscaping." These forces have produced a situation where, "from the top of the slope down to the water . . . Eurasian grasses and weeds predominate. Typical are Queen Anne's Lace, tall goldenrod, milkweed, and asters . . . (along with) willows, dogwoods and other shrubs" (Ibid.).

In addition, cottonwoods, willows, and poplars are found "along with ash, elm, maple, and box elder. The understory tends to be thickets of red-osier dogwood, gray dogwood, honeysuckle, and wild grape" (Ibid.). Crown vetch and buckthorn are becoming an increasing problem. Moreover, the stream's flow is slow, limiting the amount of dissolved oxygen in the waterway.

Nonetheless, the improving quality of the North Shore Channel's wildlife corridor has allowed red fox, deer, coyote, and beaver to live in the area. But all of this could change if proposals under consideration by Skokie planners are enacted. One idea involves moving the restricting weir farther downstream to allow powerboats from the lake to enter the channel. This proposal would not only put an end to reflective canoe trips along a tranquil waterway but also would have a negative impact on plant and animal species that have multiplied so slowly over such a long time.

The Northshore Sculpture Park stretches from Golf Road to Oakton Street along the North Shore Channel.

Golf Road

At Golf Road the border between **Evanston** to the east and **Skokie** to the west follows the east bank of the North Shore Channel. Before outside settlement began, this was a wet area where the prairies to the west met wooded areas to the east. Now the easternmost edge of Skokie between McCormick Boulevard and the channel holds the **Skokie Northshore Sculpture Park** that

extends from Golf Road south to Oakton Street. The park contains picnic areas and benches but is most distinguished by the fanciful and colorful stone and metal sculptures by local artists that adorn it from end to end.

U.S. Robotics, a high-tech manufacturer of computer modems, is located north of Oakton. This local firm was recently purchased by a West Coast company that manufactures hardware to support computer networks. As a result, the future of U.S. Robotics' Chicago operations is uncertain.

Oakton Street

South of Oakton a high rail bridge carries the CTA's Skokie Swift rapid transit line across the North Shore Channel. The Swift passes just north of the North Side Water Reclamation Plant of the Metropolitan Water Reclamation District, the oldest of seven wastewater treatment facilities in metropolitan Chicago. When it was completed in 1928, it was the world's largest sewage treatment center and served as a model for modern sewage treatment technology.

The North Side plant treats an average of 280 million gallons per day (mgd), though it has a maximum capacity of 450 mgd. It draws wastewater from a 141-square-mile area and serves the 1.3 million people who live in Chicago north of Fullerton Avenue and in the suburbs of northern Cook County. Physical and biological systems treat the wastewater and remove about 90 percent of the pollutants. Solids removed from the waste stream are diverted to the Stickney Works on the Sanitary Canal for further treatment. At the end of the treatment processes, clear, treated water is discharged into the North Shore Channel.

Today the North Side plant is tied into the Deep Tunnel system (TARP). This means that only rarely during very serious storms does untreated wastewater divert into the waterways. As the TARP reservoirs are completed, even these occasional discharges will end. It is the tie-in with the deep tunnels and the resulting cleaner stream that make it feasible to move the sluice gate. But degradation of the waterway by noise, litter, and waves

from speeding powerboats constitutes a different form of pollution that will certainly occur if the locks are moved.

East of the channel and immediately north of Howard Street, a large shopping center has replaced an old Bell and Howell manufacturing plant. Here Howard Street forms the boundary between Evanston and Chicago east of the stream. Light industry dominates McCormick Boulevard south of Howard.

From Touhy Avenue to Pratt Boulevard, the enormous **Winston Towers apartment complex** fills the area along Kedzie Avenue east of the grassy channel banks. Westward, across the stream, the **Lincolnwood Town Center** shopping mall provides shopping and services to the local population. Touhy Avenue bridges the North Shore Channel and forms the boundary between Skokie to the north and Lincolnwood to the south. Devon Avenue, which also bridges the stream, separates Lincolnwood from Chicago.

Residential development dominates the area between Pratt and Devon, and the old northern **Indian Boundary Line** cuts across the channel just north of Devon. Rogers Avenue marks this line across much of Chicago's North Side. Also north of Devon on the east side of the channel is **Thillens Stadium**, a Little League baseball park sponsored by Thillens, Incorporated, an armored transportation company. The stadium is offered without charge to nonprofit organizations that sponsor teams. The Thillens family will give a $5,000 savings bond to anyone who hits the replica of the armored car situated above the scoreboard in center field.

A **U.S. Army Reserve Center** fills the east bank of the North Shore Channel between Devon and Lincoln

West Ridge

The Chicago community of **West Ridge** lies south of Howard and east of the North Shore Channel. Brickyards were established in the area in the 1890s to take advantage of the sand and clay found there. Some of these establishments migrated to this area from Bricktown, along the North Branch around Belmont Avenue.

In 1895 there were still only 127 residences in West Ridge, and they hugged the high ground of the ridge. Land to the west was either prairie or farmland, although starting in the 1890s greenhouses were established to furnish flowers to Chicago's expanding market.

After 1900 the brickyards were very active, and they bought large amounts of clay excavated from the North Shore canal bed. By the 1930s the greenhouses began to disappear in a wave of residential construction as Germans and Scandinavians joined the Luxembourgers who first farmed the area. After World War I the population climbed to forty thousand; by 1930 there were still a few factories and brickyards in the area. But as population growth continued, the brickyards dispersed, leaving little industry in this still largely residential community. West Ridge remains one of Chicago's most diverse neighborhoods, with substantial populations of Russian and Polish Jews, Germans, Irish, English, Greeks, Koreans, Indians, Filipinos, and Chinese.

Avenues; on the west is the **Lincoln Village Shopping Center.** Lincoln Avenue bridges the channel on a north-west-southeast diagonal, forming a triangular area between Devon on the north and the North Shore Channel on the east. The northwest portion of the triangle holds a multiscreen theater complex, and another such facility occupies the southeasternmost corner.

A paved trail begins at the corner where Lincoln crosses the stream north to Devon, where an in-stream aeration station roils the waterway. Canoeists must exercise caution near this system, since it produces turbulence and significantly alters buoyancy. It is possible for canoes caught in the main agitation to lose buoyancy and sink. The best rule is to pass carefully on the opposite side from the aeration station.

Lincoln Avenue was called Little Fort Road in the days of early settlement. Today, it is a commercial thoroughfare lined with stores and restaurants, auto supply shops and vegetable markets, and a number of motels near the North Shore Channel.

Peterson Avenue

South of Peterson, residences line the west bank of the North Shore Channel, and the east bank holds Legion Park Number 2. A **riverside trail** runs along the stream in the park and passes unimpeded under the bridge at Bryn Mawr Avenue.

A new **canoe museum** is being established on the west bank at Kedzie and Bryn Mawr. The museum will occupy a currently unused building on the south side of Bryn Mawr set back about 150 feet from the channel.

A large Chicago Transit Authority storage and maintenance facility follows the west side of the stream south of Bryn

Mawr. A **U.S. Marine Corps Training Center** occupies the remainder of the west bank south to Foster, while parkland continues along the east bank.

The athletic field of **North Park University** sits on the west bank south of Foster Avenue, and **East River Park** continues the greenbelt along the east bank. A new trail along the stream allows hikers to walk from Lawrence Avenue all the way north to the confluence of the North Branch of the Chicago River and the North Shore Channel. This confluence is marked by the city's only **waterfall,** and those paddling their canoes from the North Branch toward the confluence are advised to beware. The four-foot artificial waterfall at the junction can be dangerous for inexperienced paddlers, and canoeists should pull out well before reaching the falls.

The waterfall marks the southern end of the North Shore Channel. Descriptions of the Chicago River North Branch farther south are found in the appropriate sections of the text.

CHAPTER 5

THE GREAT CIRCLE TOUR

[The Chicago River] is the lowest point on the divide between the two great valleys of the Saint Lawrence and the Mississippi. The boundless regions of the West must send their products to the East through this point. This will be the gate of empire, this the seat of commerce.

Robert Cavalier de La Salle (1682)

IMAGINE AN ENCIRCLING WATER TRIP of the entire southern portion of Chicago. Such a trip would cover seventy-five miles and would lead east out of the main stem of the Chicago River, through the inner harbor, the Chicago Lock, the outer harbor, and then onto Lake Michigan. From there the route would continue sixteen miles south–southeast down the southern lakefront to the Calumet Harbor. At that point the route would leave the open waters of the lake to enter the flowing waters of the Calumet River. The river winds south and west six miles to Chicago's International Port at Lake Calumet, the limit of deep-draft navigation.

From this point onward the journey lies westward through the inland system of the Illinois lakes to the Gulf waterway. Travel initially follows the Grand and Little Calumet Rivers, then the Cal-Sag Channel to Sag Junction near the town of Lemont. Here the route veers sharply northeastward along the Chicago Sanitary and Ship Canal back toward the center of the city. The Sanitary Canal enters the South Branch of the Chicago River at Damen Avenue. Then the course follows the channel to the forks, where the town of Chicago was born. The final leg of the voyage leads eastward—once again on the main stem of the river—to dock at Michigan Avenue, the origin of the journey.

Many people are amazed that it is possible to *circumnavigate* the southern section of Chicago. Such a trip offers a unique view of the city and provides even lifelong Chicagoans with a completely new perspective. From the water the famed lakefront is unforgettable, the heavy industry and shipping of the Calumet River is awesome, and Chicago's history comes alive. From the water, Chicago becomes an even more intensely fascinating city.

MICHIGAN AVENUE

When Native Americans were the area's only inhabitants, the Chicago River was

Amid skyscrapers, the Chicago River makes its way through the city.

The double-leaf bridge at Michigan Avenue has four bridge houses, each of which carries a distinctive bas-relief sculpture. The sculptures represent themes from the city's early history: *The Discoverers, The Pioneers, Defense,* and *Regeneration.* Pictured here is the sculpture *Defense,* which commemorates the 1812 Fort Dearborn Massacre.

very different from the stream we know today. It flowed eastward out of its main stem to Lake Michigan. Today, because of engineering triumphs, the river flows westward and carries water out of the lake toward the Mississippi River. The result is that the main stem of the Chicago River is both an end and a beginning.

This imaginary journey begins where first permanent settlement began, at about Michigan Avenue and the river. Here the original river channel curved south about one-half mile to enter the lake near Monroe Street. Here, too, **Fort Dearborn** rose on a hill on the south bank. The federal government established the fort in 1803 to safeguard the portage route to the Mississippi. Fort Dearborn is now gone and so is the hill, its earth having been used in the 1850s to help raise the central city out of the mud. Bronze markers in the pavement indicate the former location of the fort.

In 1779 Chicago's first permanent settler, **Jean Baptiste Point du Sable,** established his home and trading post just east of Michigan Avenue on the north bank of the river. When DuSable lived here, the river emptied its sluggish flow into shallows and swamps near Monroe Street east of the present Michigan Avenue.

Today, **Pioneer Court,** an open space bordered by the Tribune Tower and the Equitable Building, marks the location of Du Sable's compound. Du Sable left the area in 1800, and his house and its extensive outbuildings were eventually sold to **John Kinzie,** an Indian agent and one of the new town's principal citizens. A bronze **plaque** indicates the spot where the Kinzie mansion once stood.

Other seeds of development were planted in the area. In 1847 **Cyrus McCormick** built his reaper factory here, and the manufacture of the reaper and other farm machinery became one of the engines of Chicago's economic growth. McCormick's reaper revolutionized farming by reducing the need for manual labor on Midwestern farms. This change contributed to a mass exodus from the farms to the towns, ultimately leading to a population in the United States that is about 75 percent urban.

At this same place today stands one of modern Chicago's chief landmarks, the **Michigan Avenue Bridge,** the first double-deck bascule bridge ever built. Its construction in 1920 enabled Wacker Drive to be constructed on two levels. When the bridge was completed, it set off a land boom to the north, and quiet Pine Street became bustling **North Michigan Avenue,** now the city's most fashionable shopping area.

The Michigan Avenue Bridge, designed by **Edward H. Bennett** in the Beaux Arts style, forms the southern gateway to the **Magnificent Mile.** Daniel Burnham imagined this thoroughfare as a broad avenue modeled on the great boulevards of Paris. Flags of the United States, Illinois, and Chicago fly along the bridge railings and lend excitement to this gateway to Chicago's most urbane street. The sense of the bridge as a grand portal is further enhanced by **decorative sculptures** on its four bridge houses. These bas-reliefs symbolize themes in Chicago's history and are named *The Discoverers, The Pioneers, Defense,* and *Regeneration.* The two northern bridge houses were donated to the city by chewing gum magnate William Wrigley, Jr.

Yet even this very proper bridge has not been able to completely escape Chicago's rough-and-tumble character. The bridge was scarcely two years old when Vincent "Skimmer" Drucci, a member of the Dion O'Banion gang, attempted to elude police by darting his car around the safety gates and jumping the widening space between the leaves as the bridge opened. Apparently, the police followed suit; Drucci was apprehended when his car crashed into the south end of the bridge (Hayner 1982, 5).

In 1992 the Michigan Avenue Bridge was repaired at a cost of about $31 million. During the work, a slight mistake in balance caused the south leaf of the bridge to jump off the trunnion bearings. The final repairs could not be completed until the 6.5-million-pound leaf was lifted once again into the correct position.

The famed **Wrigley Building,** with its shining white terra cotta facade sits on the north bank of the river just west of the bridge. Its "wedding cake" architectural style impressed Joseph Stalin and influenced the design of the University of Moscow. Floodlights illuminate the building at night, making it one of Chicago's most enthralling evening sights.

Before Wrigley became world famous in the chewing gum business, he manufactured soap. Since Wrigley's soap wasn't doing very well, he switched to distributing baking powder and gave away chewing gum as a premium. Like the soap, the baking powder was a disappointment. However, the gum was in great demand, and in no time, the tail began to wag the dog. Fame and fortune came when the company forgot about soap and baking powder altogether and focused on chewing gum (Achilles 1993, 59).

Not all soap manufacturers did poorly, however. Because soap was made from slaughterhouse byproducts, many soap plants developed in Chicago alongside the city's meatpacking industry.

Notable was the firm of **James S. Kirk,** who moved to Chicago in 1859 and built a factory on the site of old Fort Dearborn. In 1867 Kirk moved his enterprise across the river and built a new plant next to the McCormick Reaper works. Kirk was persistent; after his plant burned in the Great Fire in 1871, he built a new one on the same site with a 182-foot chimney. The company claimed to be the largest soap maker in the world, but the stench of soap manufacturing clashed with the North Michigan Avenue development that had begun following construction of the Michigan Avenue Bridge in the 1920s. Kirk added another plant at North Avenue on the Chicago River North Branch, and then sold his business to Procter and Gamble a year after the main stem factory was demolished (Ibid.).

Illinois Center, the largest planned development in any U.S. city, stands east of the Michigan Avenue Bridge on the south bank. Metropolitan Structures created this eighty-three-acre project on air rights over the Illinois Central rail yards. It occupies the site where one of the city's oldest structures, a freight shed, existed from 1854 until 1971.

Starting in 1969, Illinois Center was built over a period of more than twenty or so years at a cost of over $2 billion. It now contains nineteen mixed-use buildings and a golf course. Eventually, the golf course will be converted to other uses. A daytime population of eighty-five thousand works in the complex, and nearly fifteen thousand people live in Illinois Center's 7,700 apartments. A new building houses the local operations of Blue Cross–Blue Shield. An ice-plant in the basement provides energy-efficient cooling for the Center.

All of the buildings and facilities are interconnected through enclosed

The gleaming terra-cotta facade of the Wrigley Building rises above the double-deck Michigan Avenue Bridge. Nighttime illumination provides one of the most memorable sights the city has to offer. The Wrigley Building dates from 1921 and was designed by Graham, Anderson, Probst, and White.

walkways in the lower levels lined with small shops, restaurants, and bars. The maze of passages link the apartments with the more than sixteen million square feet of commercial offices sharing the complex. In addition, there are three hotel complexes with more than 5,500 rooms, and parking for more than twelve thousand cars.

The multiple levels of Illinois Center stand back a bit from the river's edge. The developers have donated the strip of land along the river to the city

for construction of a broad esplanade that will directly connect Michigan Avenue with the lakefront.

This is the section of the Chicago River where, beginning in the 1850s, huge steam elevators rose on both river-banks. Twelve elevators with a capacity of 4,095,000 bushels stored the grain that poured into Chicago from the Illinois and Michigan Canal (Andreas 1884–86, 376). These huge elevators along the river's main stem revolutionized the grain business and helped Chicago

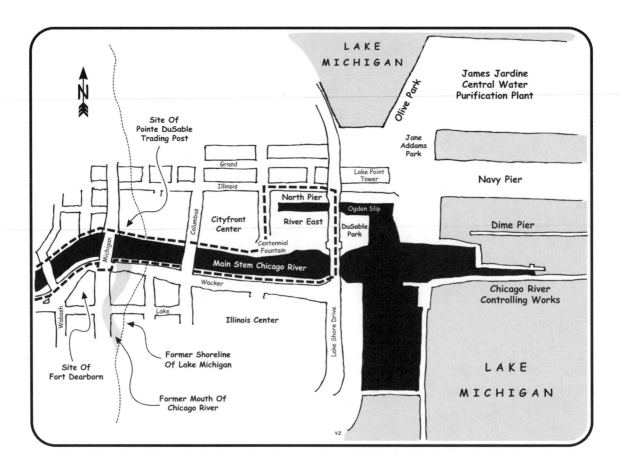

LAKE MICHIGAN

James Jardine Central Water Purification Plant

Olive Park

Jane Addams Park

Navy Pier

Lake Point Tower

Dime Pier

North Pier

Ogden Slip

River East

DuSable Park

Cityfront Center

Centennial Fountain

Main Stem Chicago River

Chicago River Controlling Works

Site Of Pointe DuSable Trading Post

Grand

Illinois

Columbus

Wacker

Lake

Michigan

Wabash

Illinois Center

Lake Shore Drive

Site Of Fort Dearborn

Former Shoreline Of Lake Michigan

Former Mouth Of Chicago River

LAKE MICHIGAN

vz

MAP 20.
Chicago River Main Stem. Note the location of the original shoreline and the natural mouth of the Chicago River. Note also the Chicago Lock and the Ogden Slip. Jean Baptiste Pointe du Sable, Chicago's first permanent settler, lived just north of the river.

become the greatest primary grain market in the world (Cronon 1991, 97–147; also Miller 1996, 106).

Another huge development, **Cityfront Center,** hugs the north bank of the river opposite Illinois Center. Prior to this development, industry still held sway on the river's north bank. Candy manufacturing and the *Chicago Tribune*'s paper docks were located here until the 1980s; earlier, this area held grain elevators, a soap factory, and McCormick's reaper works.

Like Illinois Center, Cityfront Center is a mixed-use project. It is being built on forty acres at a cost of around $3 billion. The development combines 6,000 apartments with 2,200 hotel rooms and six million square feet of office and commercial space. Major buildings at Cityfront Center now include the **University of Chicago Downtown (Gleacher) Center,** the **Sheraton Hotel,** and the **NBC Tower.** A **park** honoring Jean Baptiste Pointe du Sable is planned for the eastern end of the complex. Recently the eastern portion of this development has been renamed River East.

A **riverwalk** designed by Lohan and Associates runs along the north bank of the river. The new **Columbus Drive Bridge** was specifically designed so that the riverwalk could pass under the span. **Centennial Fountain** (now named the **Melas Fountain**) marks the eastern

The 80-story
Amoco tower
rises behind
the Hyatt
Hotel and
other build-
ings of the
vast Illinois
Center
development.

The Centennial (Melas) Fountain near the rivermouth on the north bank commemorates 100 years of the Water Reclamation District (formerly the Sanitary District). Every hour during warm weather a water canon shoots an arc of water across the channel for ten minutes.

boundary of the riverwalk and commemorates one hundred years of the Metropolitan Water Reclamation District of Chicago. This agency was established as the Sanitary District in 1889 to solve the related problems of water supply and sewage disposal for the city.

The Centennial Fountain symbolizes the fall of water through both the Great Lakes and the Illinois-Mississippi systems to the sea. It operates from 10 A.M. to midnight May 1 to October 1. A water cannon in front of the fountain shoots an arcing jet of water across the channel for ten minutes every hour on the hour (except at 3 P.M. and 4 P.M.). Boaters must beware here, lest they en-

counter an unexpected shower.

A new bascule bridge carries Columbus Drive across the river. Built in 1982 at a cost of $33 million, it is the second-largest bascule bridge in the world; only the bridge over the Bay of Cadiz in Spain is larger. Each leaf is 269 feet long and 111 feet wide. Modern welded construction produces a sleek, smooth structure. The first bridge to span the river at Columbus Drive, it connects the Illinois Center, Cityfront Center, and River East developments.

The Outer Drive Bridge, another famed double-leaf, double-deck bascule bridge, was completed in 1938 at a cost of $11 million. Franklin D. Roosevelt

CHICAGO RIVER FACT: CHICAGO HAS FOUR DOUBLE-DECK, DOUBLE-LEAF TRUNNION BASCULE BRIDGES—THE MICHIGAN AVENUE BRIDGE, THE WORLD'S FIRST, THE OUTER DRIVE BRIDGE, AND THE WELLS AND LAKE STREET BRIDGES.

Lake Point Tower, world's tallest apartment building, rises above the Chicago Lock. Its lyrical curving form makes it one of the most beautiful buildings in a city renowned for its architectural treasures.

presided over the dedication ceremonies. This bridge was constructed on two levels so that trains could cross the river on the lower level, but it was never used for railroads. In 1978, when the bridge was rebuilt, the lower level was redesigned to handle auto traffic coming from the eastward extension of Wacker Drive through Illinois Center and from the Outer Drive.

Just east of the Outer Drive Bridge is **North Pier** and the **Ogden Slip,** which was built by the Chicago Dock and Canal Company in 1869. William B. Ogden, the city's first great entrepreneur, was the company's leader, and while still practicing law in Illinois, a young Abraham Lincoln was the company's lawyer. Although the slip was built for large commercial vessels, it has been partially filled, and now small recreational boats have taken over. Restaurants and bars line this scenic old waterway, and upscale town-houses are being built along the south bank, where soap factories and grain elevators once stood.

Opposite the Ogden Slip is a turning basin on the south side of the river. In the past, slips here served coal, lumber, and grain enterprises, but today these uses are gone and the basin is used to park jumbo barges and pleasure craft. There is currently a proposal to separate this basin from the river and open it to Monroe Harbor to create additional mooring space for pleasure craft but no decision has yet been reached.

Looming over the Ogden Slip is the seventy-story **Lake Point Tower,** said to be the tallest apartment building on earth. It was built in 1968 and designed by Schipporeit-Heinrich in association with Graham, Anderson, Probst, and White, students of the famed Ludwig Mies van der Rohe, who brought his spare, less-is-more Bauhaus style to Chicago in 1938.

THE RIVERMOUTH AND HARBORS

Chicago's inner harbor lies beyond the Outer Drive Bridge. It was created in the 1870s when federal funds were made available to build breakwaters separating the harbor from the open waters of the lake. Today the area surrounding the mouth of the Chicago River is entirely artificial. The shoreline has been pushed eastward about one-half mile, and the river is separated from the lake by a delicate arrangement of piers that hold the Chicago Lock and dam.

Originally, a large sandbar diverted the river southward and blocked direct access to the lake. The mouth of the river near Monroe Street was very shallow, with a depth of about two feet. It was barely navigable by canoe, while larger vessels had to be anchored offshore and unloaded onto small craft called *lighters,* which brought the cargoes ashore.

The first federal navigation project was the construction of a lighthouse to warn ships of the shoal. It certainly was needed: the sandbar was large, totaling more than seventy acres (an acre is about the size of a football field without the end zones). Many a vessel met its end on the bar when storms swept the lake.

Jefferson Davis and other young Army engineers surveying a route for the Illinois and Michigan Canal proposed that a channel be cut through the bar to create a sheltered harbor. This channel was completed in the early 1830s when $25,000 in federal funds were matched by the State of Illinois. Soldiers from Fort Dearborn carried out the strenuous task.

But even with these improvements, "fewer than a dozen vessels dropped anchor at Chicago in 1830" (Young, in press). Nonetheless, by 1837, traffic on the river was so congested that Chicago's Common Council, predecessor of today's City Council, passed an ordinance demanding that "vessels refrain from anchoring . . . in or near the mouth of the Chicago River for more than an hour at a time" (McClellan 1966, v. 3, 2).

Water trade soon grew to enormous proportions. By 1855 more than 6,600 ships called at the river. In 1858 Caroline Kirkland acknowledged the river as "the best harbor on Lake Michigan [but nonetheless] the worst harbor and smallest river any great commercial city ever lived on" (Miller 1996, 68). But constant sand drift from the north continued to shoal the channel, making continued dredging and pier improvement necessary. Federal navigation projects followed year after year and continue to this day (Larson 1979, 59).

Today the Chicago Lock and its dam separate the Chicago River from the waters of Lake Michigan. The lock was built between 1938 and 1939 but is now too small for large lake vessels, since the lock chamber is just eighty feet wide and six hundred feet long.

The principal task of the lock is to help meter the flow of lake water into the river, a necessary function because the diversion of the water is limited to 3,200 cubic feet per second (or a little over two billion gallons per day). The original eastward flow of the river has been reversed westward toward the subcontinental divide. Literally, the river runs backward. Now it leads toward the Des Plaines River, the Mississippi River, and, ultimately, the Gulf of Mexico.

The first attempt to reverse the river came in 1871 in an effort to divert Chicago's sewage from the water intakes in Lake Michigan. This feeble effort was never very successful, and the river soon

View southeastward across the Chicago River mouth. This photograph was taken before 1930, when the Chicago Lock was built to separate the river from the lake. The old grain elevator is still there, and coal yards and manufacturing operations reach the lakefront east of the yards of the Illinois Central Railroad. (Courtesy, Illinois Central.)

resumed its lakeward flow. The herculean task was finally accomplished in 1900 with the completion of the Chicago Sanitary and Ship Canal. Even today the lock at the rivermouth usually prevents the river from backing out into the lake when heavy storms raise the river level.

When a boat enters from the lake, the water level in the lock must be lowered because the level of the Chicago River is maintained from four to six feet below lake level. Since the river is lower than the lake, lake water enters the river and flows away to the southwest.

When a lake vessel enters the lock, the lock gates behind the vessel are closed. Then the gates at the river end of the lock are partially opened. Water pours through the small opening, and the water level in the lock gradually *falls* to the river level. Strong currents in the lock make it mandatory to tie large boats against the lock wall. It is especially important for passengers to keep hands and arms inboard for safety.

When a vessel enters from the river side, after the lock gates are closed, the lakeside gates are opened slightly. Lake water then flows into the lock until the water level in the lock *rises* to lake level. Therefore, no pumps are required either to raise vessels to lake level or to lower them to the level of the river.

The Chicago Lock is a junction box, the crucial point where the open waters of the Great Lakes join the flowing inland waters. From the Chicago Lock one may sail eastward via the Saint Lawrence Seaway to the Gulf of Saint Lawrence and the North Atlantic. This route leads through Lakes Michigan, Huron, Erie, and Ontario, and the Saint Lawrence River on its way to the Atlantic. But because the surface of Lake Michigan lies 580 feet above sea level, it is necessary for ships to pass through fifteen locks to drop to sea level.

Of course, there is also a westward route to the sea. This route follows the Illinois lakes to the Gulf waterway through nine locks to the Mississippi River and the Gulf of Mexico.

North of the Chicago Lock is **Navy Pier.** This old commercial and pleasure pier dates from 1916 but it was recently rebuilt as a modern convention and recreation facility. Now tour ships line the pier's south side where in former times ships once brought cargoes from around the world.

Beyond the lock is the outer harbor that was created in 1880 by the construction of the outer breakwater system. These breakwaters provide shelter from the lake storms that sweep down from the northeast. The main entrance to Chicago Harbor through these breakwaters is 580

Navy Pier, built in 1916, stretches 3,000 feet into Lake Michigan. Its eastern end, decorated with flags, still holds the grand ballroom built as part of the original design. Now most of the pier has been completely renovated and recreational and exhibition facilities have been added.

feet wide, a happy coincidence, since lake level is 580 feet above sea level.

The **Chicago Light** guards the north side of the entrance to Chicago Harbor. For one hundred years the U.S. Coast Guard staffed this important light until automation removed the need. The old lighthouse was actually rented out as a residence for a short period in the 1980s, but it is now uninhabited.

Just to the north of the Chicago Lock is a series of pilings called City Pier Number 1. Most sailors, though, call it the **Dime Pier** because, starting in the 1930s, it was possible to fish from the pier after taking a ten-cent rowboat ride to reach it. This pier and a similar structure north of Navy Pier were built from 1914 to 1916 to protect vessels at Navy Pier from lake waves. Eventually, the northern of these two piers was removed when the artificial peninsula was built for the filtration plant.

Today a seventeen-acre artificial peninsula immediately north of Navy Pier contains the **Jardine (Central District) Water Purification Plant,** the largest filtration plant in the world, daily purifying and filtering up to 1.7 billion gallons of water for the portion of Chicago north of Pershing Road and for a host of suburban communities.

Although it was planned before World War II, the Jardine plant was not completed until 1963, and then over the objections of wealthy residents on the adjoining lakefront. The project was delayed first by World War II and then by the Korean War. In 1955–56 the site was pumped dry so that sections on the lake bottom could be constructed, where contractors discovered many

guns and knives. They also found a thirty-gallon, concrete-filled barrel from which projected two human shinbones. It appears that some of the seamier elements in Chicago's storied gangster past had used that part of the lake as a disposal area.

The Jardine plant was designed with a low profile so as not to mar lake views, and it was set amidst landscaped gardens. The foyer of its administration building holds a twenty-four-foot-long bronze bas-relief dramatizing water as the sustainer of life. Entitled "**Hymn to Water**" it was created by the late Chicago sculptor **Milton Horn.** Five circular fountains on the west side of the facility represent the five Great Lakes, and two parks grace the west end of the artificial peninsula. **Olive Harvey Park** honors a Chicago hero of the Vietnam War, and 1996 saw the completion of **Jane Addams Park,** the only Chicago park dedicated to a woman. The Jardine plant received the Outstanding Civil Engineering Achievement Award of Merit for 1965, in a national competition conducted by the American Society of Civil Engineers.

View of the North Lakefront

The north lakefront, almost all in parkland, is dominated by a wall of apartment towers. Lakeshore location has long been prized for residences, since the lake is the only scenic feature on a virtually featureless plain. In addition, the lakeshore offers cooling summer breezes and warmer winter temperatures than inland. The belt of high-value residential development continues almost uninterrupted thirty miles along the north lakeshore to Lake Forest and beyond.

Water Intake Cribs

Out in the lake are strange island structures called *cribs*, water intakes that pull lake water to the water filtration plants. The northernmost crib, built in 1915, is at Wilson Avenue. Next comes the 1892 Carter H. Harrison Crib off Lincoln Park. It was named for one of the city's most prominent and colorful mayors. This crib is paired with the William E. Dever intake (1935) named for another mayor of Chicago. Four Mile Crib dates from 1889 and stands east of Grant Park. Finally, on the city's South Side is the double-structured 68th Street Crib.

The original crib, now removed, dates from 1864. It was designed by Ellis Chesbrough, built on land, floated into position two miles from shore, and sunk to the lake-bottom clay just off Chicago Avenue. A five-foot, brick-lined tunnel was dug thirty feet below the lake bottom to connect the crib to the old pumping station on North Michigan Boulevard. At the time, this tunnel was the longest in the world (Miller 1996, 127).

Today's cribs are connected to the North and South District Filtration Plants by 16-foot tunnels in the limestone bedrock 110 feet below the lake surface. Although six cribs were built, only three currently operate. They are the Carter Harrison on the North Side and the twin cribs at 68th Street on the South Side.

Twin cribs off 68th Street on the city's South Side. Chicago pulls its drinking water from the bottom of Lake Michigan through these inlet structures.

THE DOWNTOWN LAKEFRONT

Heading south, the traveler's right-side view is of the magnificent downtown lakefront. In front of the remarkably beautiful cityscape is **Monroe Harbor.** Here a forest of sailboat masts makes it seem that the city rests on stilts. This curious illusion tells a true story because the city center literally was lifted up in the 1850s and 1860s.

Monroe Harbor is just one of Chicago's lakefront harbors. Nowadays thousands of powerboats and sailboats ply the near-shore waters of Lake Michigan. Some voyages, however, are of greater scope. Every July yachters from the nearby Columbia and Chicago Yacht Clubs and other clubs race up the entire length of Lake Michigan to **Mackinac Island.** And some truly intrepid sailors, like William Pinkney who sailed solo around the world, leave the Great Lakes altogether and test their vessels, skill, and resolve in the great world ocean.

Behind the harbor lies **Grant Park,** once called Lake Park. The western edge of the park includes the area of the old lagoon that lay between Michigan Avenue and the trestle of the Illinois Central Railroad. Much debris from the Great Chicago Fire was dumped into the lagoon, contributing to the landfill that ultimately became parkland. Some of this fire debris reemerged when the Grant Park underground garages were being built.

Grant Park now extends far to the east of the old Illinois Central trestle and includes a host of special features. At the north end of the park is an outdoor skating rink, a wildflower garden, and a special section that honors cancer survivors.

It is fitting that a section along Michigan Avenue has been set aside to honor **A. Montgomery Ward,** who worked hard and long to preserve Chicago's lakefront for all its citizens.

Many of Chicago's summer festivals are held in the park. These include the Taste of Chicago, the Blues and Jazz festivals, the Grant Park concerts, the Fourth of July fireworks, and many other events. Three underground garages provide 7,600 parking spaces.

The crown jewels of central Grant Park are the **Art Institute of Chicago** and **Buckingham Fountain.** The Art Institute houses one of the world's greatest collections of impressionist art along with a wide-ranging, world-famous general collection. The museum mounts many exhibitions of international importance that bring visitors from around the world. Its membership, the largest of any art museum in the world, now fluctuates between 130,000 and 180,000. It also operates the famed **School of the Art Institute of Chicago,** one of the premier institutions of its type in the United States.

The Art Institute occupies the site where once stood the old **Inter-State Exposition Building** or the "Crystal Palace" (Miller 1996, 178). A latter-day version has resurfaced at the new Navy Pier, where a modern Crystal Palace holds an indoor tropical garden and charming water sculptures arc above the walkways.

The southern portion of Grant Park holds many softball diamonds, where teams in a host of leagues play Chicago's own unique brand of sixteen-inch softball. This game has a long and storied history and is a hallmark of the city.

Finally, at the south end of the park, is the so-called museum campus.

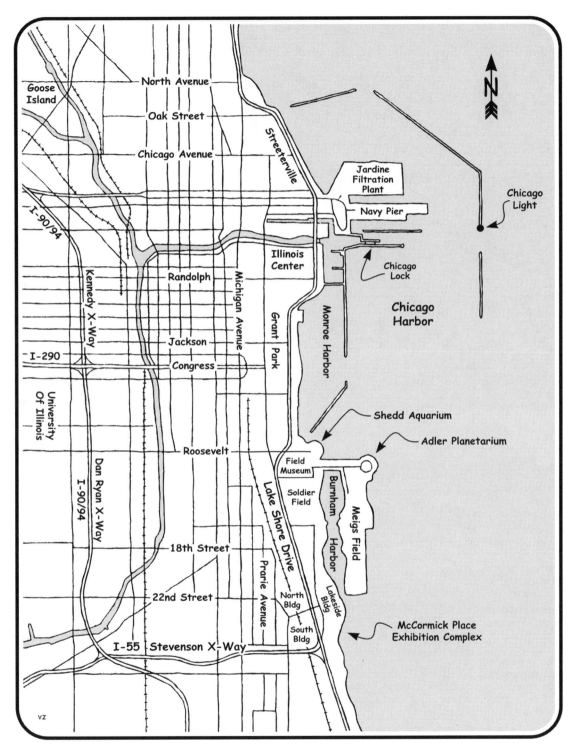

MAP 21.
Chicago's central lakefront. Note the Chicago River mouth, the Chicago Lock, and the inner and outer breakwaters.

The Adler Planetarium on the left and the Shedd Aquarium and Oceanarium on the right are two of the three world-class educational facilities of Chicago's lakefront Museum Campus. The nearby Field Museum completes the trio.

The world-famous **Field Museum of Natural History,** the **Shedd Aquarium and Oceanarium,** and the **Adler Planetarium** are located here. All are examples of the philanthropy of those few who acquired great wealth in the amazing rough-and-tumble of Chicago's dynamic commercial history.

Behind and above Grant Park rises one of the greatest urban skylines on earth. Fronting Michigan Avenue are the Art Deco buildings of the 1920s. Behind, rising high above them, are the gaunt steel-and-glass buildings of the sixties, seventies, and eighties. There is a debate among architects as to whether the skyscraper was actually "born" in Chicago. But there is no question what-

soever that much of their early development occurred here.

After the Great Fire of 1871, energetic young architects and engineers from around the world converged on the rebuilding city. **William Le Baron Jenney,** fresh from his studies at the Ecole Centrale Des Arts et Manufactures in Paris, was among them. They wrestled with the challenge of placing weighty buildings on Chicago's soft subsurface of sand and clay, and eventually found ways to support the weight by using various types of *floating* foundations.

Once techniques of foundation construction were developed, another vexing problem loomed: placing windows in walls that also had to support a building's

Buckingham Fountain

Buckingham Fountain was given to the City of Chicago in 1927 by Kate Buckingham to honor the memory of her brother Clarence. It is one of the largest fountains in the world and operates from Memorial Day to late September. Water from 133 jets bathes the intricate pink-marble decorations of the fountain, and sprays arise from the mouths of four groups of sea horses flanking the central basin. The sea horses,

designed by French sculptor Marcel Loyau, are said to represent the four states that border Lake Michigan. In addition, a huge central jet periodically pushes a column of water 150 feet into the sky.

At night the fountain is bathed in ever-changing colored lights, making it exceptionally beautiful. Nearly every day, foreign and domestic visitors come to view and be photographed (and in some cases to be married) in front of

this celebration of Chicago's water heritage. The colored lights that enliven the summer fountain are also used during the winter to make the fountain a year-round attraction.

Buckingham Fountain's water and light shows were controlled for almost thirty years by a computer in Atlanta, Georgia. Recently, however, the fountain was taken apart, reconstructed, and reassembled during

a general repair and upgrading. Computers were installed on-site, so the fountain's jets of water and play of lights are now controlled automatically by local computers. As a result of the reconstruction, the water jets are more energetic than ever, and 120 new lights bring the total to 780 for more-complex lighting displays.

The Roosevelt Road Bridge opens to allow passage of a flotilla of sailboats moving down-river toward winter storage. River City occupies the right bank, and the Sears Tower looms in the distance.

weight. Building interiors were dark because windows had to be few and small to maintain wall strength. This difficulty was finally overcome by the use of iron and, later, steel. These materials, made in Chicago, were used to create interior load-bearing skeletons that took the weight off the walls. With the weight shifted to the skeleton, walls could be opened up with larger, more numerous windows. Chicagoans improved the elevator that Elisha Graves Otis had developed, and the final piece of the puzzle fell into place (Miller 1996, 310). Tall structures became practical.

Jenney designed one of the first buildings termed a true skyscraper, the **Home Insurance Building.** Unfortunately, it met the fate of many of Chicago's historic structures: it was razed to make way for a parking lot. Happily, Chicago still hosts the tallest building ever built with load-bearing walls. It is the **Monadnock Building** (north section), at the southwest corner of Dearborn and Jackson Streets.

The building's north section was designed by John Wellborn Root of the firm of Burnham and Root. One enters this section of the building through walls eight feet thick. But adoption of the new technology was rapid, and by the time the southern section of the building was built, an interior iron skeleton had been incorporated in the design.

Of special interest is Adler and Sullivan's great **Auditorium Theater Building** on Michigan Avenue. It is a triumph of Victorian splendor. Sullivan's nature-based decoration animates the bold, forward-looking design. When it was built in 1889, its tower was the tallest structure in the city, and people flocked to its observation deck to view the spectacle of Chicago.

Chicago has three of the ten tallest buildings in the world. The **Sears Tower** was built in 1974. It is 1,454 feet high (104 stories) and dominates the southern end of the sweeping panorama of skyscrapers that mark the central city. Up until 1996 the Sears Tower bore the title of World's Tallest Building, but the new Petronas Towers in Kuala Lumpur, Malaysia, now hold that distinction.

Sears Tower illustrates perfectly the effect of the interior skeleton. Its walls are glass—just an envelope to keep out the weather, carrying no structural effect whatsoever. Thus, the original quest to increase window size in buildings with load-bearing walls has now produced buildings in which entire walls are windows.

Just north of Grant Park is the 1,136-foot (eighty-story) white **Amoco** tower, which was built in 1974. Still further north, the 1,105-foot (one hundred-story) **John Hancock Center** dates from 1970.

Chicago's panorama of great buildings is a unique treasure. Visitors come from around the world to view this living museum of architecture, featuring works from some of the most original and creative architects the nation has produced. These include Louis Sullivan, Frank Lloyd Wright, William Le Baron Jenney, Daniel Burnham, John Wellborn Root, Mies van der Rohe, Harry Weese, Walter Netsch, Helmut Jahn, and a host of others.

Because of this unique collection of architectural riches, the Chicago Architecture Foundation sponsors a host of architectural tours of different sections of the city. Information on the foundation is given in appendix B.

THE SOUTH LAKEFRONT

12th Street

The Circle Tour now heads out of the south end of the outer breakwater and passes east of the Adler Planetarium and Meigs Field. The planetarium was built on an island called **Northerly Island.** **The Burnham Plan** of 1909 proposed that a string of six offshore islands be built to house a series of parks. Only the northernmost of these islands has so far been built—hence its name. During the **Century of Progress** world's fair in 1933, visitors to the planetarium waited for hours on a wind- and wave-swept causeway that connected Northerly Island with the mainland.

Later, the island was connected to land by an artificial peninsula and extended southward to provide additional parkland. Before the park could be developed, however, the area was turned into a one-runway airport in 1948 called **Merrill C. Meigs Field.** After fifty years of operation, the airfield is now the subject of intense debate and political bickering.

In 1997 Mayor Richard M. Daley closed the airport when its lease expired, in an attempt to rebuild the area as the originally planned park. Governor Jim Edgar, however, wishes to keep the airport open, and at the time of this writing struck a peculiar compromise to keep the field operating for five more years and then allow the city to turn it into parkland.

Between the airport peninsula and the mainland lies **Burnham Harbor,** yet another of the chain of lakefront harbors that grace the Lake Michigan shoreline. It is part of **Burnham Park,** which stretches from Solidarity Drive (12th Street) south to Promontory Point at 57th Street—all landfill. This was the long, narrow site of the Century of Progress world's fair. Nowadays, Lake Shore Drive occupies the space.

Inland from the museum campus and Soldier Field is the new **Central Station Project.** This mixed-use development covers seventy-two acres and includes a variety of apartments and townhouses along with projected commercial and retail development. It is an excellent example of downtown residential development that is bringing new life to the central city.

Tucked in amidst the industrial buildings west of Soldier Field lies **Prairie Avenue.** Many of the city's richest, most influential families lived along this street, including Marshall Field, George Pullman, and Philip Armour, the Chicago Trinity, as they were called. They were also the kingpins of Chicago's emerging aristocracy of astronomical wealth and vast enterprise. William Wallace Kimball, John Glessner, and Charles Hutchinson were their neighbors.

The nicety of class distinctions that separated the Prairie Avenue crowd from the *merely* wealthy living farther south is reflected in a comment given in Arthur Meeker's book *To Chicago With Love.* He writes of a conversation with his mother in which he pressed her about the status of the people below 23rd Street. Her answer: "We *knew* them dear, but it wasn't quite the same thing. We asked them to our weddings, not our dinner parties." (Meeker 1955, 32).

Prairie Avenue life was lavish. In 1886, when Marshall Field, Jr., was seventeen, the family threw a Mikado Ball. Since the theme was Japanese, the Fields had a miniature Japanese village built inside their home, and all guests wore Japanese costumes. Sherry's from

An 1892 view north up the Chicago lakeshore from 23rd Street. Its shabby, decrepit, and rag-tag appearance underscores the magnitude of Montgomery Ward's triumph that the lakeshore should remain "forever open, clear and free of any buildings or other obstruction whatever." This decision ultimately led to Chicago's system of lakefront parks. For his efforts he was scorned by those in power and vilified by the press. But his persistence and enlightened civic zeal provided an asset beyond compare for the growing city. (Courtesy, Chicago Historical Society.)

In the late 19th century, Prairie Avenue on the city's Near South Side was "the shady street that held the sifted few."

New York City catered the affair and brought two private railcars of linen, silver, and food from the East.

Party favors were imported from Japan and two of them were designed by artist James NcNeill Whistler, famed for his mother and whose grandfather had been the first to command Fort Dearborn. The party cost more than $75,000 in 1886 dollars. (Dedmon 1983, 118–19).

Today the Glessner and Kimball homes remain along the nearly deserted avenue, echoing an age when plutocrats lived mostly in the city and on the South Side. Much of the activity on this storied street now comes from docents leading architectural tours and basking in the reflected glory of the area's fabled past.

It is curious that Prairie Avenue, "the Olympus of the great gods of Chicago" (Miller 1996, 227), developed virtually on the site of the **Fort Dearborn Massacre** of August 15, 1812. Here an uprising by a band of Potawatomi led to the slaughter of fifty-three soldiers and civilians. George Pullman commissioned a memorial sculpture of the event for the lawn of his mansion. It was dedicated in 1893 and stands there today, but Pullman's mansion is long gone.

Chicago's central position, unequalled transportation connections, and the energy of its early business leaders made the city the nation's leader for conventions and business meetings. This role began in 1847, when Ogden organized the **Rivers and Harbors Convention.**

Ogden arranged the meeting with a dual purpose in mind. He wished to marshall support for additional federal funds for harbor improvements in the Midwest, and he also wished to impress eastern investors with the benefits the new Illinois and Michigan Canal offered for railroad development.

History records the success of his plan, since the canal proved a major incentive that early-on brought railroads to Chicago. Miller states: "Chicago is the ideal example of the unassailable economic combination of rail and water. Wherever nineteenth-century railroads met an important navigable stretch of water, urban growth invariably occurred. . ." (Ibid., 93).

However, the Democratic Party platform at the time asserted that no federal monies should be expended to develop harbor improvements except on the Atlantic coast. Many felt that this position was both illogical and ridiculous, so the Rivers and Harbors Convention meetings were organized to secure federal funds for many necessary harbor and navigational improvements. More particularly, the convention provided a forum to criticize President Polk's recent veto of funds for harbor improvement in Chicago and the Great Lakes and to press for their reinstatement.

All told, more than ten thousand delegates crowded into the young city, which at that time had a population of

only 16,859. So many visitors descended on Chicago that most who came were forced to sleep and eat on the vessels that brought them. The meetings were held in an enormous tent near the center of town that had seating for about four thousand delegates. The other six thousand had to stand around the edge of the tent and try to view the proceedings over the heads of those lucky enough to be seated (Larson 1979, 70). This, then, was the first and relatively the largest gathering of the many that have since made Chicago "America's convention city" (Miller 1996, 93).

To commemorate the Fort Dearborn massacre, George Pullman commisioned a memorial sculpture that still stands on Prairie Avenue.

1919 Race Riots

The south lakefront has been witness to tragedy as well as triumph, ugliness as well as beauty. No episode was more tragic or uglier than the insanity that set off the worst race riots the city has ever suffered. In 1919, after the black population had risen due to large-scale migration from the South during World War I, racism sundered the city. Ironically, Chicago had earlier been a bastion of safety in the fight against slavery.

The greatly enlarged African-American population, which had doubled from 1916 to 1918, was confined within the very limited housing of the so-called Black Belt on the city's South Side. The suffocating segregation extended even to the beaches along the lakefront. Custom dictated that the beach at Twenty-fifth Street was for blacks while the Twenty-ninth Street beach catered to whites only.

The two beaches "were separated by a line unseen and a law unwritten. . . . An invisible line stretched the sand into Lake Michigan, parting the races . . ." When Eugene Williams, a black teenager, crossed that invisible line in the water, he was pelted with stones and was either struck and killed or drowned from exhaustion. The subsequent riots raged for five deadly days and resulted in the wounding of five hundred people and the deaths of thirty-eight (Armstrong 1997; Spear 1967).

Amidst white savagery, a black man is questioned by soldiers. (Photo by Jun Fujita. Courtesy, Chicago Historical Society.)

from

Business meetings, conventions, trade shows, and tourism bring money from outside the city to the city. This fresh capital helps to build the city, and it sets off round-after-round of additional spending. Each outside dollar works like a lever and has more than one dollar's benefit. This multiplier effect is so beneficial to the city's economy that today tourism is considered Chicago's core business.

Since the Rivers and Harbors Convention in 1847, Chicago has been the nation's premier meeting center. The city is working hard to maintain that position. An enormous new South Building with a cost of over $700 million has just been added to the already mammoth convention facilities of **McCormick Place.** The North and East Buildings attracted more than four million visitors yearly before the South Building was added. Now the combined buildings at McCormick Place give Chicago a convention and meeting center with 2.2 million square feet of exhibit space—more than any other city in the western hemisphere. This gigantic meeting center sits on the lakeshore just south of Soldier Field, a triumph of the city's spirit, geography, and imagination.

The enormous new South Building at the McCormick Place complex opened in 1997 at a cost of more than $700 million.

THE LAKESHORE

26th Street

South of McCormick Place are **Mercy Hospital** and the combined hospital facilities of the **Columbia Michael Reese Medical Center,** now operated by the Columbia Health Maintenance Organization. These hospitals are surrounded by the high-rise, middle-income apartments of **Prairie Shores, Lake Meadows,** and **South Commons,** built in the 1950s and 1960s as the first project funded under Title I of the Federal Housing Act of 1949. It had taken the federal government more than twenty years to condemn and secure title to some of the worst slum areas in the city. Once title was secured, the land was given over as a subsidy to the developers.

Next to the Lake Meadows complex on the south stands the **Douglas Monument,** topped by a statue of the statesman. Designed by Leonard Volk, this memorial marks the grave of the first nationally prominent Chicago politician: Democratic leader and U.S. Senator **Stephen A. Douglas,** "the Little Giant." Although Douglas died in 1861, his body was not placed in the crypt at the monument base until 1881 because disruption from the Civil War and a lack of funding delayed the project.

The Douglas memorial stands near Cottage Grove Avenue and 33rd Place on land that was once part of Douglas' fifty-three-acre estate, on the south lakefront. The park in which the memorial is located has the distinction of being the smallest state park in Illinois. It is slightly south of **Groveland Park,** a private residential park that Douglas himself developed before the Civil War.

The area around the Douglas tomb was at the junction of two Indian trails

that later became Vincennes and Cottage Grove Avenues. The first development in the area was **Myrick's Tavern,** at what is now 29th Street, which had pens to hold cattle that had been driven along the trails. Charles Cleaver built a slaughterhouse in 1851 on land south of the tavern. The following year he opened a soap factory and built new workers' cottages. His growing development began to be known as **Cleaverville.**

In 1856 John G. Sherman bought the Myrick property and opened a stockyard that operated on the site until 1865. Of course, the rapid expansion of Chicago toward the end of the 1800s consumed Cleaverville, and it subsequently became part of the Oakland community. Nearby was the site of the first University of Chicago, which ultimately closed because of lack of funds. This site was donated to the university by Senator Douglas.

During the Civil War, **Camp Douglas** was established immediately north of the present site of the Douglas Monument where the Prairie Shores development now stands. The camp first served as a training facility but was ultimately converted to house Confederate prisoners of war. Several thousands died and their remains lie buried today in **Oak Woods Cemetery** on the city's South Side.

The south lakeshore is very different from the shore on the city's North Side, largely because of the presence of the Illinois Central Railroad. Stephen Douglas had sold land in the Lake Calumet area to the IC railroad, which petitioned the city council to allow it to enter the city along the south lakefront. Initially, the directors of the Illinois Central wished to bring the railroad into the city from the southwest along the

Chicago River, where it would have ready access to the industries located there. But with prodding from Douglas they settled on a lakefront route, since it gave them connection to the city's river-mouth harbor.

In those days, Lake Michigan lapped at the eastern edge of Michigan Avenue. Lake storms often destroyed large portions of the parkland along the shore and swept water over the road and against the doors of the mansions that lined the avenue. It was clear that a breakwater was necessary to protect the shoreline. However, the wealthy landowners along Michigan Avenue

refused to bear the entire cost of the improvement, asserting it was for the benefit of the entire city.

Douglas, John Wentworth, and others who stood to gain from the lakefront route supported the idea that the railroad should enter along the shoreline. They believed the Illinois Central would take whatever steps were necessary to protect their right-of-way and so safeguard the lakeshore without cost to the taxpayers.

The idea of a railroad dominating the lakefront and destroying the amenity of a scenic shoreline set off legal battles over lakefront land use that continue to

A view of Michigan Avenue from Park Row in 1866. At that time, the lakeshore lay far to the west of its current location. (From a drawing by Louis Kurz. Courtesy, Chicago Historical Society.)

this day. The recent acrimonious fight over Meigs Field, the city's lakefront airport, is but the latest example.

As we have learned, Gurdon Hubbard, William Thornton, and William Archer had held back lakefront land from sale, asserting that it should be "Public ground—a common to remain forever open, clear and free." This doctrine has echoed through Chicago's history and motivated the efforts of A. Montgomery Ward, Daniel Burnham, Edward Bennett, Mayor Richard M. Daley, and today's citizen's watchdog group, the Friends of the Parks.

In 1852 a compromise was ultimately struck between the city council and Illinois Central, that granted the railroad a three hundred-foot-wide easement of lake bottom land on which to build a trestle linking its southern lines with the rivermouth harbor area. This course was supported by North and West Side property owners, who feared their taxes would rise to pay for a breakwater if the railroad could not be induced to do it. Wealthy landowners along Michigan Avenue, on the other hand, asserted that they paid high prices for their land precisely because it was to remain forever clear and free. Finally, after many complex maneuvers, the compromise was enacted (Wille 1972, 28).

The Illinois Central Railroad entered the city via a trestle along the lakefront that created a lagoon that stabilized the shore. It was granted additional land, however, and turned the trestle into a causeway. This created not a bucolic lagoon but a debris-filled industrial basin that cut off Michigan Avenue from the lake and prevented high-quality residential construction along the shore. To make matters worse, the railroad itself was an eyesore, and rail authorities steadfastly refused to fill in the land between the causeway and the shore to create a park.

Members of the state legislature ultimately agreed to let Illinois Central purchase all of the area between the trestle and the shore, thus effectively ending the idea of a lakefront parkland. Apparently, the legislators were persuaded to arrive at this decision by the railroad's disbursements of monies to these public-spirited officials. After continuing public uproar, the legislature voided the sale, and the railroad took them to court. The matter was finally resolved during the early years of this century by the U.S. Supreme Court, which ruled that the state did have the right to void the sale (Miller 1996, 102).

In the meantime, the railroad had filled in the old lagoon, so the deal finally benefited Chicago's citizens by enlarging the park. However, the presence of the railroad with its smoke, vibration, and noise was part of the reason that wealthy residents in the area ultimately followed Potter Palmer to the North Side.

Beginning about 1871, the Illinois Central was placed in a below-grade cut along the shore south to about 47th Street. From there it was eventually placed on an elevated embankment to eliminate grade crossings in east Hyde Park. Yet even with this accommodation, the presence of the railroad inhibited residential construction on the south lakefront.

35th Street

The low-lying shoreline from 35th to 47th Streets is all artificial; Lake Shore Drive and Burnham Park continue along this stretch of man-made land. The adjoining communities of **Douglas, Oakland,** and **North Kenwood** began as wealthy neighborhoods but now are among the poorest in the city.

THE GREAT CIRCLE TOUR

In the fifties and sixties, slum clearance and public housing construction was concentrated here. Unfortunately, the high-rise public housing structures built by the Chicago Housing Authority proved to be a security nightmare and costly to maintain. Today most of these units are vacant and awaiting demolition as the area struggles to renew itself.

Meanwhile, older and more interesting homes along the interior boulevards are being restored, and new housing is making its appearance, especially along Lake Park Avenue, King Drive (formerly South Parkway), and Drexel Boulevard. The city has recently installed planters in the median on King Drive and adorned the boulevard with statuary and charming bus-stop benches, each of which is a unique artwork.

In addition, subareas such as **the Gap** still contain structures of outstanding quality and serve as centers for renovation. This small neighborhood, situated between 33rd and 35th Streets on Calumet Avenue, boasts many distinguished homes designed by prominent architects and includes a group of apartments designed in Tudor style by the young Frank Lloyd Wright (Pacyga and Skerrett 1986).

Today the first steps are being taken to renovate the Oakland community and nearby sections of Douglas and North Kenwood. One indicator of an upturn is that many of the worst structures have been razed—almost 70 percent of the area stands vacant. With its lakefront vistas and excellent public transportation intact, the future of the area looks brighter. Perhaps deconcentration of the poor through scattered-site public housing and sensitive redevelopment of these old lakefront communities will, at last, provide residents with safer and more appealing neighborhoods.

LAKE MICHIGAN

The Circle Tour continues south on the broad back of Lake Michigan. This is the third largest of the Great Lakes and the only one that lies entirely within the United States. It is, therefore, an inland waterway and not covered by the Boundary Waters Treaty with Canada. Consequently, antisubmarine warfare exercises were conducted on the lake during World War II. Recently, divers have found and raised fighter aircraft of that period from the lake bottom.

The Great Lakes are a priceless resource, since they contain 95 percent of the total freshwater supplies of North America. They furnish drinking water for twenty-four million people in eight states and two Canadian provinces. Lake Michigan, Chicago's almost unlimited freshwater resource, is celebrated locally with a number of large fountains.

By contrast, water-starved southern California has had to bring water from the Colorado River and from the mountains of northern California to serve its growing populations. Even so, supplies are barely adequate. For more than twenty years, regional committees have studied various ways to increase the water supply. Amazingly, their ideas have included building a pipeline two thousand miles across mountains, plain, and deserts to divert water from the Great Lakes, a plan being actively reconsidered today.

Lake Michigan is approximately 307 miles long and about 118 miles across at its widest point. Its 22,300-square-mile surface lies 580 feet above mean sea level in New York State, and its level rises and falls approximately 6 feet through an 11 1/2-year cycle.

Lake Michigan is made up of two basins separated by a boundary slightly

The *Windy*, a high-tech four-masted excursion ship operating in Chicago, with the Loop skyscrapers in the background.

north of Milwaukee. The deep northern basin is swept by strong currents. At its deepest point, its rugged bottom lies 923 feet below the surface, that is, about 340 feet *below* sea level.

By contrast, the southern Lake Michigan basin is much shallower. Its bottom is smooth, and its currents are weak. This presents a problem, since one of the world's largest concentration of industry lines the lake's southern shore. Industrial pollution entering the southern basin takes many years to disperse northward by natural processes. And because Lake Michigan alone supplies drinking water to more than eleven million people, a major pollution event could imperil this resource and the populations that depend upon it.

Lake Michigan is linked with Lake Huron, and the two operate as a single hydraulic unit. From time to time it has been claimed that the Chicago diversion of lake water has adversely affected lake levels. But while the Chicago diversion is limited to 3,200 cubic feet of water per second, average evaporation alone from the two lakes removes 87,000 cubic feet of water each second.

The Great Lakes' Unwanted Residents

The Great Lakes are connected by the Saint Lawrence Seaway to the world's oceans. Because of this connection, the lakes have been invaded by a variety of exotic plants and animals over the past forty years. The sea lamprey was such an invader; it took a heavy toll on lake salmon until a method was found to control it. In addition, alewives, water fleas, the European ruffe, and the goby have entered the lakes' ecosystem, negatively affecting native species of lake fish.

But the most notorious of the invading species so far is the **zebra mussel.** This small, striped shellfish, one to two inches across, entered the lakes in 1984, when a ship from the Baltic region accidentally carried zebra mussel larvae in its ballast water. When the ballast was pumped into the Detroit River, the larvae were unwittingly introduced into the lakes.

These small creatures attach themselves to any hard surface underwater. Unfortunately, this means that they attach to the hulls of ships, rendering them less efficient and seaworthy. It also means that they cover underwater sections of docks and piers, sometimes making them unusable. Further, they attach themselves to water intake pipes that lead to public water supplies and to atomic reactors. In the latter case, they may block essential cooling water from reaching the reactors with possible catastrophic consequences.

These creatures breed at an alarming rate: one female may lay as many as thirty thousand to forty thousand eggs in a single year. As a result, the mussels are present in all of the Great Lakes and, through the Chicago diversion, the Mississippi River system and its tributaries.

A meeting organized in Ann Arbor, Michigan, by the U.S. Fish and Wildlife Service and Detroit Edison in 1989 concluded that since there is no known way to control these pests as yet, water intakes, ship hulls, and dock facilities must be designed to minimize their impact.

47th Street

At 47th Street a red buoy marks a shallow area known as the **Hyde Park Shoals.** This street also marks the northern boundary of the **South Kenwood–Hyde Park** communities. Although one of the most racially integrated communities in the nation, it is much less integrated economically. The Hyde Park–Kenwood community focal point is the **University of Chicago.** It includes middle-class families and many students, but overall it remains an island of high income in a sea of poverty.

Also at 47th Street, the character of lakefront development changes dramatically. Instead of high-rise public housing units, there are high-quality apartments serving the university community. A collection of particularly distinguished cooperative apartments stands along 49th Street. These include the Art Deco masterpieces the **Powhattan** and the **Narragansett.** Because of the presence of these two buildings, the whole area became known as Indian Village.

Up to the end of World War II, the **Chicago Beach Resort Hotel** stood on Hyde Park Boulevard at 51st Street. Its swimming beaches disappeared in the 1920s, when a road that became Lake Shore Drive in the 1940s was extended to Hyde Park. During the war, the old hotel became a hospital and later the headquarters for the U.S. Fifth Army. After the war the building was razed, and an apartment building took its place.

Late-summer swimmers crowd the beach at 56th Street and the lake. Chicago's almost unbroken system of lakefront parks provides many swimming beaches and other facilities for the city's residents.

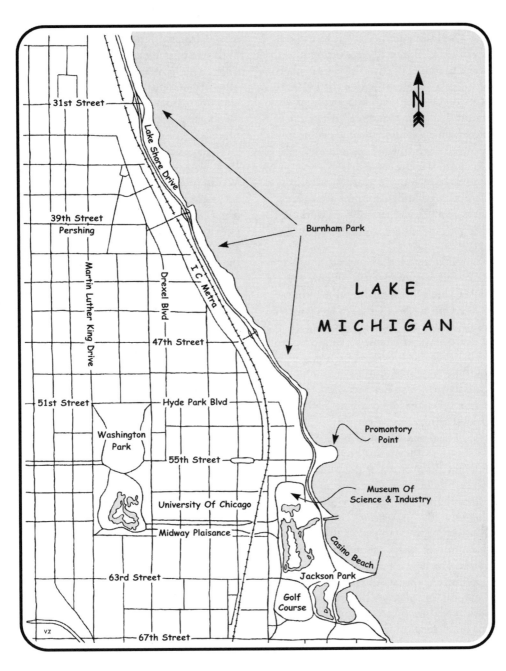

31st Street

Lake Shore Drive

39th Street
Pershing

Burnham Park

I. C. Metra

Martin Luther King Drive

Drexel Blvd

47th Street

LAKE

MICHIGAN

51st Street

Hyde Park Blvd

Washington
Park

55th Street

Promontory
Point

University Of Chicago

Museum Of
Science & Industry

Midway Plaisance

Casino Beach

63rd Street

Jackson Park

Golf
Course

vz

67th Street

MAP 22.
The mid-
south
Chicago
lakeshore.
An unbroken
park rims the
shore.

Beginning in the 1890s, Kenwood became, like Prairie Avenue before it, home to some of the wealthiest members of Chicago's mercantile elite. In 1910 the Kenwood branch of the elevated rapid transit line (now abandoned) was completed, giving middle-income people access to the Kenwood community. Subsequently, starting around 1920, wealthy residents began moving to the suburbs as increasing pollution from the stockyards and steel mills and an influx of working-class people changed the character of the neighborhood.

After a period of decline, South Kenwood reasserted itself as home to highly paid professionals and members of the University of Chicago faculty. It also contains the mansions of the leaders of the **Nation of Islam,** organized by the late Elijah Muhammad. His regal dwelling is located at 49th and Woodlawn, with homes of similar design for other high-ranking leaders located nearby.

The development of both Kenwood and Hyde Park was greatly aided by the decision of the Illinois Central Railroad in the 1850s to operate commuter trains on its right-of-way along the south lakefront. Town centers formed near the stations. At first, both communities were rural retreats or summer resorts near the mushrooming metropolis. They were both parts of the Township of Lake, which extended from 39th Street southward and included a few other small towns. Hyde Park and Kenwood became part of the new Township of Hyde Park in 1861 after some of these small settlements were given separate township status. Hyde Park then extended from State Street to the lake and from 39th to 103rd Streets (Pacyga and Skerrett 1986, 372–77).

Ultimately, the Township of Hyde Park voted for annexation to Chicago in 1889. This outcome, however, came only after acrimonious debate between patrician forces from Hyde Park and Kenwood and working-class residents from other sections of the township.

Paul Cornell, who developed Hyde Park, worked assiduously after the Civil War to promote the development of parks south of Chicago. After a number of defeats, park proponents finally won support from the state government to create the parkland; Cornell became known as the Father of the South Park System. Ultimately, Jackson Park, the Midway Plaisance, and Washington Park—all designed by Frederick Law Olmsted—framed Hyde Park with parkland.

Today the University of Chicago dominates Hyde Park. It extends for a mile along both sides of the **Midway Plaisance,** and its towers rise behind the apartments that line the lakeshore. In addition to being one of the great universities of the world, the university is one of the largest employers in Chicago. Its mix of characteristics illustrates both its international prominence and its urban location. On the one hand, it has been home to more nobel laureates than any other university on earth; on the other, its private police force was, for a time, second only to that of the City of Chicago and was larger than the force of the State of Illinois. Today it numbers about 115 full- and part-time patrol officers and supervisors.

In the 1950s the university felt threatened as decaying neighborhoods encroached upon Hyde Park. It spearheaded a massive urban renewal program that resulted in the demolition of more than 140 acres of buildings. Gone was the **57th Street artists' colony,** which occupied charming wooden structures built for the 1893 World's Columbian Exposition. Also razed were many of the small bars, restaurants, and theaters that gave Hyde Park its gritty but exciting texture. Gone, too, were old four- and five-story walkups that housed increasing numbers of the urban poor.

While many were bitter over the drastic renewal effort, Hyde Park and the university weathered the storm. New restaurants and stores have appeared, returning some of the neighborhood's former character. Within the past five years, housing has been developed on nearly every piece of vacant land in Hyde Park, and many of the oversize lots in the neighborhood have been subdivided for development.

Clearly, Hyde Park benefits from its lakefront location and the amenities offered by the university and **Jackson Park.** The park begins at 57th Street, where a promontory locally called the Point juts into the lake. It features beaches, harbors for pleasure craft, an eighteen-hole golf course, and a driving range. Tennis courts and soccer fields provide additional sports opportunities.

The wooded island designed by Olmsted for the World's Columbian Exposition is now the **Paul Douglas Nature Preserve.** In warm weather, docents from the Audubon Society conduct early morning bird walks here. During the world's fair, the Japanese government built a large teahouse on the island, where it remained until World War II, when it burned down mysteriously. It was replaced by a smaller facility and later by a small Japanese garden. The garden fell into disrepair until, in spring 1996, Chicago's Sister City of Osaka donated $250,000 to build a magnificent

entrance gate and to reconfigure and refurbish the garden. It is now an almost unknown gem of the Chicago Park District, and many special events are held there each summer.

Jackson Park is a key element in Chicago's remarkable network of parks and boulevards encircling the innermost city. Recent federal grants have renewed these historic, but deteriorating boulevards through the **Boulevard Restoration Plan** of 1994. Today planters, street sculptures, antique street lamps, and banners proclaim this ongoing effort.

The southern portion of Jackson Park holds the **La Rabida Children's Hospital and Sanitarium.** It is named for a replica of the monastery of La Rabida, Spain, which was featured at the World's Columbian Exposition in 1893. A longtime resource for neighboring communities, the hospital treats chronically ill children from low-income families.

The classical entrance gate to the Osaka Garden in Jackson Park. This garden, rebuilt with funds from Chicago's sister city Osaka, Japan, occupies the site where Japan built the classical Japanese building, the Ho-o-den, during the World's Columbian Exposition in 1893.

The World's Columbian Exposition

Jackson Park was created by **Frederick Law Olmsted** on land originally developed as the site of the fabulously successful 1893 World's Columbian Exposition. Because of its "reputation as a convention center, its unrivaled rail connections, [and] its proven capacity for carrying through big municipal projects" (Miller 1996, 379), Chicago won the coveted honor of hosting the event. The citizen's planning committee, formed in the summer of 1889, was a pantheon of Chicago's moneyed elite. The committee appointed Daniel Burnham director of works, and their shared mutual leadership, intelligence, audacity, political influence, and wealth created "an American Venice out of an unsightly split of sand and swamp water" (Ibid., 381). The Beaux Art architecture of the fair was an effort by Chicago's "self annointed urban elite . . ." to reinstate classical virtues through harmonious surroundings (Ibid., 492).

The fair was a miniature city, with its own "sewage, water, and electric-power plants; fire, police, street cleaning, and governing bodies; and the most advanced urban transportation system in the world" (Ibid., 491). Because Chicago's water supply was often polluted and always unpleasant to the taste, water for the fair was piped from near Waukesha, Wisconsin, and then passed through a highly advanced purification system.

An almost imperial entrance connected the fair with Lake Michigan and led to a Court of Honor surrounding a reflecting basin. Olmsted designed lagoons, islands, and channels for the grounds so that every major building fronted on water. Many visitors arrived at the fair by lake vessel, and thousands rode on gondolas imported from Venice through the canal dug along the Midway Plaisance.

The World's Columbian Exposition was one of the most significant events in post–Civil War America. It was also the greatest tourist attraction of its time and represented a turning point in Chicago's history. With its stupendously successful fair, Chicago had vanquished the effects of its devastating Great Fire and had come of age.

The **Palace of Fine Arts** was the only major building that remained after the fairgrounds were razed. It later became the first Field Museum until 1919. After the museum moved into its new building on 12th Street, Julius Rosenwald donated $7.5 million to renovate the structure and transform it into the Museum of Science and Industry, now the world's busiest museum. At this writing, the museum is constructing a large underground garage and adding southeast and southwest wings to its already huge building.

Chicago's 1893 world's fair—the World's Columbian Exposition—symbolized the city's recovery from the devastating fire of 1871 and its arrival as one of the great cities of the world. The area that was to become Jackson Park was transformed from swamp-like conditions into the "White City" of the fair. This is a view across the west end of the central basin surrounded by the spectacular but temporary fair pavilions. (Courtesy, Chicago Historical Society.)

The South Shore Country Club has gained a new lease on life as the South Shore Cultural Center, operated by the Chicago Park District.

67th Street

Sixty-seventh Street forms the southern boundary of Jackson Park and the northern edge of the **South Shore** community. For many years it also formed the northern boundary of the exclusive **South Shore Country Club.** The club occupied a beautiful location where the lakeshore turns slightly toward the southeast. As a result, the view from the elegant ballrooms was to the north, toward the heart of Chicago. The club catered to some of the richest families of the city, including the Potter Palmers and the Marshall Fields. It also was, in the custom of the times, restricted so that neither Jews nor African Americans were permitted to become members.

In the later stages of the club's history, membership rules were relaxed as white flight from the area reduced the pool of potential members. Eventually, the club was sold to the Chicago Park District and added to the city's magnificent system of lakefront parks. The beautiful clubhouse was restored to its former glory. Though it reopened in late 1984, the full restoration took several more years and cost about $11.5 million. Today the old country club is called the **South Shore Cultural Center.**

Now the patrician clubhouse rooms that front on the lake may be rented for weddings, business functions, and other events. And the building hosts art exhibits, musical performances, community functions, and many other gatherings. In the summer, jazz, blues, and gospel festivals are staged on the broad lawns and the lovely beaches are filled with swimmers from the South Shore community.

South Shore occupies the area between 67th Street and 79th Street along the south lakeshore. This fascinating community was developed after the World's Columbian Exposition closed in Jackson Park, immediately to its north. The entire area was low-lying and swampy, with a great deal of surface water. One section of the community was found to be a few inches higher than the general level and was immediately and, ironically, named "The Highlands." **The Highlands** area today boasts homes that would not be out of place in the most expensive suburbs of the north lakeshore. Doctors from the University of Chicago are neighbors to musicians such as Ramsey Lewis, and Jesse Jackson has long made his home in the area.

Chicago's lakefront is entirely parkland, with the exception of industrial development at the mouth of the Calumet River and in small areas on the far North and South Sides of the city. Private lakeshore ownership on the North Side stretches from Hollywood Avenue (about 5600 North) to the Evanston line. But even there the shoreline features seventeen public parks that occupy about half of the shoreline.

Two sections on the south lakefront also remain in private hands. A four-block residential area runs from 71st to 75th Streets, where private residences and rental and cooperative apartments occupy the shore along **South Shore Drive,** the southern extension of Lake Shore Drive. But even this section contains a small "vest-pocket park" at 74th Street with

tennis courts, a walking track, a picnic area, and a swimming beach.

Rainbow Park and Beach at 75th Street continues Chicago's lakefront park system. Generations of Chicagoans have enjoyed the extensive beaches here, and Mayor Harold Washington saw to it that new softball diamonds, tennis courts, and playground equipment were added to this and other parks throughout the city. Additional features of Rainbow Park

South Shore Bank

Perhaps the most intriguing aspect of the South Shore community is the presence of the **South Shore Bank.** Long a fixture in the area, the bank was on the brink of closing during the late 1960s, when the community underwent rapid racial change. A group of investors from Hyde Park Bank became interested in it, and took over the ailing business in August 1973. They believed that if the bank could successfully remain in the community in the midst of its changes, the quality of the community could likewise be maintained.

After twenty-four years of operation, the new South Shore Bank continues to keep the financial taps flowing for this middle-class, predominantly African-American neighborhood. The community is stable and

has not suffered the massive decline in land values and building conditions that occurred in other similar areas. Where South Shore was declining, the bank provided loans that helped to stabilize and redevelop the area. The bank is well known nationally and has carved out an international reputation.

South Shore Bank is trying to recreate its South Shore success in rural Arkansas and in the Austin neighborhood on Chicago's West Side. Bank officers regularly work in special projects worldwide, such as helping the Polish government move toward a market economy, assisting the Lakota Sioux with economic initiatives on their western reservations, and coordinating microloan programs in India.

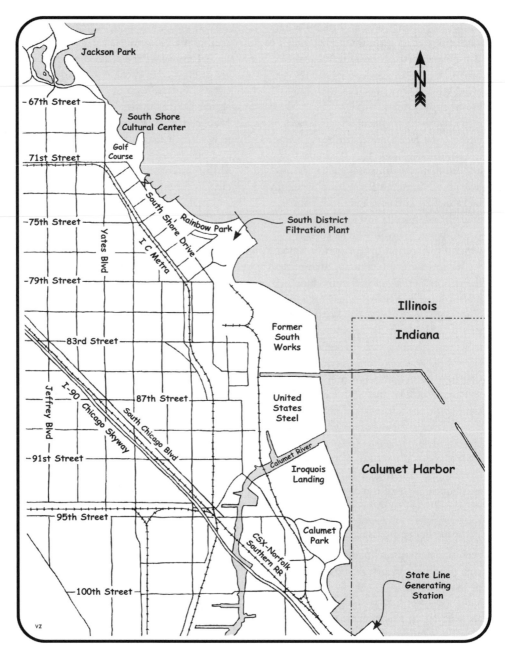

MAP 23. Chicago's far southern lakefront. The nearly continuous lakefront park is interrupted only by the four-block area from 71st to 75th Street and the mile-square artificial peninsula that held the former South Works of U.S. Steel. South of the Calumet River entrance, past Iroquois Landing, is Chicago's southernmost park, Calumet Park, stretching to the Indiana state line.

Life on the Lakeshore

The author is privileged to live on the shore in this area where fossils of creatures from ancient tropical seas punctuate the sandy beaches. Intimate round-the-clock involvement allows one to feel the lake as a living presence. At dawn, a path of light streaks the immensity with gold. At dusk, shimmering azure floors the darkening skies. Sometimes the lake edge is frozen and silence sits upon the shore. More often, the myriad sounds of wind and waves fill the air. Herons flap, geese pass in chevrons, and gulls wheel and shriek and slice. Ever-changing views provide a kaleidoscopic beauty. But always there is the sense of awesome power.

On February 8, 1987, a massive storm combined with record high lake levels and a northeast gale to produce waves of nearly oceanic proportions. Massive shoreline erosion occurred, and Lake Shore Drive was flooded and closed on both sides of the city. National newscasts detailed the flooding of basements in lakefront buildings that knocked-out electricity, elevators, and heat. In some cases, lakeshore residents had to be evacuated to nearby hotels until the storm relented and power and heat could be restored. Large sections of Chicago's lakefront had to be repaired, and some of the lakefront parkland had to be elevated to protect the Drive from renewed flooding.

Waves break on Promontory Point at 55th Street on the south lakefront. The "point," as it is known locally, divides Burnham Park to the north from Jackson Park to the south.

include public gardens, basketball courts, and an outdoor handball court.

The low gray building on the shore at the south end of Rainbow Park is the **South District Filtration Plant** that provides drinking water for the portion of Chicago south of Pershing Road (3900 S.). Chicago's walter filtration system is the most extensive in the nation, and increasing numbers of Chicago's ringing suburbs also get their water from the city due to declining quality and volume of the wells that originally supplied their drinking water.

Construction of the filtration plant began in 1938 but wasn't completed until after World War II, in 1946. The plant receives lake water from a pair of water intake cribs located two miles offshore at 68th Street. A major disaster occurred while the second crib was under construction:

> At about 8 o'clock on the morning of January 20th, 1909, the crib was the scene of of an appalling and disastrous fire which resulted in the loss of . . . sixty workmen who were on the crib at the time . . . the fire developed with great rapidity and enveloped the entire structure. . . . A number of workmen saved their lives by jumping overboard into the Lake and by then reaching the cakes of floating ice. . . . Some of the men who reached the water were drowned before they could be rescued (Public Works 1909, 106–7).

Seventy-ninth Street marks the southern boundary of Rainbow Park. It also marks a land-use change from parkland and residential development to a zone of heavy industry centered on the Calumet River, which extends south to the northern boundary of Calumet Park at 95th Street.

At 79th Street, an artificial peninsula juts into the lake. This was the former site of the **United States Steel South Works.** The South Works was one of the world's greatest hot-metal factories, and became, for a time, the largest employer in Chicago. Plant construction began in 1882, when it was part of Captain E. B. Ward's North Chicago Rolling Mill Company.

The North Chicago Rolling Mills developed in 1856 on the North Branch of the Chicago River at 1319 Wabansia, just north of Goose Island. The first steel rails produced in America were rolled at this mill in 1865. Replacings of iron rails with high-strength steel rails revolutionized the railroad industry, which, in turn, was a major force in Chicago's ascent to industrial and commercial greatness.

The almost insatiable demand for steel rails by the expanding railroad industry soon made it necessary for larger mills to be built. After the Great Fire in 1871, more and more steel producers left the congested, expensive inner city for expansive, cheap land along the Calumet River, where water frontage and a fine harbor were complemented by excellent rail connections.

The steel industry itself underwent many changes as it grew. In 1889 the North Chicago Rolling Mills merged with two other steel companies to form the Illinois Steel Company, then Chicago's largest and most modern steel-making facility. The 260-acre plant at the Calumet came to be known as the **South Works** because the old North Chicago Mill was called the **North Works.** As a result, when the North Works were dismantled in 1907, the northernmost steel mill operating in Chicago was, ironically, the South Works (McClellan 1966, 19; Miller 1996, 42).

View eastward toward the mouth of the Calumet River. The fabled South Works of U.S. Steel occupies the north bank (*left*) of the river. Across the stream on the south bank is the Youngstown Sheet and Tube Company steel plant. (Courtesy, Chicago Historical Society.)

The Illinois Steel Company subsequently became part of Federal Steel Company, then Carnegie Illinois Steel Company, and finally, after J. P. Morgan bought out Andrew Carnegie in 1901, part of the newly incorporated colossus, United States Steel. Operations continued until the South Works closed on April 10, 1992.

As the Great Circle Tour proceeds, it enters the Indiana shore of Lake Michigan and continues in the Hoosier state almost to the Calumet River entrance. A word of caution: here the lake surface is often choppy as one approaches the Calumet Harbor breakwater because of so-called reflection waves, which often result from east and northeast winds.

A Giant's Demise

By the late 1970s, the **United States Steel South Works** occupied 575 acres on an artificial peninsula constructed of fill and slag. Employment was at ten thousand, having peaked during World War II, when the plant employed twenty thousand workers. In 1976 South Works produced iron in seven blast furnaces and made steel in a basic oxygen process shop with three steel-making vessels.

During this period, water tours near South Works were spellbinding as giant ore boats jockeyed for position in the restricted channel of the Calumet River and brought iron ore from the northern lakes to be mixed with limestone ballast and coke and fired in the astonishing alchemy of the blast furnaces to produce iron.

South Works was a major producer of beams and structural steels used in the construction of bridges and skyscrapers. Much of its production was intended for the Chicago market, which led the nation in construction of office buildings in the 1970s and 1980s. The John Hancock Center, the Prudential Building, Sears Tower, and many other famed Chicago buildings were built of structural steel manufactured at the South Works.

Nonetheless, changing markets, foreign competition, obsolete facilities, high energy costs, and stubborn union and management actions ultimately led to the giant plant's demise. During the late 1970s, many facilities were closed and dismantled. Employment shrunk from 10,000 to 6,800. The final years showed the plant operating with about 700 workers as a scrap reprocessing facility that recycled scrap from the area to make structural steel for Chicago's burgeoning office market. When that market quieted, the plant closed.

Today the nearly mile-square peninsula sits virtually empty on the lakeshore just north of the Calumet River. Only the power plant, some transformers, and the concrete walls that once supported giant gantry cranes remain. The site has begun once again to resemble the desolate fishing village that preceded industrial development.

Many plans have been advanced for the future redevelopment of the property, but as of this writing, none has come to the fore. One proposal suggests that the northern part be converted to a modern community of townhouses, with marinas and wetlands. The area along the Calumet River would remain industrial.

Calumet Harbor

The Circle Tour enters **Calumet Harbor** through the north entrance in the breakwater. Large ships cannot enter here because a submerged wreck near the entrance and sand accumulation have reduced the depth so much that these vessels are forced to move around the outer edge of the breakwater and enter the harbor along a deep channel.

Calumet Harbor is part of the fragmented Port of Chicago, which also includes the **Chicago, Indiana, Buffington and Gary (U.S. Steel), and Burns Harbors.** In 1906 Calumet Harbor received more tonnage than did Chicago Harbor and since that time it has been the city's principal port. In Calumet Harbor's natural state, there was no protection outside the rivermouth. Breakwaters were built to create a one-half-mile-square harbor of refuge for vessels entering and leaving the river, and one often sees ships lying at anchor awaiting their turn at the docks.

The view south from Calumet Harbor encompasses a portion of the southern shore of Lake Michigan and one of the greatest concentrations of heavy industry on earth. It also embraces one spot of green to relieve the otherwise uninterrupted industrial development. On the shore south of the river is **Calumet Park,** an all-but-unknown gem and the southernmost of Chicago's lakefront parks. Just beyond the park is the state line power station of Commonwealth Edison of Indiana. Slightly to the southeast, the **Inland Steel** plant sits on an artificial peninsula jutting out two miles into the lake. The largest blast furnace in North America is visible at the left edge of the plant. A huge furnace, forty-five feet in diameter, is one of the five largest blast furnaces on earth and symbolizes both the rebound of the Chicago steel-making district and the application of high technology to the production of steel.

West of Inland Steel is the **LTV Corporation** plant on its own artificial peninsula. Slightly inland from the shore is the refinery of the **Sinclair Oil Company** and the huge **Amoco** refinery in Whiting, Indiana. This refinery complex at the south end of the lake is one of the world's largest. These mammoth industrial facilities have spawned a host of related industries that use the products of the mills and refineries to create additional products. For this reason, paint, metalworking, chemical, and other industries crowd the area.

All of the steel-making operations along the Indiana shore of Lake Michigan are considered to be in the Chicago District. Although total steel production in this district has fallen somewhat over time, its *proportion* of American steel production has *risen.* As of this writing, fully one-third of all steel produced in the United States is made in the Chicago District.

The Bureau of the Census links northwestern Indiana and northeastern Illinois into a single Consolidated Area because so many industrial and commercial activities cross state lines and bind the areas together. The integration of the area is further encouraged by the increasing numbers of people from both states who cross the state line to work.

Development of Harbor Facilities at the Calumet River

We have already seen how much the mouth of the Chicago River was changed from its natural state. Similar efforts were made to create a harbor at the mouth of

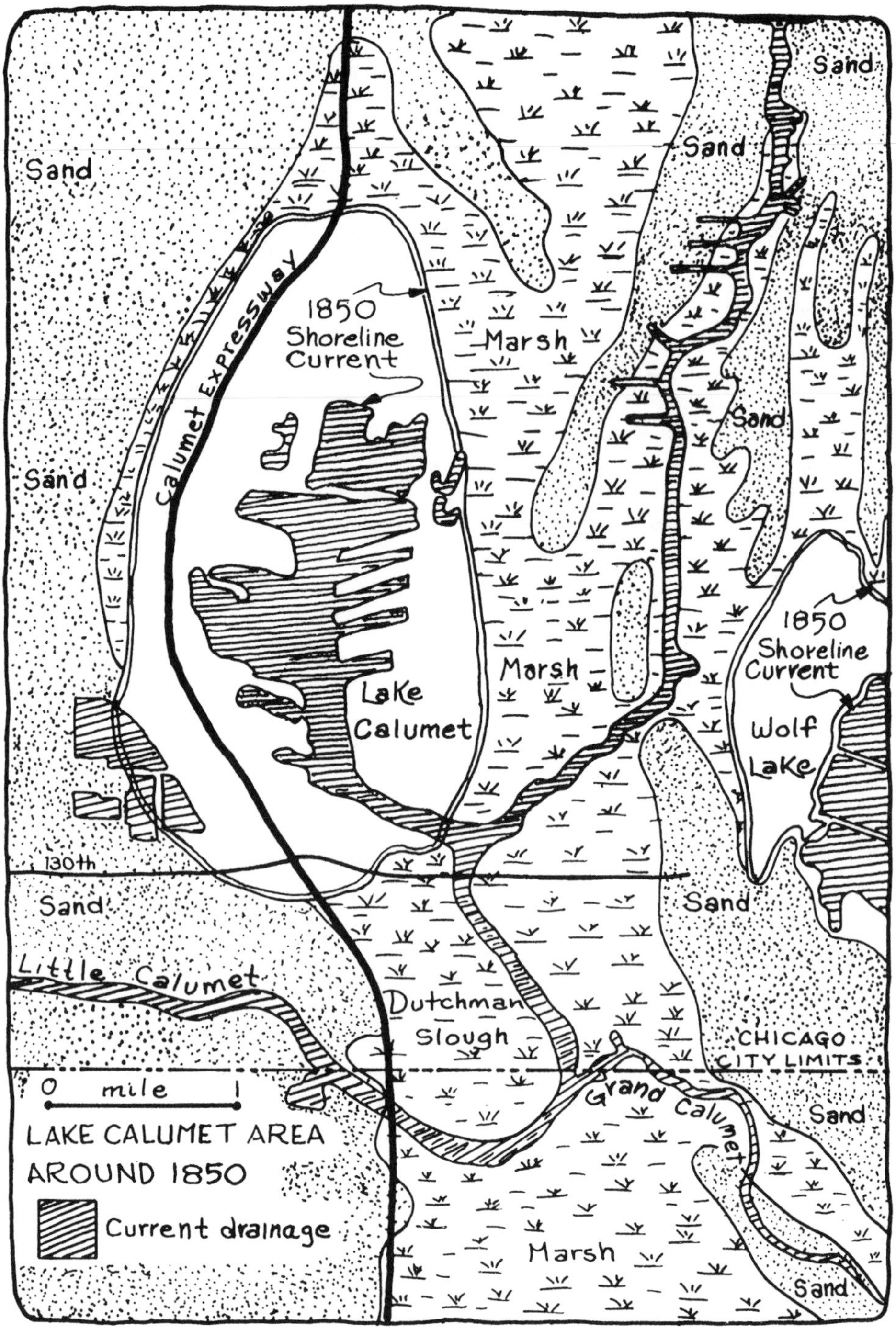
Sand
Sand
Sand
Sand
Sand
Sand
Sand
Sand
Sand
Marsh
Marsh
Marsh
Calumet Expressway
1850
Shoreline
Current
1850
Shoreline
Current
Lake
Calumet
Wolf
Lake
130th
Little Calumet
Dutchman
Slough
Grand Calumet
CHICAGO
CITY LIMITS
0 mile 1
LAKE CALUMET AREA
AROUND 1850
Current drainage

MAP 24. Lake Calumet area, 1850 to the present. Once a morass of marshes and shallow lakes, the area around Lake Calumet has suffered massive change due to human action.

Salties and Lakers

Ships that call at Calumet are of two types: *salties* and *lakers*. Salties are general-cargo vessels that arrive from anywhere in the world, operating where and when cargo requires. That is, they are not scheduled liners, which keep a regular route at set times. These ships average about 550 feet in length, with a beam width of about 50 feet. They draw about twenty-seven feet of water and carry from five thousand to seven thousand tons of cargo.

In 1959 as many as forty-eight shipping companies paid regular call at the Port of Chicago. But deregulation, *containerization* (placing cargoes in standard containers), the increasing size of vessels (many now are too large for the Saint Lawrence Seaway), infrastructure obsolescence, and

out the Great Lakes (Young 1992, 1).

Laker is the local name for a lake bulk

competition from coastal ports and railroads have decimated foreign trade not just in Chicago, but through-

freighter—an ore boat. These huge ships are often 1,000 feet long and 75 feet wide amidships. They are owned

by a variety of marine transportation and steel companies and carry low-value (but very

important) heavy and bulky commodities useful for industry. Such ships are the workhorses of the lakes, regularly shuttling iron ore from the Mesabi Range in Minnesota or from Quebec to the mills at the south end of Lake Michigan. Similar ships carry coal from Chicago north to Milwaukee, and still others carry grain, limestone, portland cement, quartz, coke, petroleum, corn, flat-rolled iron and steel, steel scrap, ferrous alloys, soybeans, iron and steel bars, and slag.

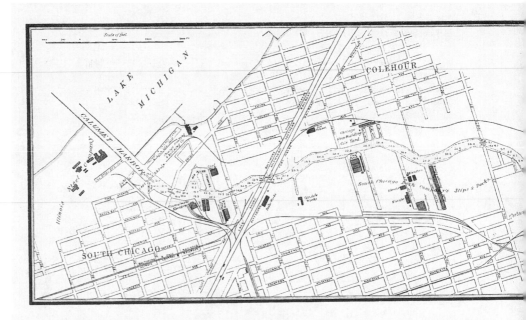

the Calumet River. Actually, it is something of a misnomer to call what came before by the name *river,* because the Calumet River turned back to the east without forming a distinct mouth in this area. In fact, there was *no real river* where the mouth of the Calumet now flows. Rather, there was a series of sloughs—lakes set amid marshes—through which a channel was cut artificially.

The already weird path of the Calumet River was further interfered with by human action. A closer look at what we now call the Calumet River is given by the map of the Lake Calumet environment around 1850 (Map 24). Where the present-day Calumet River flows, we see only extensive marshland interrupted by occasional sand ridges and water lying between Lake Calumet and Wolf Lake. Note also that two islands existed in the Calumet that are no longer present on the landscape.

It is clear that within the marsh there was a fairly deep channel, since the Chittenden trail (Map 25) had a toll bridge where the trail crossed the narrowest part of the marsh between sand ridges. The current river channel passes through here.

There was, however, something of a rivermouth and, as early as 1836, army engineers spoke of improving the channel and building piers like those built at the mouth of the Chicago River. In early times, this area was a favorite camping ground for the Potawatomis, and, later, it was the site of **Ainsworth**, a small fishing village.

Industrial development got off to a slow start. In 1867 the Northwestern Fertilizing Company set up shop in the Calumet where it was joined by two lumberyards and some small grain elevators. Irish and Swedish workers began to filter into the area as a few jobs became available.

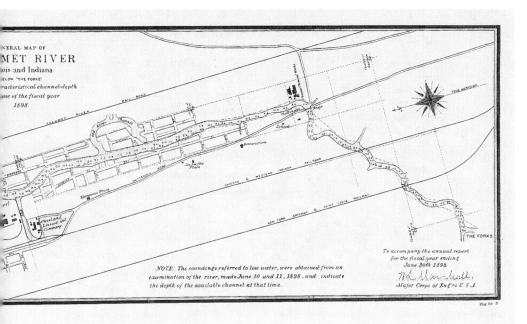

NERAL MAP OF
MET RIVER
ois and Indiana
LOW "THE FORKS"
racteristical channel-depth
ose of the fiscal year
1898.

NOTE: The soundings, referred to low water, were obtained from an
examination of the river, made June 10 and 11, 1898, and indicate
the depth of the available channel at that time.

To accompany the annual report
for the fiscal year ending
June 30th 1898.

Major Corps of Eng'rs U.S.A.

But it was a private firm, the Calumet and Chicago Dredge and Dock Company, that began the river improvement around 1870. This firm cut a channel from the Calumet River to Lake Michigan, dredged Lake Calumet, installed pilings, and constructed docks and artificial harbors. Cargo ships began using the newly created harbor as early as 1871. The creation of the new channel led to an upsurge in development so that by the mid-1870s, small steel works and car shops for the Baltimore and Ohio Railroad were established in the area.

The tour now turns west, reenters Illinois and passes into the man-made entrance of the Calumet River, gateway to one of the greatest concentrations of industry on earth. Like the Chicago River, the Calumet's flow has been reversed so that lake water moves westward *into* the rivermouth. To the right is the derelict area where, for more than one

hundred years, huge blast furnaces lined the river and steel production flourished. On the left stood the Iroquois Steel Company Plant, which later became part of Youngstown Sheet and Tube. Youngstown subsequently closed the mill, and now the site is home to the **Iroquois Landing**, container and general cargo facility of the Chicago International Port District.

In the past, this terminal facility handled many kinds of general cargo—one could occasionally see hundreds of Volkswagens sitting on the wharf. Today, although some general cargo arrives here, most of the shipments consist of various forms of imported steel. On any given day during the shipping season, the wharf and nearby yards are crowded with rusty steel coils, steel bars, and semifinished steel billets.

Often, when an area has a manufacturing specialty, it is a primary point

Plimsoll Marks

The midsection of cargo ships exhibit a peculiar symbol located on the painted waterline of the vessel. This symbol is called a *Plimsoll mark*, and it shows how deeply a ship may be loaded to qualify for insurance. The approved load level varies by the time of year and the route to be followed.

This insurance symbol appears on ships because of the single-minded work of **Samuel Plimsoll** (1824–98), a British politician who spent his life fighting for the safety of seamen. He aroused public opinion against "coffin ships," overloaded and unseaworthy vessels. These ships were sent out without regard for the safety of their crews. When they foundered, often with the loss of all hands, their owners collected large sums from the insurance companies.

As a result of Plimsoll's tireless fight, ships were required to conform to safe loading practices to *qualify* for insurance. The marks that indicate safe loading were named for this champion of sailors.

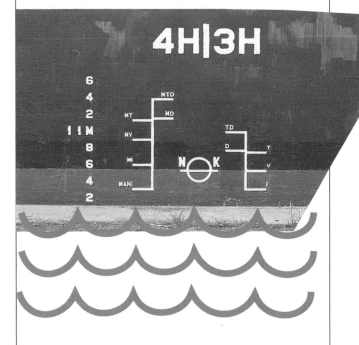

for import of similar products. So it is with steel. Chicago has the storage facilities, the sales offices, the customers, and the transportation that make it a logical place to import foreign steel. Imported steel now provides something of a benefit to domestic producers.

Most modern mills in the Chicago District strive to create high-tech facilities to handle about 85 percent of peak demand. This means cost savings, since plants can be kept to a size and workforce that meets demand most of the time without the expensive extra equipment and extra labor required to meet the 100-percent demand level. This also means fewer layoffs when demand fails to reach the unusual peak levels.

These days, about one-third of U.S. demand is met by producers in the Chicago District. Another third is supplied by the rest of the American steel industry. The final third comes from imported steels furnished by trading partners in the global economy.

Despite the overwhelmingly industrial character of this area however, tour visitors have told the author how they and their sweethearts would come down to the Calumet River to watch the ships and the fiery glow from the furnaces. Apparently not all the sparking came from the mills.

Waterway travelers frequently see foreign vessels tied up alongside Iroquois Landing, unloading steel from Brazil, Japan, Germany, or Mexico. In 1994 tonnage records were set in the port because of a surge in imported steel made necessary by the temporary shutdown of a number of blast furnaces along the

Lift bridge spanning the Calumet River near its mouth east of Ewing Avenue.

Indiana shore. At the same time the furnaces were being relined, they were being outfitted with new, highly sophisticated instrumentation and controls. Now that these furnaces are back in action demand for import steel has eased. Because of the furnace upgrades, the Chicago District has the world's most modern steel production facilities.

Vessels tied alongside Iroquois Landing fly the flag of their country of registry on their stern. Often the country of registry is not the country of the ship's owners. Rather, it represents what is called a "flag of convenience." A few countries have less stringent regulations concerning labor and other costs. As a result, many ship owners register their

vessels in those countries to avoid high taxes and other costs associated with U.S. registry. Favorite countries for flags of convenience include Panama, Cyprus, and Liberia.

Up ahead is the first bridge to be encountered on the Calumet River, a center-span lift bridge. Its entire center span is lifted vertically by counterweights attached to cables on supporting towers on each bank. This bridge carries the tracks of the Elgin, Joliet and Eastern Railway, a wholly owned subsidiary of United States Steel. When the South Works was operating, unit trains brought coal from the Ohio Valley to the blast furnaces at Calumet. A *unit train* is an industry term for a train that achieves scale economies by carrying a single cargo (in this case coal) from a single origin to a single destination.

On the right bank, just past the bridge, is the **Nalco Chemical Company** plant, where industrial water treatment and specialty chemicals were manufactured and distributed for the oil refining, steel, metalworking, and pollution control industries. In 1995 Nalco merged with Exxon Corporation and the plant was subsequently closed and put up for sale.

On the left (south) bank, **Cozzi Company** operates one of its many scrap yards. Here electromagnets lift ferrous (iron-bearing) scrap into barges for ship-

ment to the steel industry at the south end of the lake. Scrap is an important input for steel making. So, by locating near major markets, steel producers are also near sources of scrap.

An unexpected link with the area's past is found on the site of the Cozzi scrap yard: a grave. It turns out that the property now occupied by the scrap operation was once owned by one **Andreas Von Zirngibl.** Herr Von Zirngibl decreed in his will that he should be buried on his property facing the lake. He further stipulated that any sale of the property should contain the provision that his grave was to remain in place and be available for visits from friends and relatives.

The Cozzi (Metal Management) scrap metal yard on the Calumet River. The grave of Andreas Von Zirngibl appears in the foreground.

The tomb-
stone of
Andreas Von
Zirngibl.

As the property has been transferred since Herr Von Zirngibl's passing
in the 1850s, various owners have found
these provisions in the title somewhat in-
convenient and have sought in court to
move the grave. Apparently, the matter
has, on one occasion, reached the Illinois
Supreme Court. Unfortunately for the
current owners, the court upheld the
conditions of the deed. So today the
grave sits in the middle of a scrap yard,
protected by four large concrete posts at
its corners. The inscription reads:

> *In Memoriam*
> *Andreas Von Zirngibl*
> *Born March 30, 1797*
> *Died August 21, 1855*
> *A Veteran of 1816* [sic]
> *Battle of Waterloo*

At 93rd Street, the Ewing Avenue
double-leaf bascule bridge spans the waterway. This is a very active bridge due to
heavy water traffic, and drivers often find
themselves waiting while the bridge is up
to accommodate ships or barge tows.

The right bank past the Ewing
Avenue Bridge is the location of the
North American Salt depot. Here piles
of salt the size of small hills are covered
with black plastic tarpaulins. This road
salt arrives by lake-bulk vessels from
salt tunnels that extend under Lake Erie
almost all the way to Canada. It is stored
here for winter use on Chicago's streets.

Salt that is stored indoors is *grocery
salt,* which comes by barge from the
lower Mississippi Valley. Until the
1970s, a grain elevator occupied this site,
but it perished in a spectacular explosion
and fire. Grain dust is highly flammable,
and many derelict elevators in Chicago
have made spectacular exits as their grain
dust ignited.

On the east bank is the Calumet facility of the **Hannah Marine Company,** a
major operator of barge tows through the

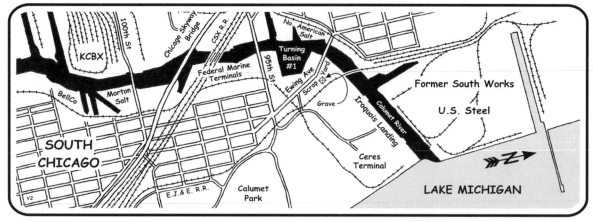

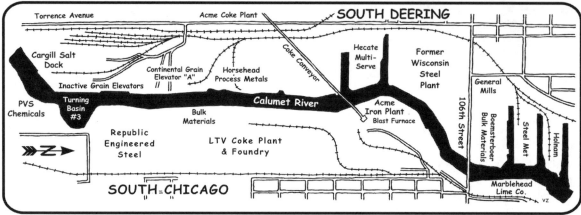

MAP 26.
Calumet
River, Turning
Basin No. 1.

MAP 27.
Calumet
River, South
Deering. This
artificial chan-
nel has been
repeatedly
straightened,
widened, and
deepened.

Illinois lakes to the Gulf waterway and
on Lake Michigan as well. The site the
company occupies was the location of
one of the oldest companies in the area,
Great Lakes Dredge and Dock Company.
It was the surviving form of the company
that first cut a channel through the
sloughs to link the Calumet River and
Lake Michigan.

The **Great Lakes Towing Company**
operates marine and river towboats and
occupies another section of Turning
Basin No. 1. The towboats with the
sharp bows are used on the open waters
of the lake. The rectangular towboats

with square bows are used on the flowing
waters of the rivers and canals inland.

Federal Marine Terminals Company
operates dock and warehouse facilities at
the southern end of Turning Basin No. 1
that stretch southward to the rail bridges.
It is common to see foreign vessels off-
loading steel here. Coils of imported
steel can often be seen in open storage,
awaiting shipment to purchasers. However, Federal is cutting back its Calumet
operations and shifting to Burns Harbor,
Indiana.

Most of the bulk cargoes moved by
water can be stored outdoors, open to

Barges

A common sight in the Calumet are barges of many different types. Some are open and carry crushed stone or scrap, while others are covered to ship grain, cement, chemicals, or sugar. Still others are tankers for moving petroleum and petrochemicals. Nearly all conform to a standard size, which is 35 feet wide, 109 feet long, with a draft of 9 feet.

At maximum draft, these barges hold between twelve hundred and fifteen hundred tons of cargo. They may not be pretty, and they are surely less romantic than the foreign cargo ships, but they are the real backbone of Chicago's water transportation. If one sees a tow of four barges, it represents roughly the same cargo capacity as one of the general

cargo ships. Slips cut in the banks are used to park barges out of the stream to relieve congestion.

The barges are mostly used on the twelve thousand miles of connecting inland rivers and canals, which provide water transportation over a vast area. These inland waters are maintained at a standard project depth of nine feet by the U.S.

Army Corps of Engineers. Standard barges are designed specifically for use on this system. Recent changes in water commerce regulations have allowed small barge tows to be used to transport materials on Lake Michigan.

A standard 1,500-ton covered barge loading cement. Such barges average 105 feet in length and are 35 feet wide.

the elements. Piles of such bulk materials are generally separated by large cast-concrete blocks, which are moved about by crawler cranes to increase or decrease storage for any one commodity. In this section of the waterway, crawler cranes often can be seen loading scrap, unloading salt and coal, or shifting limestone.

Next, one passes under the double-leaf bascule bridge at 95th Street that carries U.S. Highways 12 and 20 across the waterway. These highways generally follow Indian trails that ran along sandy ridges above the marshes and wetlands formerly in the area. Immediately after the 95th Street Bridge, on the right bank, are the silos of the **Holnam Company** terminal, which is typical of the plants using the waterway. They work with large amounts of bulky, low-value materials that would be prohibitively expensive were they to be transported long distances overland.

Just past an old bridge remnant are two center-span lift bridges that carry Conrail tracks across the channel. Although the northern bridge is permanently open, the southern one carries very busy tracks, so trains full of raw materials or finished products are a common sight here. Since steel production is a mainstay of this industrial zone, many trains haul finished coils of steel in specially built railcars for the local and national markets.

Often one sees railcars especially designed to hold standard containers. These rectangular boxes allow general cargoes to be handled with automated equipment, and they can be transferred easily between railcars, barges, ships, or flatbed trucks for final delivery.

At the time of this writing, the Conrail system is about to be bought out by CSX and Norfolk and Southern

Railway. It is too soon to tell which railroad will take over the lines through the Calumet.

High above the waterway soars the fixed toll bridge of the **Chicago Skyway.** This 125-foot-high bridge was built to link the Indiana Toll Road (I-90) to Chicago's Dan Ryan Expressway (I-94). When the toll road was nearing completion, it was observed that the high-speed superhighway would dump traffic onto Chicago streets. At that time it was illegal to build tollways in Illinois, but the law said nothing about *toll bridges.* This loophole established, the 7 1/2-mile Chicago Skyway Toll Bridge was completed in 1958.

The bridge has been a financial failure since the number of vehicles using it has never been sufficient to pay off the debt (Heise and Frazel 1987, 138). Nonetheless, the huge structure provides a magnificent elevated view of the industrial areas along the Calumet River and the working-class neighborhoods of Chicago's Southeast Side.

A double-leaf bascule bridge crosses the Calumet River at 100th Street, and just south of the bridge on the east bank is an additional large open-storage area of the **Morton Salt Company.** It is easy to tell whether a salt storage or terminal facility belongs to Morton Salt, because the firm dyes its salt blue. Almost all road salt that is stored in the open will look a bit blue if it becomes wet or reflects the sky. However, Morton's salt is a very distinctive blue color under all conditions. The salt storage yard follows the bank southward to the slip north of **S. H. Bellco,** a firm that distributes bulk materials.

Horsehead Resource Development Company processes copper on the west bank of the river across from LTV, and **Continental Grain Company** operates its

6.8-million-bushel Elevator B south of the Horsehead operation. This elevator handles soybeans, corn, and soft red wheat. Just south of Continental is the now unused group of elevators of **Cargill Corporation.** Said to be the largest private elevator complex in the world, the aging facility proved less efficient and more costly to operate than newer facilities at Burns Harbor in Indiana. Cargill continues to operate its salt storage operation at the south end of the property where the river bends westward.

PVS Chemicals, Inc. of Illinois manufactures sulphuric acid at its plant on the riverbank south of Turning Basin No. 3. Sulfuric acid is sometimes referred to as the king of chemicals, since it is the largest tonnage chemical produced in the world and has many manufacturing applications.

In the past, piles of bright yellow sulphur filled the wharf. Open storage is avoided today because of environmental concerns but also because neighborhood children loved to set the piles on fire. Such piles are no longer necessary since the sulphur now arrives in molten rather than solid form and is delivered by insulated tanker trucks or one hundred-ton

A lake bulk carrier vessel loads grain at Continental Elevator B.

Industrial Strength

On the west bank, just about two miles from Lake Michigan, rises the dark, angular mechanisms of the **KCBX Corporation,** which operates the only multimodal dry-bulk transfer terminal on the Great Lakes and serves as a good example of the complexity of cargo movement through the Port of Chicago. KCBX is equipped to handle all lake vessels, even two at a time, except for the one thousand-foot self-unloaders, which cannot navigate through the winding Calumet River.

Coal is the principal commodity transferred here, but petroleum coke, bentonite clay, iron ore pellets, potash, and other bulk materials are shifted between railcars, trucks, barges, and lake vessels. The huge, fascinating machinery offloads barges, dumps railroad hopper cars at one hundred tons per minute, shifts coal onto conveyors, or drops coal into the giant holds of lake bulk carriers. This facility helps Chicago keep its status as one of the largest coal-shipping ports on the Great Lakes. In 1996 KCBX handled a total of 7.4 million tons of cargo; 5.5 million tons were coal.

KCBX operates twenty-four hours a day, 365 days a year but is busiest during the Great Lakes shipping season from late March through January when ice in the northern lakes limits navigation. Round the clock operation is necessary because lake vessels make money only when they are moving; in port, they cost nearly $1,200 an hour and it takes about twelve hours to load a 25,000-ton laker.

At KCBX, bentonite clays from Wyoming are transferred to ships bound for Europe. The coal that arrives from Montana, Wyoming, Colorado, New Mexico, and Utah is either sent by six-barge tons to local utilities (*six-packs*) or moves uplake on ships that carried taconite or limestone on their downlake voyage.

For an outsider, it is hard to comprehend the variety and complexity of the industries associated with iron and steel production. The west bank of the Calumet River south of KCBX is the location of several such operations. **Holnam Chicago** has another plant here that grinds slag to be used as an additive for concrete and, farther south, **Steel Met,** recycles stainless steel scrap.

The extensive property of **Beelman Trucking Company** lies south of Steel Met; north of 106th Street on the west bank of the river is the **Beemsterboer Bulk Terminal,** which crushes and screens rock to make uniform sifted limestone ballast and ore for blast furnaces. Across the river, **Marblehead Lime Company** operates a huge cement plant.

The considerable turnover, realignment, and downsizing in U.S. industry is well illustrated by the recently expanded and upgraded manufacturing facility of **General Mills.** Despite this upgrade, General Mills has sold its adjoining elevator facility and razed its factory, which once had the largest flour mill in Chicago. A windowless, prefabricated plant with automated equipment replaced the old plant, but now even this ultra-modern factory is being closed.

One Hundred and Sixth Street is a major route through the Calumet area. The double-leaf bascule bridge that spans the Calumet River at 106th Street is the busiest of all the movable bridges in Chicago: in 1987 it was lifted 5,805 times. The next-busiest bridge in the region is the single-leaf bascule span at Kinzie Street, which opened 3,100 times in 1989 and is described in detail earlier in chapter 4.

At this writing, the 106th Street Bridge is undergoing a complete rehabilitation.

A small section of the west bank of the river south of 106th Street is occupied by the **Repusto Truck** parts facility. Surrounding the facility and reaching from 106th Street south along the bank to the Wisconsin Slip is the derelict **Wisconsin Steel Mill.** This desolate, shuttered plant occupies the site of the first steel-making facility in the Calumet area.

After the Great Fire of 1871, industry began leaving the Chicago River in the central city. Not only was there concern over future fires, but redevelopment caused central city land to become too expensive for large manufacturing plants. In 1875 Joseph H. Brown Iron and Steel Company built a plant on the west side of the Calumet River near 109th Street.

In 1882 the company was sold to Calumet Iron and Steel Company, and when this firm failed, the plant was sold to South Chicago Furnace Company. Deering Harvester Company, second-largest manufacturer of harvesting equipment at the time, then acquired controlling interest in the company. Consequently, the entire area began to be known as **South Deering.** In 1902 Deering Harvester merged with McCormick Harvesting Machine Company to form **International Harvester,** and the mill was then renamed **Wisconsin Steel.**

The South Deering area was a magnet for immigrants after the turn of the century; first Yugoslavians, then other groups of southern and eastern Europeans. For a time, so many Polish immigrants flooded the area that it was nicknamed the South Pole. Later, Mexicans and then African Americans moved in.

Wisconsin Steel continued operation as a wholly owned subsidiary of International Harvester, with roughly one-half of its production used by the parent company and one-half sold on the open market. From the 1970s onward, the old mill began to lose large sums of money. On March 28, 1980, three years after the mill was sold to Environdyne Industries, Inc., holding company of the Economic Development Administration, Wisconsin Steel was closed forever.

When the mill closed after 105 years of operation, it idled 3,500 workers and crippled the many small businesses that served them and their families.

The closing of Wisconsin Steel started a chain reaction that engulfed the entire area. After Wisconsin Steel, every other major steel company pulled out by the end of the decade. In 1980, for example, Southeast Chicago employed roughly one out of every five steelworkers in the United States. By 1990 the number was near zero. Only one small integrated mill— **Acme Steel**—remains within the city limits.

Yet today, the Chicago District still leads the nation in steel production, and the entire area has rebounded. Now, in addition to Acme Steel, **Republic Engineered Steel** operates a bar and rod mill. Nonetheless, the days of huge integrated steel mills in Chicago appear to be over. Time after time, as changing economic currents have challenged the city's infrastructure, its diverse economic base has provided the springboard for new economic growth. As a result, Chicago has maintained its economic power through the closing of the stockyards and steel mills and the decline of the passenger rail business.

The iron plant of Acme Steel Corporation, occupies the river's east bank between 106th and 111th Streets, and offers the waterways

explorer a close-hand look at a working blast furnace, the last remaining blast furnace in Chicago. (The only other blast furnace in Illinois is at Granite City Steel, near St. Louis.)

Since this furnace produces about one million tons of iron each year—more than 2,700 tons every day—it consumes huge amounts of ore, coke, limestone, and water. To serve the furnace's enormous appetite, giant gantry cranes move mountains of iron ore, limestone ballast, and coal.

Coke for the furnace is made at the Acme coke plant west of the river on Torrence Avenue, a recently rebuilt facility that is said to be the cleanest plant in the world. Conveyors carry the newly-made coke directly from the coke ovens to the blast furnace over a fixed bridge 130 feet above the Calumet River.

The molten iron produced in the blast furnace is poured into special 180-ton "torpedo" or "bottle" rail cars that are like giant thermos on wheels. Then the 2,400-degree liquid metal is carried about six miles by rail to the Acme steel making plant at Riverdale. During the half-hour trip, the temperature of the liquid iron drops by about 300 degrees.

Opposite Acme's blast furnace on the west bank is **Hecate-Multi-Serv,** which adjoins the coke plant to the west and supplies bulk materials to Acme and processes slag aggregates.

Giant facilities continue along the river's east bank. Two huge dark triangular Wellman unloaders, sitting at the water's edge, unload coal barges. These machines are part of the coke plant and foundry operated by LTV Corporation. Reserve Marine Bulk Terminals Company adjoins the LTV facility on the south.

Still farther south on the east bank, from 116th to about 120th Streets, is **Republic Engineered Steel,** producer of steel bars and rods. As of this writing, the fate of the plant is uncertain. Republic Engineered Steel is planning a major expansion, but whether this will be in South Chicago or elsewhere is as yet undecided. Turning Basin No. 3 marks the southern end of the Republic mill. Here, as at Wolf Lake, one may occasionally see swans swimming placidly amidst the titanic structures that line the industrial waterway.

insulated railroad tank cars. These cars are fitted with steam coils to liquify the sulphur in case it solidifies during shipment.

PVS produces more than one hundred tons of sulfuric acid per day. Before 1957 sulphur arrived by water from Louisiana, but now sulphur needs are met at nearby refineries that harvest the element as a by-product from their stack gasses. In earlier times this sulphur was simply flared into the atmosphere, producing foul-smelling, eye-stinging sulphur dioxide. Now it is caught, collected, and sold. The harvesting and sale of fugitive sulphur illustrates how more-stringent environmental regulations have spawned profitable new by-product industries.

PVS no longer uses the Calumet River regularly for transportation, but it does use the water as a noncontact cooling agent. The firm carefully monitors water quality at its outfall to ensure that there are no leaks in the system and that water returned to the stream meets all environmental requirements.

West of PVS Chemicals on the south bank of the river is **Arrow Terminal,** which handles bulk materials, ferro-alloys, and pig iron. Some of these materials arrive by rail or truck, but most are delivered by barges that come up the Mississippi from New Orleans and through the Illinois lakes to the Gulf waterway. Two center-span lift bridges cross the channel: one carries Torrence Avenue and the other, the tracks of the Chicago and Western Indiana Railroad, a part of the belt railway system of Chicago. Waterway explorers on one of the author's tours had the good fortune of viewing the center span of the **Torrence Avenue Bridge** being floated into position on the backs of two barges. When it was in place, the cables were connected and the span was lifted.

Widening the Calumet River required that new bridges be built. Here, the central span of the Torrence Avenue Bridge is being floated into position on the backs of two barges.

Hegewisch

The area south of the Calumet River lies in **Hegewisch,** the southernmost community in Chicago. There was no settlement in this extensive marshland before 1880, and even then populations remained small. Polish-Americans and Mexican-Americans are among the largest ethnic groups in the blue-collar community, home to many workers at the nearby steel mills and to many Chicago police officers and firefighters. The median family income of $37,000 exceeds the city average of $31,000 by about 20 percent.

Community organization and activism have grown in Hegewisch ever since 1990, when a plan proposed by Mayor Richard M. Daley would have demolished the community as part of a grandiose scheme to develop a third major airport in the Calumet region in an attempt on the part of the city administration to deal simultaneously with environmental and economic problems in the area. The creation of the airport, it was felt, would help clean up industrial "brownfields" and simultaneously provide many new jobs.

Unfortunately, the plan would have required the relocation of the Calumet River and most of the local industrial concerns at a cost that was as astronomical as it proved incalculable. Hegewisch residents argued that even if they received fair market value for their homes, those funds would not be sufficient to purchase comparable housing elsewhere. Further, aviation experts indicated that such an airport would cause major traffic overlap with Chicago's O'Hare Field, the nation's busiest.

These and other obstacles ultimately killed the airport proposal.

The death of the airport plan gave Hegewisch residents new hope and new resolve. Since then they have been very active in opposing the creation of new landfills in their already heavily polluted area. They have also been among the chief sponsors of a proposal to create a **Lake Calumet National Ecological Park** focusing on the unique wetlands on Chicago's far South Side. This proposal recently passed Congress and was signed by President Clinton as part of an omnibus parks bill. Whether the park becomes a reality depends upon receiving funds for the project.

Cleaning Up the River

The SEPA stations use high-capacity screw pumps to lift water from the river into elevated pools on the banks. The water then cascades back into the stream over a series of artificial waterfalls, which have the effect of cooling the water and increasing its oxygen content. With cooler, oxygen-rich water, natural aerobic decomposition processes are enhanced. These processes literally help the stream to clean itself. The five SEPA stations have made remarkable differences in the cleanliness of the Calumet and connected streams. Their combined capacity is 1.3 billion gallons per day. The five stations cost close to $35 million, with estimated savings over chemical water treatment facilities of roughly $265 million.

SEPA Station No. 1 is designed as a prairie wetland and bird sanctuary. The screw pumps at this facility can handle more than 370 million gallons of water each day—more than one-half the stream's flow. It is heartening to find a relatively low-tech approach to stream cleanup that not only helps to clean the stream but also provides wildlife habitat and recreational opportunities. In the few years that these facilities have been operating, it has become common to find fishermen along the river near the artificial waterfalls. Today steelheads, bass, and other fish that have not been seen in these waters are regularly found here.

This bridge replacement is just one example of the many modifications that have been made in the channel of the Calumet River and in the structures that surround it. The river was widened, deepened, and straightened so that, when the Saint Lawrence Seaway was completed in 1969, ocean vessels could pass unimpeded through the river to the port facilities at Lake Calumet. But, as we have already noted, the Calumet River, which connects the Grand Calumet River with Lake Michigan, is itself artificial and resulted from dredging that began in the 1870s.

During the cycles of changes to the river, many bridges have been built and then replaced. The old center-pier swing bridges that originally connected adjoining land areas impeded traffic on the river, and so were replaced to accommodate large vessels. Some of the old bridge abutments can still be seen on the north side of the channel. Ironically, many of the waterway improvements occurred after traffic began to fall because of the decline of the local steel industry.

Another lift bridge looms ahead. This is the bridge for the Norfolk and Southern Railway Company. On the north bank of the river, between this bridge and the two just described, is a facility called **SEPA** (Sidestream Elevated Pool Aeration) No. 1. This facility and four others are part of a waterway cleanup project undertaken by the Metropolitan Water Reclamation District.

Opposite the SEPA station is the **Ford Motor Company Assembly Plant,** which assembles the popular Ford Taurus and Sable automobiles. Had plans for a third airport materialized, Ford would have moved its plant from the Chicago area. Ford's strong stand was one of the main reasons the airport plans were scrapped.

Ford operated its Chicago facilities at 39th Street and Wabash Avenue from 1911 to 1923 before moving to 130th Street, where the current plant was opened in 1924. The first product produced was the Model T Touring Car. Since that time the plant has also made the Torino, Elite, Thunderbird, Granada, Cougar, LTD, and Grand Marquis car models in addition to government and civilian trucks.

Ford is a major employer, with 2,815 employees and an annual payroll above $152 million. The success of the Taurus car and Chicago's retraction of its airport plans led Ford to invest $360 million to create a new Body-Side assembly plant, increasing the plant size to 2.5 million square feet on 106 acres of land. The assembly lines stretch for twenty-two miles, and 253 robots toil along with the production line workers.

The **Lafarge Corporation** operates a cement distribution plant west of the Ford assembly plant. It is a break-of-bulk or transshipment operation, bringing in shiploads of cement from its manufacturing operation in Alpena, Michigan, off-loading it into a cement storage barge, and selling it to local ready-mix concrete contractors.

MAP 28. Calumet River, international port at Lake Calumet.

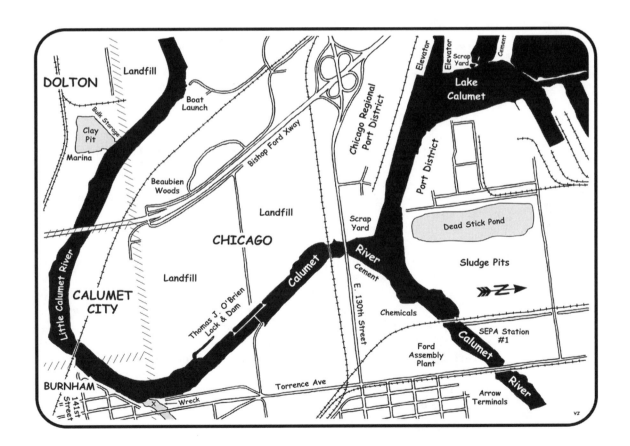

Despite land-fills of solid waste, the Lake Calumet area still holds a signif-icant number of wetlands.

Marsulex maintains a transshipment facility for sulphuric acid just west of the Ford plant. Here, acid is transferred from railroad tank cars to trucks for local distribution.

Lafarge has just put in service the newest ship on the lakes: the *Integrity,* a tug-barge combination vessel that consists of a jumbo barge fitted with a tugboat as a power unit. The result is a lake-bulk car-rier vessel with a detachable power unit.

Lake Calumet
At this point the waterway explorer has traveled six miles inland from Lake Michigan through the winding course of the Calumet River to Turning Basin No. 5, the junction of the Calumet River with **Lake Calumet.** Now to the right can be seen the expansive surface of the

Chicago International Port at Lake Calumet, the southwesternmost point ac-cessible to ocean ships coming through the Saint Lawrence Seaway into the heart of the continent.

Besides Lake Michigan, Lake Calumet is the largest remnant lake left after waters from glacial Lake Chicago drained away to the west. Other small remnant lakes in the area were part of a vast assemblage of shallow lakes and cat-tail marshes that extended over twenty-two thousand acres. These lakes were known as Berry (or Bear), George, and Wolf Lakes. Today **Berry Lake** is a mem-ory, having been completely filled in; **Lake George** is essentially gone; and **Wolf Lake** has had its western arm— Hyde Lake—reduced to a single drainage ditch. Overall, the original area of nearly

34 1/2 square miles has been reduced to slightly less than one square mile (five hundred acres).

Although Indian trails and then roads and railroads traversed the marshland on long sand ridges, little other development or settlement occurred near Lake Calumet before **George Pullman** built his model community on the west shore of the lake in 1881. Even then, the lake and its extensive marshlands were mostly used for hunting and fishing until after World War II, when a large portion of the wetlands area was used as a dumping ground for industrial wastes.

In 1940 the City of Chicago began to convert the northern third of the lake to a garbage dump, an ugly, malodorous source of pollution that inhibited nearby development for decades. Today the old dump had been converted to a golf course, not the kind of development the port district should undertake, many feel, since it fails to generate jobs. On the other hand, the golf course has been successful enough to improve the image of the area.

The dredging of the huge marsh between Lake Calumet and Lake Michigan began in 1870 and was gradually extended to create what is now known as the Calumet River. Eventually, this river reached Lake Calumet so that Lake Michigan and the shallow inland lake were reconnected. Shipping traffic and industrial development were attracted to the extensive low-cost sites along the waterway, and by 1906, the Calumet River handled a greater volume of water traffic than did the older historic section of the Port of Chicago at the Chicago River. In 1909 the Chicago Harbor Commission urged that work start toward "creating an inland harbor on Lake Calumet."

Pullman

In 1880 **George Pullman** built the ultimate company town on an empty stretch of marshland on the northern shore of Lake Calumet and named it after himself. Lake Calumet was then much bigger than it is today, and Pullman established his town along its northern shore. The town of Pullman, designed jointly by Solon S. Beman and Nathan F. Barrett, was built with bricks made from clay dug from the bottom of Lake Calumet.

The community bordered the factories of the **Pullman Palace Car Company.** A wooden bridge connected Pullman to the five-acre "Athletic Island," which was situated in the lake. Although Pullman was world famous for its enlightened planning, it ultimately became a symbol of corporate paternalism and greed and was the focus of a devastating and violent strike in 1894. Three years later, in 1897, the Pullman Company was forced to divest itself of ownership in the town.

The storied Florence Hotel in Pullman—the ultimate company town—on the shore of Lake Calumet. (Courtesy, Paul Petraitus.)

In 1911 the Chicago City Council enacted ordinances designating harbor districts that included the Calumet River and Lake Calumet. Ten years later the city secured title to the lake from the State of Illinois. On July 22 of that year, the city council adopted the **Van Vlissengen Plan,** which called for excavation of the harbor area and filling sections of the lake to create sites for industries and terminals.

Little actual work on the harbor was done between 1924 and 1953, when an updated plan for harbor development was adopted. The federal government deepened the southern end of Lake Calumet as authorized by the Rivers and Harbors Act of 1935 by creating a basin 3,200 feet long and 670 feet wide with a depth of 21 feet, to give access to a steel dock wall that the City of Chicago planned to build as part of a water-rail-highway terminal.

The wall was completed in 1940, but the terminal facility was never built. However, the basin proved useful during World War II, when the **Pullman-Standard Car Manufacturing Company**

operated a shipyard at the south end of Lake Calumet that built small navy craft for the war effort. After the war, the shipyard was converted to a major terminal facility (Mayer 1957, 184–85).

The Regional Port District (later named the Illinois International Port District) was approved in June 1951 as an autonomous, self-supporting body. Finally, on September 29, 1955, with the completion of the Saint Lawrence Seaway looming, underwriting was secured for bonds to support port development. The day after the bonds were issued, construction began on more than one mile of wharves for ocean vessels, three fireproof transit sheds, a warehouse, two 6.5-million-bushel grain elevators, and infrastructure.

Traffic began at the port in 1956, and the first stage of port development was completed in 1957, two years before completion of the Saint Lawrence Seaway. The first oceangoing ship reached Chicago in April 1959, when the seaway came on stream. Today major commodities through the port include portland cement, ethylene glycol, iron and steel wire, ferrous scrap, soda lye, maize, isopropyl

CHICAGO RIVER FACT: MORE THAN 50,000 VESSELS PASS THROUGH THE CHICAGO RIVER EACH YEAR, INCLUDING COMMERCIAL, RECREATIONAL, AND PASSENGER BOATS.

alcohol, iron and steel bars and angles, and other iron and steel products.

Initially, port traffic rose quickly, but has declined greatly since 1975. Nonetheless, the revenue bonds were paid off in 1991, some 4 1/2 years early.

To meet its revenue obligations, the port district became an aggressive industrial development agency, and today income from leaseholds exceeds revenue from maritime operations. Land development holds the key to the port's future although there are still some special opportunities in the maritime sector. Leases on the port's two grain elevators recently expired, and, as of this writing, negotiations are under way to secure new ones.

Also at the head of the lake is the facility of the **Medusa Cement Corporation.** This firm owns and operates two bulk carrier vessels. The more-modern vessel, placed in operation in 1996, is a tug-barge named the *Medusa Conquest.* The older is the well-known *Medusa Challenger.* Built in 1906 and refitted in 1967, the ship is 552 feet long at 11,300 gross tons. In the 1970s the *Challenger* was a frequent visitor to the main stem and North Branch of the Chicago River. It developed a reputation

The notorious *Medusa Challenger.* In the past, this 552-foot long, 11,300-ton vessel often jinxed the usually reliable bascule bridges on the Chicago River's Main Stem.

as a jinx because it seemed to turn Chicago's dependable bascule bridges to stone when in the river. These days, the *Medusa Challenger* calls only at Lake Calumet, and the bridges have far less trouble.

Many residual ponds and sloughs still exist near Lake Calumet. One of them is **Dead Stick Pond,** made famous by the Chicago mystery writer **Sara Paretsky.** The wetlands that remain in the area form the basis for the proposed Lake Calumet National Ecological Park, which holds promise to save not only a unique area but also many endangered species of birds that nest there.

On the west shore of the lake are transit sheds and a building near the port entrance that is a designated free trade zone. Materials may be brought into this facility, worked on, and shipped out without paying duties. Of course, the North American Free Trade Agreement means that products from Canada and Mexico already enjoy duty-free status.

A wide variety of activities cluster at Lake Calumet. These range from firms that handle imported nonferrous metals or steel and steel specialties to scrap yards, pollution control firms, and a variety of bulk storage, break-of-bulk, and transshipment facilities. The mix has recently been joined by metal fabricating firms such as Welded Tube Company which is a major success story in this rebounding industrial district previously hard-hit by plant closures.

All told, employment at the International Port at Lake Calumet and along the Calumet River exceeds eight thousand. According to John Galvin, public relations director for the port, future industrial development looks promising.

THE CALUMET RIVER

130th Street Bridge
The **130th Street Bridge** is a major boundary on the Circle Tour, for it marks the navigation limit for deep-draft, oceangoing vessels. From here on, one passes through flowing inland waters available only to small craft and to river towboats and barges. The depth of the Calumet River conforms approximately with the Saint Lawrence Seaway standard of 26 1/2 feet. After this bridge, however, the channel depth maintained by the U.S. Army Corps of Engineers is nine feet, the standard depth for inland waterways in the United States.

Soon the river flows beneath another fixed bridge, which carries the tracks of the Chicago, South Shores and South Bend Railroads. The last remaining interurban rail line in the United States, it has survived repeated financial crises. Today it carries hosts of commuters who work in Chicago but live across the border in Indiana.

Immediately after passing under the rail bridge, the river veers off to the southeast toward the **Thomas J. O'Brien Lock and Dam.** As mentioned earlier, the river is an artificial channel that connects Lake Michigan and Lake Calumet with a natural stream. The stream is the previously east-flowing Grand Calumet River and the previously west-flowing Little Calumet River. The Grand and Little Calumets are really one stream that curves back on itself.

But not only is the Calumet River artificial, its flow is *reversed.* Instead of flowing *toward* Lake Michigan, it now flows *away* from the lake and toward the Mississippi River. A lock and dam was built to monitor the flow and prevent stream backup. In 1922, when the

Calumet River was first connected through the nine-foot Cal-Sag Channel with the Sanitary and Ship Canal, the original lock was located near Blue Island. Then, in 1956, a larger lock was authorized as part of the Cal-Sag Project to enlarge the waterway, for more-efficient barge transportation.

The original Cal-Sag canal was cut along the line of an 1848 feeder canal that brought water into the Illinois and Michigan Canal. The Cal-Sag was dug for the same reason as the Sanitary and Ship Canal: to reverse the flow of the surface streams and divert sewage westward away from Lake Michigan, the city's water supply. It followed the channels of the Calumet River, the Grand Calumet River, and the Little Calumet River, and included a section of the channel of a small stream known as Stony Creek. The Cal-Sag also proved useful for barge transportation, but on a limited scale.

The Thomas J. O'Brien Lock was completed in 1960 with a width of 110 feet and a length of 1,100 feet. Since standard barges used on the inland waters are 35 feet wide and 109 feet long, the lock can accommodate barge tows of six or more barges. In practice, most barge tows using the locks are two barges wide and three to four barges long.

One enters the lock chamber when so indicated by the lock tender, who

Pleasure boats and commercial barge tows are lowered by the Thomas J. O'Brien Lock before entering the Little Calumet River and the Cal-Sag Channel.

Calumet Area Plants and Animals

Proof of the revival of the area's waters is given by the plants and animals that live in and near the lakes and streams. Their numbers are increasing, and species of fish that have never been observed in these waters are making an appearance. From this point onward, there are many opportunities to see waterbirds along the stream. The **Hegewisch Marsh,** just to the east (left) of the O'Brien Lock, teems with life. Look for the great blue heron, the great egret, the black-crowned night heron, the green heron, and myriad ducks, cormorants, gulls, killdeer, and kingfishers. Occasionally, one may observe bald eagles, goshawks, fish eagles, turkey vultures, red-tailed hawks, and many other types of birds.

A great blue heron awaits its prey.

signals using a red-green traffic light at the end of the lock and by sounding a short blast on an air horn. It is important to tie boats to the lock wall so that the surging currents won't throw the craft against the wall. It is also *very* important to *keep hands and arms inside the boat.* A slight shift in the position of all but the smallest craft could result in serious injury. Play safe; be extra careful in locks.

In the case of westward travel, the water in the lock is gradually released by opening the southern lock gate, allowing the excess water to pour out of the lock into the surface stream beyond. As the lock chamber empties, boats in the lock are gradually lowered to the exit river level. This done, and the air-horn sounded, vessels in the lock chamber may proceed to the waiting river beyond. The stream in this area grazes the communities of Burnham, Calumet City, and Dolton, all blue-collar suburbs.

On the right (north) bank of the river rises a very large hill, quite a thrill if one is from Chicago. Alas, the hill was not given to us by nature but rather was built for us with our donations. It is, of course, a hill of garbage from Chicago. The companies that construct such landfill say that space in the old landfills is running out, so we should allow them to fill in the rest of the area's wetlands (on our behalf) for waste disposal. Serious recycling and more-reasonable packaging will certainly slow the rate at which we destroy additional areas with landfills. When one views these enormous hills of refuse, the urgent necessity for a lower level of consumption becomes palpable.

Fortunately, most who tour the waterways live far from these pestilential piles. But there are people who live all the time in their shadow. The residents of nearby Altgeld Gardens think that the high incidence of cancer in their neighborhood might relate to their proximity to these landfills.

Wonderfully, amazingly, these waters, for so long severely polluted, are on the mend. This is partly attributable to the new side-stream aeration pools along the waterway and partly due to better construction of landfills, better sewage treatment, and stronger environmental regulations.

When the author arrives at this section of the waterways, he regrets that the excitement of the Calumet industrial area is past, yet is relieved that the intensity level has dropped. Now along with occasional industrial plants—some of them quite imposing—are pleasure-boat marinas, second-growth forests, and wildlife. Sailboats and power craft operators—a few all too ignorant of good manners or physics—appear on the river along with the almost omnipresent barge traffic.

One might wonder why, in the absence of obvious traffic on the river, large tour boats occasionally slow to a crawl. There is a no-wake rule for areas where heavy wakes could damage boats, destroy docks, or cause barges to break loose. No-wake zones are growing in number because of the multiplying facilities along the water, especially small-boat marinas.

Just beyond the O'Brien Lock, no fewer than three marinas put in their appearance. All told, the Circle Tour will pass more than a dozen of these facilities. The number of marinas and boats on the water gives the explorer some appreciation of the economic impact of the estimated 60,000 boats registered in Cook County.

The natural stream called the **Grand Calumet River** flows into the waterway from the left, under the fixed bridge at Torrence Avenue. Curiously, there is a boat sunk right in the middle of the channel. Apparently the vessel, the *Baby Doll*, floated to this position, where it sank. Nobody claims responsibility, even though the U.S. Army Corps of Engineers has tried to find its owner.

The craft itself has had a rather colorful history. For a time, we are told by tugboat skippers and other "old hands" on the waters, the *Baby Doll* sailed Lake Michigan and offered illicit pleasures to businessmen out on the lake. Whatever its actual history, its inglorious end places it smack in the Grand Calumet channel, where it does no harm—the one-foot-deep stream is no longer navigable.

After passing the confluence with the Grand Calumet, the waterway becomes the channel of the **Little Calumet River.** Like the Grand Calumet, the Little Calumet is a natural stream, and it continues for about six miles as part of the Cal-Sag route to the west. At the Grand Calumet confluence, the Little Calumet turns sharply southwest for about one-quarter of a mile before it turns westward once again. Landfills dominate the right bank of the stream. Many short pipes protrude from them to flare off natural gas (methane) that is produced by the decomposition of organic materials. Flames occasionally appear at the tips of these pipes. At this point the stream passes beneath the Conrail Bridge.

The Conrail Bridge is about 141st Street South, and just beyond it, around 142nd Street South, is the southernmost point of the Circle Tour. Nearby on the left is the Ashland Chemical plant where the company manufactures industrial adhesives. Overall, the river flows almost due west from this point, although it winds back and forth and makes a very sharp set of turns at Acme Bend.

Multiple bridges span the Calumet River. In the background is the bridge of the Chicago Skyway. Only the closest bridge, formerly of Conrail, is still in use.

Up ahead, the twin fixed bridges of the Calumet Expressway, now named the **Bishop Ford Expressway** after a local clergy member, cross the stream. It is interesting to view the intensity of traffic on the expressway from the quiet smoothness of the river.

The right bank is built up with ridges of earth that were spoils from digging the original channel. It is overgrown now and part of the Forest Preserve District of Cook County. A small boat-launching ramp and marina provide access to the stream. The left bank also features a small-boat marina and bulk-cargo storage facility made out of what was formerly a clay pit. This clay bed was used for brick making well into the 1970s. Now the old brickyard has been closed and the clay pit converted to new uses.

The Indiana Avenue fixed bridge lies ahead, and just past it are the bridges that carry the Illinois Central Gulf Railroad over the Little Calumet River. These bridges give water travelers an opportunity to see for themselves the previous limitations that plagued this water route. On the left is the dark original bridge that spanned the old channel. It is sixty feet wide, the width of the former restricted channel. To the right is the light-colored bridge over the enlarged channel. This clear-span fixed bridge was built on dry land, and then the 225-foot channel was excavated beneath it.

The main line of the Illinois Central is very busy and one may observe firsthand the almost continuous flow of trains on the bridge, often with trailers or standard containers on rail-road cars—so-called piggyback operations. Trains here also regularly carry newly assembled automobiles, tank cars of agricultural sugars and oils, fertilizers, steel coils, and fabricated metal products. These highly varied cargoes speak of the complexity and diversity of industrial activities in the Chicago metropolitan area.

Past the bridges, the stream enters the sharp turns of Acme Bend, with Chicago on the north bank and Riverdale on the south. **Acme Steel** is the destination for the torpedo cars of molten iron that were produced at the blast furnace along the Calumet River. It produces specialty low-carbon high-strength steels using basic oxygen furnaces for various

MAP 29.
Little Calumet River, Acme Steel.

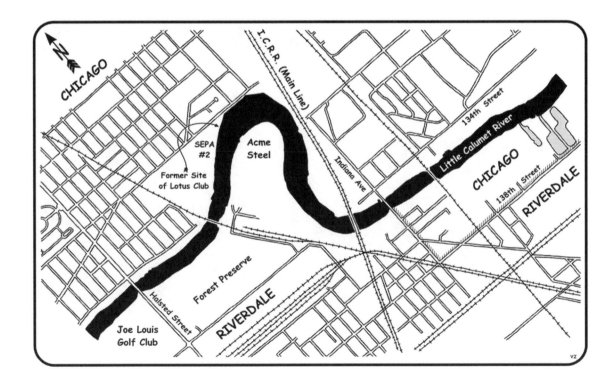

Acme Iron
Plant along
the Calumet.

"niche" markets including its own three manufacturing divisions.

In August 1994, Acme invested $300 million to build a new continuous caster and compact hot strip mill. This cutting edge facility has dramatically increased quality and productivity by cutting steel casting and rolling cycles from ten to twelve days down to about one hour. It is expected to project Acme into a new era of steelmaking.

Acme Steel is interesting and picturesque. The large blue building seen behind the dark, older rolling mills contains the new continuous caster and hot strip mill. Torpedo cars and slag-handling operations are also readily seen from the river, and oxygen storage facilities can be viewed. Conscious of its environmental responsibilities, Acme has water-recycling operations set up near the riverbank. The new mill should also reduce the environmental impact of the company's operations.

On the north bank of the river, directly opposite Acme Steel, is the second SEPA station built to resemble a waterfall amidst oak trees. Once again, the additional recreational space and the beneficial effects on the waterway make this a very effective facility. In the 1870s, before industry came to the Calumet, the young **Louis Sullivan** and his friends had a clubhouse called the **Lotus Club** near this site. Sullivan kept meticulous records of their swimming and diving competitions.

The Conrail Bridge marks the western limit of the operation. It is now used to move materials between Acme and its subsidiary firm, Nacme, north of the river. The western side of the bridge is being rebuilt so that it can carry a bike trail over the stream. Beyond the rail bridge, the character of the stream changes radically. On the left bank is a section of the **Forest Preserve District of Cook County**, and just beyond is the **Joe Louis Golf Club**, past the Halsted Street fixed bridge.

Small, privately owned bungalows now line the right side of the channel. These modest homes are in various states of repair, but all of them enjoy the beauty of the stream. Waterbirds are their neighbors, and barge tows and pleasure craft glide by on the stream's green pathway. Many of these homes have private docks, which once held boats. But times have changed, and few boats are seen today.

About one-half mile past the **Halsted Street Bridge**, the stream reaches another confluence. A marina occupies the left bank just before the channel of the Little Calumet River turns off to the southwest. Here, too the old Milwaukee fireboat, the *Deluge,* is docked. Through this stretch Little Calumet is tranquil and quite beautiful, and herons and other waterbirds are regularly sighted along its winding course. It is a very pleasant stream for canoe enthusiasts.

The community of **Calumet Park** sits on the right bank, where the remnant north wall of the old **Blue Island Lock** may be seen. When the channel was widened, the narrow sixty-foot lock chamber was destroyed and the south wall obliterated. Nonetheless, the north wall still exists and contains niches matching the shape of the lock gates.

After the lock was replaced by the much larger O'Brien Lock, the property was rented for a time to Material Service Company, but it seems that this yard has been closed. Raceway Park Speedway lies just to the north of the old lock area.

THE CALUMET-SAG CHANNEL

Blue Island Lock

From this point onward, the west-flowing stream is the artificial **Calumet-Sag Channel.** It follows the route of a feeder canal for the Illinois and Michigan Canal, cut through the southern of two drainage "sags," or low valleys made by the draining waters of glacial Lake Chicago. One small stream, Stony Creek, once wandered through this area: the canal occasionally follows a portion of its winding course.

This route through the southern sag was once considered for the Illinois and Michigan Canal. The plan might have been approved had not Gurdon Hubbard pointed out that if the southern route was chosen, Illinois would have had to pay the entire cost while Indiana would reap most of the benefit. Hubbard's argument proved decisive, and the northern route to the Chicago River was immediately affirmed.

Hubbard was a very important personage in the young city. He served as a canal commissioner and helped to ensure that Chicago's lakefront would remain clear and free of development for all the people. He also lived long enough to see the transformation of Chicago from a frontier fur-trading post to a city of more than one million. Hubbard lost virtually his entire fortune in the Great Fire of 1871, but he struggled on and wrote a remarkable autobiography that provides an on-the-scene account of the city's early days.

The Rivers and Harbors Act of 1946 authorized the enlargement of the Cal-Sag route from a 60-foot-wide channel to a 225-foot width. These modifications were done to relieve con-gestion and increase the scale of barge transport. When the Cal-Sag was sixty feet wide, barge tows had to be broken up so that a maximum of two barges could be towed, one behind the other, upstream toward the Calumet. No wonder barge operators called this stretch of stream "sixteen sad miles."

The stream modifications had the desired effect; cargo tonnages rose dramatically from 1955 onward. But the changes weren't accomplished quickly, and they weren't cheap. In addition to widening the channels and building a new lock, it was necessary to replace fourteen rail and seventeen highway bridges and to remove six steel highway bridges. The 1970 price tag was almost $270 million.

The Cal-Sag Channel now passes under the Ashland Avenue Bridge and the twin bridges of the **Dan Ryan Expressway** (I-57). The speed and intensity of the traffic overhead reminds the traveler that although the stream seems bucolic and remote, urban life surges on just beyond the trees.

Barge tows are often seen along the Cal-Sag, with the most common type consisting of tows two barges across and three in length. Often these tows move coal from the KCBX terminal along the Calumet River to various power stations along the waterway. Large triangular structures at the front of the towboats, called towing knuckles are used to secure the barge tows to the forward end of the towboats—vessels that, in reality, push the barges from behind.

Notice the crews working on the barges. They always wear life jackets because theirs is a difficult and dangerous occupation. Barges frequently carry hazardous or explosive materials, and they

operate around the clock in all seasons. Citified folk who work hard in offices rarely encounter the dangers that are the everyday experience of the men and women who work on the waterways.

Both banks of the stream are now in the community of **Blue Island.** To the left, a trailer park has been developed next to the canal. On the right, the high center of Blue Island may be seen. Blue Island, or, more properly, the Blue Island Ridge, was an island when Lake Chicago lay over the land sixty feet higher than the level of Lake Michigan today. After the lake receded, the ridge remained a well-drained high point above the marshes of the lake plain.

The Cal-Sag Channel now passes under a succession of bridges at Division Street and Chatham Street and then the high bridge at Western Avenue, which soars almost forty-five feet above the water. Between Chatham Street and Western Avenue on the north (right) bank is the third SEPA station, this one built to resemble a turn-of-the-century urban park. The graceful curve of the waterfalls lends beauty to an otherwise undistinguished section of the stream bank, while the SEPA station provides needed parkland that is well used during the summer.

Almost immediately after the stream passes beneath Western Avenue, it flows below the twin rail bridges of the

The SEPA station (side-stream elevated pool aeration) at Blue Island. Five SEPA stations along the Calumet River and Cal-Sag Channel cool the water and increase its oxygen content, allowing the stream to clean itself.

Baltimore and Ohio Chicago Terminal Railroad and those of the Canadian National Railroad. Soon thereafter, the span at Francisco Avenue is passed, and then the Kedzie Avenue Bridge. West of Kedzie Avenue are three graceful suspension bridges that carry petroleum products over the water. They feed the Clark Oil Refinery on the north bank and the nearby Martin Oil Company storage terminal just to the west.

To the left (south) is the community of **Robbins,** a bedroom suburb with very few commercial services. The population is overwhelmingly African American and poor, with an unemployment rate approaching 30 percent. Robbins has an interesting history. In 1917 it became the first incorporated African-American town in the United States, and it operated the first black-owned airport.

Irene Brody, the mayor of Robbins, fought hard to establish a new waste incinerator facility in an effort to provide taxes to the cash-starved community and bring jobs. The facility was in compliance with state environmental regulations, and state subsidies in the form of tax breaks were granted.

However, the moment that neighboring communities heard of the proposal they began a massive campaign to kill it, arguing that such a potentially dangerous facility in an all-black suburb constituted environmental racism. And, in truth, landfills, toxic waste dumps, and similar activities tend to be concentrated in poorer neighborhoods. Hence, the neighbors objected on behalf of the citizens of Robbins and for themselves.

The citizens of Robbins felt the irony and wondered where this concern for their welfare was *before* the incinerator project was announced. They seemed to feel that jobs, even disagreeable ones, were preferable to no employment at all. The facility is now operating and the ironies continue as a number of black employees have filed a civil-rights complaint, charging that they were harassed and verbally abused.

Forested ridges of spoil dug from the canal continue on both sides of the channel. Behind the spoil bank on the right, just before the Crawford (Pulaski) Avenue Bridge, is the nearly hidden plant of **FSC Corporation.** This Australian-owned firm recycles paper collected from a large area in the Midwest. The primary product is newsprint although Kraft paper and a patented, white-coated writing paper are also produced. FSC pumps in water from the canal, cleaning and treating it for manufacturing processes. The process water is returned to the waterway via the Alsip sanitary treatment plant.

Alsip is the community along the north bank as the canal flows west of Crawford Avenue. Next to the bridge on the right is a drop shaft for the Metropolitan Water Reclamation District's Deep Tunnel Project. Many such drop shafts line area waterways and carry excess stormwater from the streets and sewer overflow. This water falls three hundred feet to thirty-foot-diameter tunnels in the limestone bedrock. After the storm has passed, the stored water is sent to the treatment plants before being returned to the waterways.

The Northern Illinois Toll Highway leaps the canal on twin bridges that angle to the northwest. **Crestwood** is the community to the south of the stream. The second-growth forest on the spoil banks is quite beautiful, especially in autumn. Outcroppings of dolomitic limestone show where coral reefs stood above the

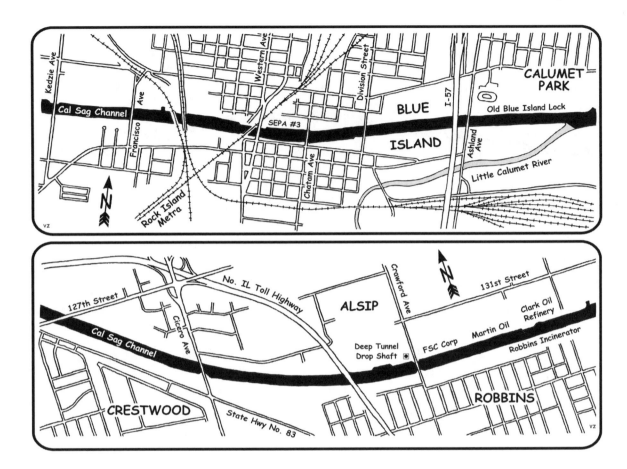

floor of the shallow, tropical sea that blanketed this area 400 million years ago.

The canal at the Cicero Avenue Bridge is about 130th Street South. Considerable development of the canal banks is evident at Cicero Avenue (Illinois 50). From here the channel shifts a bit to the northwest, and the east-west 127th Street crosses the stream. Immediately after the canal passes under the 127th Street Bridge, Tinley Creek joins the canal from the south. By the time the canal forms the division between Worth to the north and Palos Heights to the south, it has moved north to about 120th Street.

The fourth SEPA station is found on the north bank of the canal in the community of **Worth**. Once again the recreational land generated by this facility seems to be very popular for picnicking and fishing. Ridgeland Avenue crosses the stream at about 120th Street, where it forms the approximate eastern boundary of Worth and **Palos Heights.**

The **Eidelweiss Development** of stacked townhouses occupies the south bank west of Harlem Avenue in **Palos Park.** Here the canal is used as a scenic amenity, and terraced landscaping with picnic areas enhance the development. Harlem Avenue (Illinois 43) bridges the

MAP 30.
Little Calumet River, Blue Island.

MAP 31.
Cal-Sag Channel, Alsip.

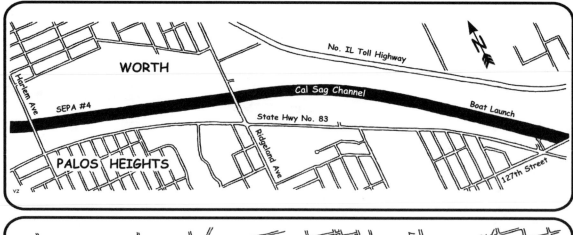

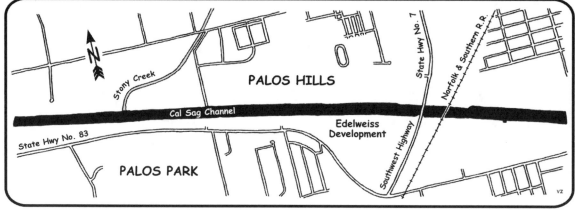

canal at about 117th Street. Slightly to the northwest, twin bridges carry the Norfolk and Southern Railway and Southwest Highway (Illinois 7) over the channel near the four corners of Worth and Palos Heights to the east and Palos Hills and Palos Park to the west.

In **Palos Hills,** Stony Creek's wandering course once more intersects the Cal-Sag. Here it joins the canal from the north, and a development of attractive homes is tucked along the creek.

Now the land to the north (right) slopes upward and is called **Mt. Forest Island.** It is the triangular section of the moraine that is cut off by the northern and southern sag valleys. Virtually all of this high ground lies in forest preserves, golf courses, and cemeteries. The rolling uplands form alternating hills and depressions filled with lakes and sloughs— typical morainic topography, where residual lumps of ice from the retreating glacier melted and formed undrained depressions. This type of landscape is called *kettle and kame topography,* where the *kames* are the hills and the *kettles* the undrained depressions.

Many trails are available here to the hiker or the cross-country skier. Wildlife is abundant: deer and coyote make their appearance along with a host of smaller

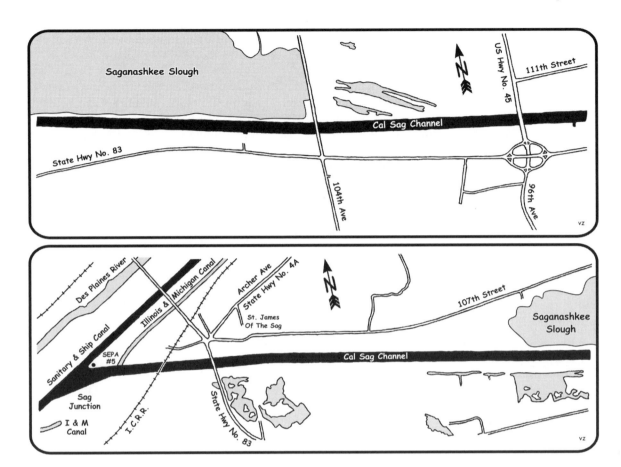

creatures. Waterbirds favor the quiet sloughs, which have colorful names such as Boomerang, Buttonbush, Bellydeep, and Horsecollar. The largest of them all, the great **Saganashkee Slough,** stretches for 1 1/2 miles north of the Sag Channel.

Two major roads cross the canal and give access to the area. They are 96th Avenue (U.S. Route 45) and 104th Avenue. Forest growth on spoil banks and rocky outcrops of limestone make this tranquil section of the canal a place of great beauty.

On the right bank are a number of tall, dead trees. Their bare, white branches are favorite perching places for the turkey vultures that are often seen

there, especially in wet weather. The high ground ahead is a continuation of the moraine upland. It holds the **Waterfall Glen Forest Preserve** that wraps around the **Argonne National Laboratory.**

The end of the Cal-Sag Channel approaches. On the right, two miles before the junction of the Cal-Sag and the Sanitary and Ship Canal, the rocky bank has been fortified with concrete. Two bridges are ahead. The first is the fixed span of the **Sag Highway Bridge** (Illinois 83). Then, about one-quarter mile further along, just beyond an automobile junkyard, the **Illinois Central Gulf Railway Bridge** crosses the channel.

MAP 34.
Cal-Sag Channel, Saganashkee Slough.

MAP 35.
Cal-Sag Channel, Sag-Junction.

On the right bank immediately after the bridge is the place where the old Illinois and Michigan Canal crosses the Sag Channel. Of course, the canal preceded the Cal-Sag Channel and went straight across the area. It should be visible on both sides of the channel, but its southern continuation has been filled in and obliterated by spoil from the widening of the Cal-Sag Channel. So, the view to the right provides the only opportunity on the Great Circle Tour for a direct look at a remnant section of the old canal.

It is virtually impossible to overstate the importance of the Illinois and Michigan Canal to Chicago's growth and rise to power. As mentioned earlier, the notion of such a canal occurred to French explorer Louis Joliet in 1673 on his portage from the Des Plaines to the Chicago River. By 1816 topographical engineers were actively considering the canal route. In 1818 the northern boundary of the proposed state of Illinois was moved northward before the state was formally admitted to the Union. This boundary change was done expressly to give Illinois a shoreline on Lake Michigan and to ensure that the planned canal would lie entirely within the state.

In 1822, during the presidency of James Monroe, Congress authorized the State of Illinois to construct the canal. The canal project fired the imaginations of settlers, would-be settlers, and land speculators who helped touch off several frenzied episodes of land speculation in the Chicago area. Actual construction of the canal began in 1836, but work was temporarily suspended in 1841 due to a financial panic. Work finally resumed in 1845, and the canal was completed on April 16, 1848. On that day the passenger packet *General Fry* made the first ceremonial trip along the canal. A week later, the canal boat *General Thornton* carried a cargo of sugar from New Orleans to Chicago, where it was loaded on a steamer bound for Buffalo, New York. When the sugar reached Buffalo, its arrival was considered such an event that it was announced in Congress by Abraham Lincoln.

The impact of the Illinois and Michigan Canal was immediate and profound:

> . . . the canal brought striking changes to the regional economy. During its first season of operation, eastern corn shipments from Chicago multiplied eightfold as farmers in the Illinois River Valley suddenly discovered an alternative to St. Louis as an outlet for their produce. . . . Over 90 per cent of the new corn shipments came to Chicago via the canal, which was henceforth the city's chief source of corn until after the Civil War. Lumber receipts at Chicago from the forests of Michigan and Wisconsin nearly doubled in 1848, and one-fourth of this wood moved south down the canal, to be used for houses, fences, and farm buildings on the Illinois prairies. . . . It was as if a corridor of relatively cheap transport has suddenly appeared . . . (Cronon 1991, 64 and 65).

In addition, the canal was largely responsible for the ascendancy of Chicago as a rail center. Because the canal brought the produce of the western lands to Chicago, eastern railroads became interested in lines between Chicago and the East Coast. Within ten years, Chicago became the "Big Junction," the center of rail transportation in the United States.

As the canal and railroads increased the flow of grain into Chicago's warehouses, they simultaneously encouraged an expansion of shipping out of its harbor, contributing to a general reorientation of western trade toward the east and away from the south. Between 1850 and 1854, the net eastward movement of freight shipments via the Great Lakes finally surpassed shipments out of New Orleans (Miller 1996, 110).

It seems difficult to reconcile a regional reorientation of trade from a north-south to an east-west axis with the tiny ditch called the Illinois and Michigan Canal. But the canal, having been accountable for Chicago's founding, then became heavily responsible for its rampant growth and rising economic importance.

The **Illinois and Michigan Canal** stretched ninety-six miles from the South Branch of the Chicago River at Ashland Avenue to the La Salle-Peru community on the Illinois River. It was sixty feet wide and six feet deep. In several places it had to cross natural streams, often at a different elevation, requiring construction of dams and aqueducts.

Overland travel in general was so bad at the time that passenger service on the canal, moving at a very leisurely four to five miles per hour, was considered suitable—and decidedly more comfortable

A remnant section of the old Illinois and Michigan Canal as seen from the Cal-Sag Channel near Sag Junction. This 60-foot wide channel helped establish Chicago as the great market of the Midwest.

An aerial view of the waterways near Hodgkins. The large stream in the middle is the Sanitary and Ship Canal. To the left is a small remnant section of the Illinois and Michigan Canal and to the right is the Des Plaines River.

than the faster, but jarring stagecoach. Starting in 1867, the canal was widened and deepened. It "carried 1,011,287 tons . . . during its peak year in 1882 before the decline set in" (Young, in press). But the canal's peak tonnage year was not its peak year for tolls. In the early days, the canal carried all kinds of general freight, which paid high tolls. Later, from about 1867 onward, it carried principally bulk cargoes, which raised tonnage figures but produced lower tolls. As a result, tolls on the canal peaked in the late 1860s and then fell steadily. The old canal was finally abandoned for navigation in 1932.

In the late 1950s, the State of Illinois considered selling canal lands to raise revenues, but citizen opposition prevented this course of action (Howe 1956, 7). A sixty-one-mile **Illinois and Michigan Canal State Trail** was set up by 1974, and citizen support led to federal efforts to protect and enhance the Canal Corridor's cultural and natural resources. Thus was born the **Illinois and Michigan Canal National Historic Corridor,** the first of a new form of "partnership parks" linking the state and federal governments.

The corridor encompasses more than forty cities and towns in five

counties and many Chicago neighborhoods. It includes state and local parks, forest preserves, and rare natural lands, and helps to open these areas for recreational activities such as cross–country skiing, fishing, canoeing, and camping. The corridor also preserves many historic sites that played critical roles in the growth of Illinois and the nation. And the canal corridor connects to the east with the proposed **Calumet Ecological Park.**

Now it is possible to hike or bicycle along an excellent, very flat trail from **Channahon** most of the way to the canal's west end at **La Salle-Peru.** Where the canal holds water, canoeing is pleasant. The scenery is lovely, and there is no competing water traffic.

As soon as the I & M Canal remnant is passed, the fifth and final SEPA station becomes visible, also on the right bank. This station is designed around a lighthouse that marks the junction of the Cal-Sag Channel with the Sanitary and Ship Canal. Water from the Cal-Sag is pumped to a small retention pond and then cascaded over artificial waterfalls into both canals. The result is a very attractive, effective facility that sits at a critical junction of the waterway system.

A beautiful trail follows the towpath along the old Illinois and Michigan Canal southwest of Chicago near Channahon.

THE SANITARY AND SHIP CANAL

Sag Junction

Now the Circle Tour makes a sharp turn to the right and enters the **Sanitary and Ship Canal** for the return trip to the heart of Chicago. The canal was the means by which the flow of the Chicago River was finally reversed. Opened for traffic in 1900, it was the culminating effort capping years of indecision and makeshift attempts to safeguard Chicago's water supply. When it was built, it was by far the largest municipal undertaking in the United States.

As the tour vessel makes the turn, one may look downstream to see various barge docks and suspended pipelines crossing the channel. This tends to be a busy section of the waterway, so barge tows are often seen here.

On the left side of the sanitary canal, out of sight behind the spoil banks, is the Des Plaines River. On the right bank, past the SEPA station, is a shipyard run by the **Hannah Marine Corporation.** The firm has operated at this site for forty-eight years, cleaning and doing topside repairs to barges and other vessels. For a time, Hannah rented a floating dry dock so that it could make vessel repairs below waterline.

Just inland from Hannah is a remnant section of the Illinois and Michigan Canal, but it cannot be seen from the sanitary canal. This is the northern sag valley and three parallel streams now flow through it.

Almost immediately the water tour passes under the bridge of Illinois 83, which we met a short time earlier where it crossed the Cal-Sag. Now on the right, it is just barely possible to see the steeple of **Saint James of the Sag** where it sits

on a high ridge overlooking both waterways. The church is almost entirely obscured by forest, but the steeple does appear momentarily.

Saint James of the Sag is the oldest functioning Roman Catholic church in the Chicago area operating at its original site. It is located near the junction of Archer Avenue and 107th Street, where it sits surrounded by the Argonne Forest Preserve. The congregation dates from the period 1833 to 1837, the dates of Chicago's incorporation, first as a town and then as a city. The present church edifice was built in the 1850s and is surrounded by its burying ground.

The cemetery is very interesting, since it contains the graves of many Irish laborers who perished while digging the Illinois and Michigan Canal. Many of the individuals buried here were born in the eighteenth century; the oldest grave is dated 1816. Before the church occupied this ridge top, the site was the location of a French lookout post, and before that, an Indian village.

Silos of a Dundee Cement distribution facility are located on the right bank, and this stretch of the canal runs ramrod straight through surface limestone formations that overhang the stream. In many places the stream has dissolved the stone and chunks of the overhanging bank have collapsed into the water. This is a very beautiful section of the canal and for a considerable distance there are few indications of the urban development nearby. Now a curious concrete structure is seen on the left (north) bank. It is a spillway intended to remove high water from the Des Plaines River and shunt it into the sanitary canal.

Since commodities ranging from corn to calcium chloride are transported on this waterway, one may expect to see

The church of Saint James of the Sag and its cemetery occupy the high ridge between the Cal-Sag Channel and the Sanitary Canal near Sag Junction. Many Irish laborers who died digging the I & M Canal are buried here.

facilities that use or transport these items. As the canal leads closer to the city, more and more petrochemical storage operations appear.

Bridges over the inland rivers are fixed, so the pilothouses on the towboats are retractable. They can be raised for easier steering and maneuvering, or they can be lowered to fit beneath fixed bridges. It is quite common on the Great Circle Tour to see a towboat's pilothouse being moved down and up as the tow reaches a bridge. These towboats are usually fitted with "twin screws"—that is, they have two fifteen-hundred-horsepower engines and two propellers. As a result, they can maneuver in tight spaces and exert massive turning power on the tows by rotating their engines in opposite directions. The

propellers are set in grooves in the hull to generate maximum thrust.

It takes a barge tow about one week, moving against the flow of the stream, to proceed from the lower Mississippi River near New Orleans to the Chicago area. By contrast, barge tows moving with the stream downriver toward New Orleans take about two weeks to make the trip. This curious situation results from the difficulty of holding barges against the force of the stream.

At the **Willow Springs Bridge,** the three streams flow very close together. The Des Plaines River, the Sanitary and Ship Canal, and the I & M Canal are all contained in a strip of land just fifteen hundred feet across.

This storied section of the canal in Willow Springs is cut through a high

A barge tow of crushed limestone moves along the Sanitary and Ship Canal. The pilot house of the towboat is lowered to safely pass under the fixed bridge.

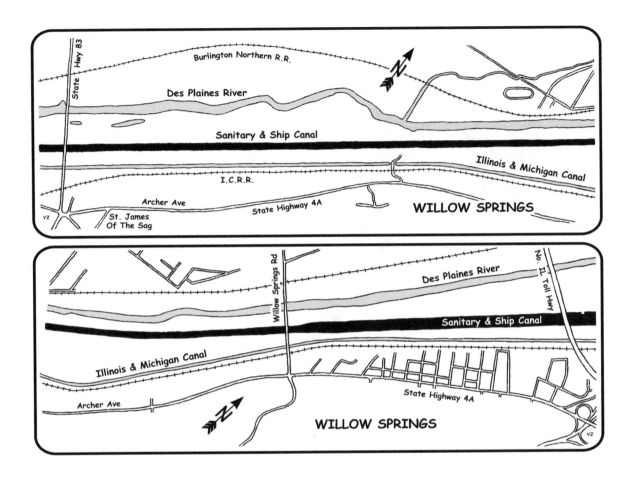

portion of the dolomitic limestone bedrock. Where the canal is cut through rock, the top and bottom dimensions are about the same. But east of the Willow Springs Bridge, the channel is cut through a mixture of rock and earth. Because earthen walls cannot stand vertically, the banks are angled, increasing the surface width of the canal. So, just beyond the bridge the canal widens dramatically.

Twin bridges carry the Northern Illinois Toll Highway over the channel, and the sudden appearance of high-speed, high-intensity traffic reminds the traveler of the sprawling urban develop-

ment that encircles the quiet waterway. Immediately past the tollway bridges is the La Grange Road Bridge (U.S. Routes 12, 20, and 45). These same highways were encountered in the Calumet District and are the modern expressions of ancient Indian trails. The high ground of **Mt. Forest Island** on the right side of the channel begins to decline as the tour proceeds out of the northern sag valley and onto the broad lake plain. The community of **Willow Springs** lies on both sides of the channel at the bridges about 7900 south.

Between the tollway bridges and La Grange Road is the **Willow Springs**

MAP 36.
Sanitary and Ship Canal, Saint James of the Sag.

MAP 37.
Sanitary and Ship Canal, Willow Springs.

The Masters Murder

The south-west suburbs sit on the rolling morainal hills, and the hummocky terrain includes many small lakes and ponds. Forest preserves, golf courses, and cemeteries fill the region. Growth has been slow and the area has retained a feeling of remoteness. Because of this rural character, the region around Willow Springs has long been a favorite dumping ground for all sorts of things. These "things" have been quite diverse and have included everything from stolen cars to murder victims.

Since the 1920s many bodies have been dumped in the forest preserves, the Cal-Sag, and the Sanitary and Ship Canal. The most sensational case of this kind occurred in the fall of 1983 when Alan Masters, a prominent attorney with offices in Summit, reported to the police that his wife Diane was missing. As a trustee of Moraine Valley College, Diane was an elected public official. Her disappearance set off a long and feck-less investi-gation. Unfortunately, **Diane Masters** was not found and little evidence was discovered that shed light on her disappearance.

The break in the case came unexpectedly six years later in connec-tion with a completely unrelated matter. In 1989 barge operators on the canal reported that their vessels were striking submerged ob-jects. When the reports were investigated it was discovered that these objects were automo-biles reported stolen in a scheme to defraud insurance carriers. A virtual reef of these car bodies had built up on the floor of the canal just west of the Willow Springs Bridge.

Contractors were hired to retrieve the ve-hicles and, in the course of removing them, dis-covered a blue Cadillac that belonged to Diane Masters. Her body was subsequently found in the trunk of the vehicle. She had been struck on the head and shot.

A celebrated con-spiracy case, based on circumstantial evidence, developed since the murder couldn't be at-tributed directly to any-one. Alan Masters and his accomplices were tried in federal court and found guilty of conspiracy to de-prive the victim of her civil rights by killing her. The theory was ad-vanced that Diane Masters had re-turned home after an evening meet-ing of the Moraine Valley College trustees and stopped at a local bar. Apparently, she and her husband quarrelled out-side their Palos Hills home and Alan struck Diane, knocking her un-conscious and possibly killing her.

According to the prosecution's theory, Masters panicked and asked a friend to help dispose of the body.

The friend, in turn, called on yet another friend who placed Diane in the trunk of her Cadillac. Then the car was driven to the south bank of the Sanitary and Ship Canal just west of the Willow Springs Bridge. Here, someone fired several shots into the trunk and drove the car down the bank into the stream.

What riveted pub-lic attention on the case was not just the sordid crime but also that the two accomplices were Michael Corbit, former chief of police of Willow Springs and his friend, a lieutenant in the Cook County sheriff's office. All three conspirators are currently serving ex-tended sentences in a federal penitentiary al-though there is a possi-bility that Corbit will be released in 1998 for turning state's evidence in a number of cases.

Terminal, the local off-loading and storage facility for the Marathon Oil Company. It is the first of a great many barge terminal facilities and petrochemical tank farms that line the canal. In fact, there are so many tank farms along the canal from this point onward that, for many years, this stretch of the waterway was nicknamed Gasoline Alley after the famous comic strip.

At La Grange Road, the canal begins a gentle curve to the left, where it is due south of the community of **Hodgkins.** This is the location of the main pumping station for the Deep Tunnel Project (Tunnel and Reservoir Project). Tunnels converge three hundred feet down in the bedrock, where a huge pump room has been carved out of the limestone. Some of the largest pumps in the world are located here, shifting 1.8 billion gallons of water from the tunnel system to the Stickney Works for treatment. One may tour this fascinating facility through the Metropolitan Water Reclamation District.

Justice is the community on the south bank of the canal, and Hodgkins sits on the north bank. On the south (right) bank one may see a few short electric transmission towers. These once carried electricity to Chicago from a hydroelectric plant at Lockport.

A powerhouse at the controlling lock and dam marks the southern end of the Sanitary and Ship Canal. Here the burden of waters diverted from Lake Michigan and the flows of the natural portions of the Chicago River system pass through turbines that recover some of their energy as electricity. In earlier times this electric current moved toward Chicago along wires carried by those old towers. Today, the Metropolitan Water Reclamation

District continues to generate considerable amounts of electric power. In 1995 MWRD produced fifty-nine million kilowatt-hours of electricity valued at $2.66 million.

About one mile past La Grange Road, also on the right bank, is a small diversion channel that leads from the Sanitary and Ship Canal to the Illinois and Michigan Canal less than two hundred feet inland. Just upstream from this small channel is an unseen but very important device in the waterway. It is a submarine air barrier that pumps compressed air to the surface of the water in case of an oil spill. This air barrier is set at a sharp angle to the bank so that surface oil will be shunted along one bank for easier removal.

Meanwhile, a rail line appears on the left bank, part of the thirty-mile, short-line railroad owned and operated by the Metropolitan Water Reclamation District. It has four locomotives and 156 railcars to carry dewatered solids to sludge-drying areas.

Sludge is the inert, left-over solid material from the sewage treatment process. It is water-soaked and thus very heavy. Before it can be carted away for use it must be dewatered, or dried. This organically rich material makes outstanding fertilizer, but may not be used for food growing because it is also rich in heavy metals. It is used, however, to revegetate strip-mined lands and so reclaim severely damaged areas.

The sludge-drying beds are vast, and they are clearly visible from the Stevenson Expressway (I-55), occupying almost all of the area between the sanitary canal and the Des Plaines River for a distance of about three miles. The Metropolitan Water Reclamation District maintains a barge-loading facility on the left bank so that the sludge can be shipped by water.

Barge transportation continues to be important for the shipment of petroleum and petrochemical products, graphically illustrated by the large numbers of docks and tank farms along the canal. In quick succession the tour passes the dock and tank farm of the **Shell Oil Company,** followed by the similar facility of GATX— the **General American Transportation Company.** Then slightly ahead, but again on the right bank, is the **Argo pumping station,** which handles effluent from the Argo Corn Starch Company.

Across the canal but out of sight beyond the Des Plaines River is the **McCook Quarry** that had been scheduled to become one of the reservoirs for the Tunnel and Reservoir Project. The proposed reservoirs would hold excess storm water beyond the 1.8 billion gallons the tunnels can contain, representing the final phase of this enormous and enormously expensive project. Unfortunately, the issue has become politicized in the little town of McCook, where incendiary rhetoric leads to statements that they "don't want the largest toilet in Illinois" in their neighborhood.

MAP 38.
Sanitary and Ship Canal, Justice.

MAP 39.
Sanitary and Ship Canal, Summit.

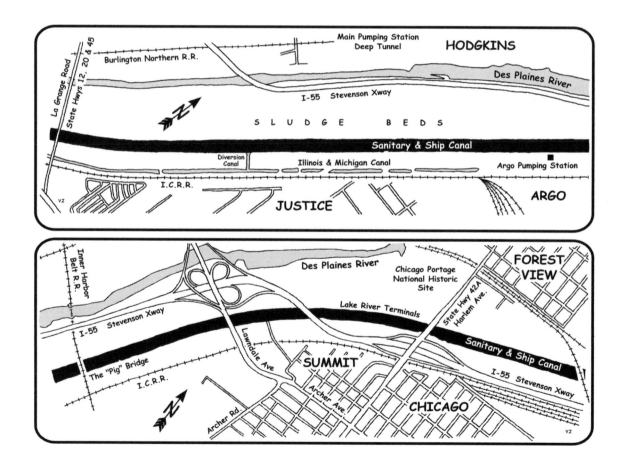

Actually, the water stored in such reservoirs would be mostly storm runoff from the streets, with only a small amount of sewage. Further, the oxygenation of the reservoir should cancel odors through aerobic decomposition and the water would be promptly moved on for treatment after storms abate. As an alternative approach, the MWRD has advanced another proposal that a quarry be excavated in the area of the current sludge beds to hold excess water. This proposal seems unrealistic, since the district still needs sludge-drying beds. And this idea, too, has met with community resistance.

The tour proceeds against the current and passes under the bridge old-timers call the **Pig Bridge.** It carries the B & O Chicago Terminal Railway (the Inner Harbor Belt Line), which connects the Barr rail yards in Blue Island with the huge, busy Clearing Yards. The bridge carries double tracks, so trains are almost always seen. Freight hauled by the trains speaks to the state of the economy, the level of imports, and the economic diversity of Chicago. These days one sees many standard containers, usually double-stacked and often from our Far Eastern trading partners.

The rail bridge marks a change in the character of the waterway. West of the bridge, despite the presence of a few terminal facilities, the Sanitary and Ship Canal seems remote from the city as it quietly flows through woodlands. East of the bridge, there is a sudden rise in the industrial development along the banks, and the voyager becomes acutely aware that the canal follows a transportation route that has been important since prehistoric times and is today even more intensely used.

South of the canal and parallel to it is one of the lines of the Illinois

Central Gulf Railroad. To the left, the **Stevenson Expressway** (I-55) runs between the Des Plaines River and the canal. A bit farther north, but again paralleling the canal, are the tracks of the Santa Fe Railroad. Barge tows move up and down the channel, pipelines follow the water route, and commercial aircraft pass overhead on their way to and from **Midway Airport.**

The south (right) bank features yet another cement distribution facility and the docks and tank farm of the **Trumbull Asphalt Company.** Asphalt is a very thick and viscous material that has to be heated to flow freely. So it is necessary to heat asphalt to offload it from tanker barges. Tour visitors fortunate enough to see an asphalt barge being unloaded often glimpse the activity through clouds of steam.

Slightly farther along the right bank is the attractive, small-boat launching facility grandly named the **Port of Summit.** It seems curious amidst the flatness of the lake plain to run into a town called **Summit.** Yet the name is appropriate because the town sits astride the subcontinental divide separating the Great Lakes and the Mississippi River drainage. The divide rose no more than twelve feet above the waters of Lake Michigan, and rainy periods often caused the Des Plaines to overflow the divide and split its drainage between the Atlantic and the Gulf of Mexico.

Up ahead the twin bridges at Lawndale and First Avenue cross the canal and link with I-55 just to the north. Then, about one-half mile beyond the first bridge group, the twin fixed spans of the Stevenson Expressway traverse the waterway at an angle as I-55 crosses from the north to the south bank of the canal.

The Pig Bridge

Since a 1964 accident that dumped livestock into the canal, the old B&O Bridge has been dubbed "The Pig Bridge." (From the private collection of Richard Sutphin.)

In 1964 a bizarre accident occurred at the B&O Chicago Terminal Railway bridge that lead to its nickname, the **Pig Bridge.** A railroad gondola car with extra-high metal sides was overloaded with scrap, and a portion of one side broke and hung over the side of the car. As the car went over the bridge a chunk of overhanging metal damaged various parts of the bridge, up to the center tower. Here the metal piece broke off and flipped into the stream.

The next train across the bridge was loaded with pigs and was pulled by two locomotives. The tremendous weight of the locomotives caused the damaged bridge to buckle and settle toward the stream. The freight cars of the train became jammed together like bricks in an arch, and kept the train from plunging into the stream. At this point the bridge looked a little like a metal basket hanging down to the surface of the canal. In the process, many pigs were either killed or dropped into the stream. For weeks, oil-covered pigs could be seen floating or swimming in the canal and washed up against the banks.

The surviving animals were eventually rounded up and put in a corral. But people from the area came at night and stole the oil-covered animals—often putting them in the backseats of their cars.

Meanwhile, since the bridge outage meant that connections were severed with the Clearing Rail Classification Yards and the canal was blocked, engineers and their crews worked around the clock to repair the damage. A used but functional bridge was brought in sections from the East Coast and modified to serve the new location. The bridge replacement was accomplished in a record thirteen days.

As soon as the bridges of I-55 are passed, the left bank holds one of the drop shafts that carry excess surface water down three hundred feet into the Deep Tunnel. It is an imposing structure with a louver set in a concrete tower. The louver allows air to escape as water plummets down into the tunnels, so that the compressed air does not rupture the drop shaft.

Now the extensive break-of-bulk facilities of the **Lake River Terminal** crowd both banks. On the right are the silos, storage sheds, and rail spurs that comprise the dry cargo section of the terminal. On the left bank, one sees the beginning of the large tank farm and the network of pipes and pumps constituting the fifty-million-gallon liquid storage portion of the terminal facilities.

Lake River Corporation operates facilities for off-loading and storing bulk chemicals, for blending and mixing these chemicals into proprietary products, for making and filling containers with those products, and for labeling and shipping the finished products to customers. Computers that keep secret formulas secret also automatically control all process steps for tenant companies.

Twin fixed bascule bridges mark Harlem Avenue, which divides Lake River Corporation in two. Harlem closely follows the ridge that forms the subcontinental drainage divide. And about one-half mile north of the Stevenson Expressway on the west side of Harlem Avenue is the **Chicago Portage National Historic Site.**

The site was established in 1952 to commemorate the old Chicago Portage at its western end where **Portage Creek,** the westernmost part of Mud Lake, drained into the Des Plaines River. Here the canoes carried around Mud Lake could finally be floated on the Des Plaines waters. The actual length of the portage depended critically on the water levels in Mud Lake and the Chicago and Des Plaines Rivers. High water sometimes meant no portage was necessary. On the other hand, low water levels led to a long and miserable overland carry.

Constructing the Stevenson Expressway

One of the major costs associated with expressway construction comes from the purchase of land for the highway right-of-way. By crossing from the north to the south side of the Sanitary and Ship Canal, the Stevenson Expressway (I–55) was able to use a corridor of land that was already in public ownership: the route of the old Illinois and Michigan Canal. Since the canal was already owned by the State of Illinois, title could simply be transferred without having to purchase large tracts of land. With the land acquisition problem solved, the canal could be filled in and the highway constructed. So it is that when entering or leaving Chicago via the Stevenson Expressway, one rides atop the filled-in channel of the Illinois and Michigan Canal.

A large steel sculpture at the Chicago Portage National Historic Site shows the explorers Joliet and Marquette and an Indian guide dragging their canoe through the shallows of Mud Lake.

The Portage Historic Site features a remarkable rusted-steel sculpture of Marquette, Joliet, and an Indian companion as they drag their canoe through the shallows. The sculptor of this notable work is Ferdinand Rebechini, a Chicago native. The historic site is being further improved. Plans now call for a major interpretive center to include a museum, archaeological center, and library in nearby **Ottawa Trail Woods** as well as a replica of **Laughton's Trading Post** at the rocky ford named after this pioneer.

Easy level trails lead one-quarter mile west into the forest. Sloughs and thickets alive with deer and other animals give visitors an opportunity to step back in time to glimpse the way the Chicago area looked about three hundred years ago. This "time machine" allows visitors to appreciate the difficulties of travel in the Chicago region before the Illinois and Michigan Canal, railroads, and highways made travel easy.

The site may seem wild but otherwise unremarkable. Yet this place is the key to the water route that unlocked the commercial potential of the region. When visitors walk along the trails here, they are very likely walking through the exact area where the Potawatomi, Joliet, Marquette, Hubbard, and countless

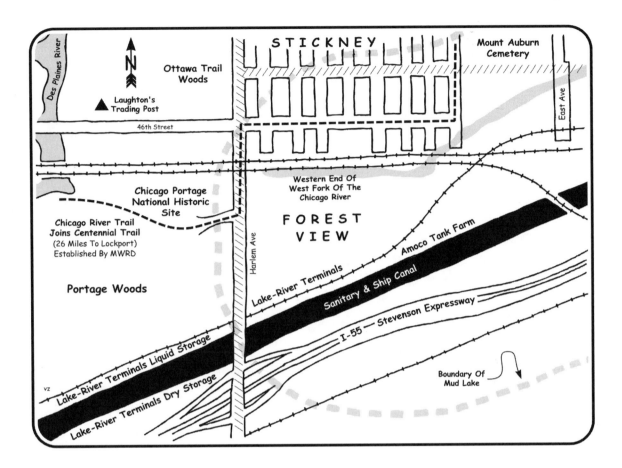

others walked. These early residents and explorers then either prepared themselves for the upcoming rigors of the portage or heaved a sigh of relief that the ordeal was past and the way to the West lay unimpeded before them.

Harlem Avenue

The tour moves east along the waterway, and heads upstream since the reversed Chicago River and its westward connection through the Sanitary and Ship Canal now flow toward the west.

Of course, two hundred years ago, an eastward trip on the Chicago River would have been downstream. Further,

there was no stream immediately east of Harlem Avenue. Rather, there was a large wetland that stretched almost all the way to Damen Avenue, a distance of about six miles.

There was often a stretch of open water in the midst of the marsh, a shallow pond called **Mud Lake**. The extent of the lake varied greatly with the seasons and with the amount of rainfall. In periods of wet weather, it was common for the Des Plaines River to overflow the low divide near Harlem Avenue and to drain simultaneously into both Mud Lake to the east and into its regular course to the west. So, the Indians of the area found

MAP 40.
Sanitary and Ship Canal, west end of the Chicago Portage. Gray area indicates the former channel of the Chicago River West Fork and the boundary of Mud Lake.

MAP 41.
Sanitary and
Ship Canal,
southwest
treatment
plant. Gray
area shows
the former
channel of
the Chicago
River West
Fork and the
boundary of
Mud Lake.

that there were times when they could paddle their canoes directly over the divide and on to the Illinois River with no portage at all.

Eventually, Mud Lake was drained and a single deep channel wriggled westward across the former marshland, which came to be known as the west fork. This channel was an avenue of commerce for about fifty years after Mud Lake was drained. When the Sanitary and Ship Canal was dug during the 1890s, a connecting collateral channel was created between the canal and the west fork.

As demand for land intensified and as the Sanitary and Ship Canal took more and more of the area's waterborne commerce, the usefulness of the west fork declined drastically. First its eastern portion was filled in; later the western section was placed in city sewers. Today the entire west fork has disappeared from the landscape—drainage is entirely within the sewer system. Some vestiges of the old channel still remain in the form of odd lot and fence lines and a few portions of old bridges that once crossed the stream.

The accompanying map shows the former channel of the west fork, and the

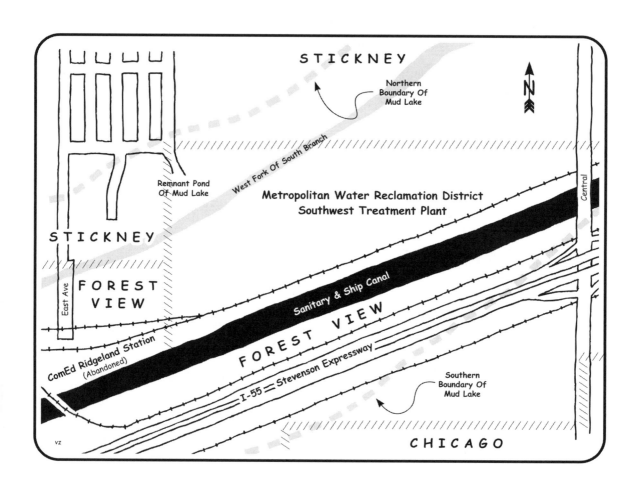

traveler may take a fascinating hike through the areas where it once flowed. But only the collateral channel remains today as a direct reminder of the old watercourse.

Chicago recently lost a part of the upper reaches of the Ogden Slip for the development of the Cityfront Center property. In addition, a plan was advanced to fill in the North Branch Canal on the east side of Goose Island. The continuing loss of useful waterway is a source of great concern, since waterways provide habitat and recreational space that would be very hard to duplicate.

Despite its splendid lakefront parks and historic boulevard and park system, Chicago is still considerably deficient in park space in terms of its population. Existing waterways provide a great deal of open space that must be preserved.

With Mud Lake now long gone and the west fork of the Chicago River a memory, intense industrial development fills the area east of Harlem Avenue and along the canal banks. Oil storage facilities of the Lake River Corporation continue along the north bank east of Harlem, and an Amoco tank farm adjoins that facility. The south bank carries

MAP 42. Sanitary and Ship Canal, Cicero Avenue. Gray area shows the former channel of the Chicago River West Fork and the boundary of Mud Lake.

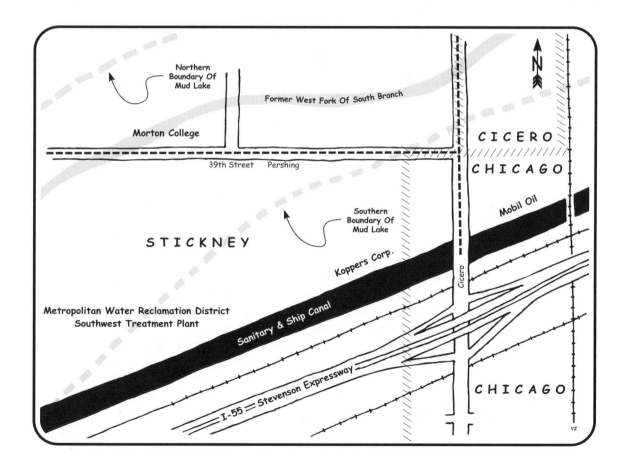

A center-pier swing railroad bridge over the Sanitary Canal.

the Harlem Terminal of Badger Pipeline Company, the waterway terminal and tank farm for the Tropicana Energy Company, and another cement distribution facility of the Lafarge Corporation. Note that pipelines join the other transport modes in this intense corridor. The terminal operations typify activities that have been seen all along the waterways.

Now the waterway explorer has a chance to see a modified, relatively modern version of the type of bridge that once ruled the waterways: the **center-pier swing bridge.** The bridge pivots on a pier set in the middle of the channel so that vessels can pass on either side. The first such bridges in Chicago were much smaller and lighter than this Santa Fe bridge. They were turned by hand with large T-bars that gave a great deal of

leverage. Later, as bridges became larger to accommodate heavier loads, electric motors swung the spans.

This bridge, and three others like it on the canal, have long been inoperable; their machinery has been removed. Nevertheless, their old gears and wheels are still fascinating and photogenic.

The left (north) bank contains a virtually empty area crisscrossed by high-voltage electrical cables. This is the **former site of Commonwealth Edison's Ridgeland Station,** once the most modern thermo-electric power plant in the area. The facility was dismantled, however, as ComEd chose to rely more heavily on nuclear power—a decision that has haunted the company ever since.

The high cost of nuclear electric power in Chicago has had an inhibiting effect on industrial development. Now that deregulation of the electric supply is on the horizon, ComEd may lose market share to competitors who operate less-expensive coal- or natural-gas–fired power plants.

Originally, it was thought that oxidation processes and dilution would be adequate to treat Chicago's sewage before it was a threat to downstream communities. There was even an extraordinary test in the first decade of the twentieth century in which live typhoid bacteria were introduced into the Sanitary and Ship Canal to test the stream's cleansing properties! Results of the test were inconclusive because of the generally high levels of bacteria in the stream. To be sure, there was a marked improvement in the condition of the water downstream, but it took the installation of the Stickney Water Reclamation Plant to assure downstream communities of a reasonably safe water supply.

As the tour boat passes the water outflow from the plant, the force of the outrushing water pushes the heavy vessel emphatically toward the opposite bank. Watch for herons and other waterbirds here. The warm water returning to the stream apparently attracts food for these birds, so they are often present along the banks. The many small boats and barges docked near the east end of the Stickney Works are water cleanup and pollution control vessels.

Immediately east of the Water Reclamation District's Stickney Plant is the forty-acre chemical plant of **Koppers Industries.** Here 150 employees make a variety of chemical products, mostly derived from coal tar. The **Chicago Block Company** sits opposite the Water Reclamation Plant on the south bank, a large cement block manufacturing

Stickney Water Reclamation Plant

Immediately east of the old Ridgeland power station site is the **Metropolitan Water Reclamation District's Stickney Water Reclamation Plant,** the world's largest sewage treatment operation. This gigantic facility covers 570 acres and resulted from the joining of the old 1930 West Side plant with the Southwest plant in 1939.

The plant treats more than 800 million gallons of wastewater every day, well below its designed capacity of 1,440 million gallons, covering a 260-square-mile area and a population of 2.4 million people. When heavy rains fill the deep tunnels, the effluent is shunted to the Stickney Works for treatment before being placed in the surface waterways. In 1955 the Stickney plant was named one of the Engineering Wonders of the United States by the American Society of Civil Engineers.

operation that was spun off by Material Service Company. Its bulky materials and finished products are shipped by barge and truck. Almost all of a group of companies that specialize principally in the transportation, storage, and distribution of liquid bulk cargoes stretch all the way from west of Central Avenue to Cicero Avenue.

The Sanitary and Ship Canal enters Chicago just west of Cicero Avenue, and the number of petrochemical terminals and tank farms falls off dramatically once the city limits are reached, since restrictive zoning for the storage and handling of flammable and explosive materials limits their development. One of the few exceptions is the **Mobil Oil Corporation** dock and terminal facility, on the north bank next to the Alpha Portland Cement Distribution operation.

East of Cicero, the tracks of the Chicago Belt Railway cross the canal on the second of four center-pier railway swing bridges that span the waterway. Like the others, this bridge is now fixed, with its machinery removed.

At one time there was a plan to construct a crosstown expressway to re-lieve congestion on the Dan Ryan and Kennedy Expressways. It was proposed that this highway follow the route of the Chicago Belt Railway over a considerable portion of the city's West Side. Despite its support by many transportation experts, the project was scrapped after West Side residents objected.

A transformer yard of Commonwealth Edison is on the west side of Pulaski Road, and next to Edison is a remnant operation of Peoples Gas along with the **Institute of Gas Technology's Energy Development Center.** Here studies are under way to find methods of converting high-sulphur Illinois coal into clean-burning natural gas.

The bridge at Pulaski Road is a new span completed in 1995. Like all of the newer bridges, it is a fixed structure that will not impede barge transportation and costs much less to build and maintain than a drawbridge. Many trucking firms and their terminal facilities are located nearby in the transportation corridor.

The Crawford Avenue plant of Commonwealth Edison sits on the north bank east of Pulaski Road. It generates

CHICAGO RIVER AND WATERWAYS FACT: DEEP TUNNEL CONSISTS OF A SERIES OF TUNNELS THAT LIE 250 TO 300 FEET BELOW THE CHICAGO RIVER AND RUN PARALLEL TO IT. THESE TUNNELS, UP TO THIRTY FEET IN DIAMETER, CONVEY STORM WATER AND SEWAGE OVERFLOW TO THE STICKNEY WATER RECLAMATION PLANT, WHERE THEY ARE TREATED AND DISCHARGED INTO THE SANITARY AND SHIP CANAL.

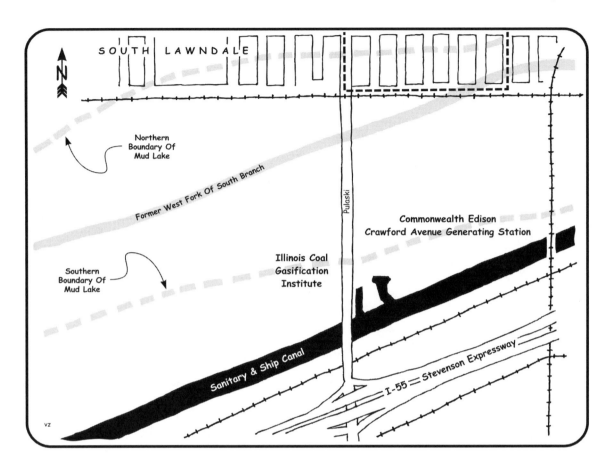

MAP 43.
Sanitary and Ship Canal, Pulaski Road. Gray area shows the former channel of the Chicago River West Fork and the boundary of Mud Lake.

electricity by burning coal and natural gas. A huge gantry crane sits along the waterway to offload the coal barges usually seen parked along the dock. This plant uses canal water to cool its turbines and, as a result, raises the stream's temperature. The increased temperature diminishes the stream's ability to clean itself through aerobic processes.

Now a local switching rail line, the Illinois Northern Railway, crosses the canal on a center-pier swing bridge. **La Preferida Foods Company** uses the property on the south bank as a base for its food distribution facilities. Just beyond this point, Kedzie Avenue

crosses the water on a graceful fixed bridge made of Cor-Ten steel, which creates its own anticorrosion coating as it oxidizes. Radio station **WVON** has its transmitter on the north bank west of Kedzie Avenue

Immediately east of Kedzie in the **Brighton Park** neighborhood, the fourth and final center-pier swing bridge over the canal carries the Illinois Central Railroad. The **Apex Motor Fuel Company** dock on the north bank sits on the west bank of the collateral channel that once connected the west fork of the Chicago River South Branch with the Sanitary and Ship Canal.

Close to the junction of the collateral channel and the canal is an interesting rail bridge that is unique in the city.
When it was operable, this retractile
bridge could be pulled back onto the
west bank to allow large vessels to pass.
During World War II, most of the
bridges over the sanitary canal were movable so that naval vessels, built on the
Great Lakes, could be safely moved to
the Gulf coast free from enemy fire. After
the war's end, the canal bridges were converted to fixed spans.

Illinois Brick, which sells antique
and modern brick to the Midwest market, occupies the south bank east of

Kedzie. Officers of the firm say that there
is a great demand for antique Chicago
brick as far away as Texas and a good
deal of old brick is exported. This firm
imports new brick from Utah for use in
Chicago, which was once was a national
leader in pressed-brick manufacture.

At California Avenue the new high-
rise court building of the **Cook County
Jail** rises to the north over the sheds
of two scrap-processing operations.
The large building is a steel mill of the
J. Pitt Melting Company, which melts
down steel scrap in electric furnaces and
re-forms the metal into billets up to
thirty feet long. The operation has been

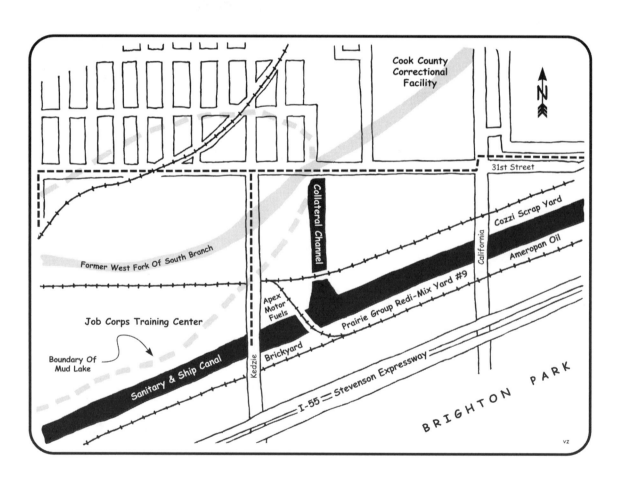

on standby for more than a year as of this writing. Pitt shares the property with the scrap yard of **Cozzi Iron and Metal Company,** which operates five scrap yards along area waterways.

East of California on the south bank of the canal is **Ameropan Oil Company,** one of the few petrochemical storage operations inside the city limits. An unexpected feature of this oil terminal is the presence of llamas, apparently kept as animal lawn mowers. Although a tour of the waterways shows the explorer almost every facet of the city, one hardly expects to see llamas!

Ahead loom four unusual, dark bascule bridges—now fixed—that carry the Baltimore and Ohio, Chicago Terminal Belt Line. Their seventeen-foot

height above the water is the limiting clearance for the entire Illinois lakes to Gulf waterway. If a vessel trying to reach Lake Michigan can't fit under these bridges, it has the unfortunate choice of either going back to Sag Junction and up the Cal-Sag, or heading down the Mississippi, through the Gulf of Mexico, up the Atlantic seaboard, and through the Saint Lawrence Seaway to Chicago.

The first cargo to pass the length of the Illinois and Michigan Canal in 1848 was a boatload of sugar from the lower Mississippi River en route to Buffalo, New York. It is fitting then, that the **Domino Sugar Corporation** should have a terminal on the Sanitary and Ship Canal. Here the water traveler sees

Twin B & O Chicago Terminal bascule railway bridges. Their machinery has been removed and these fixed bridges, 17 feet above the water, make the limiting vertical clearance on the entire Illinois lakes-to-Gulf waterway.

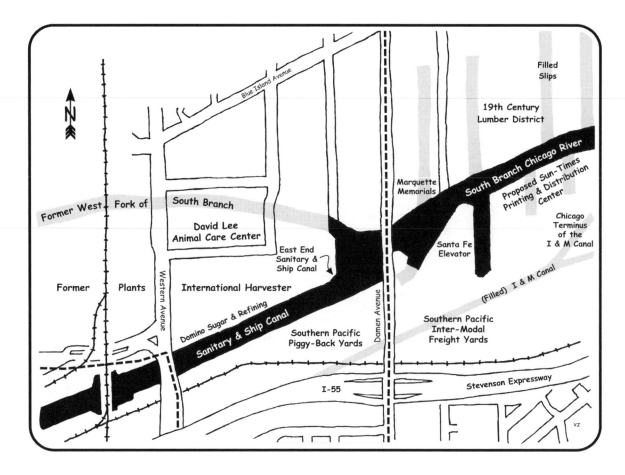

The map shows labels including: Blue Island Avenue, Filled Slips, 19th Century Lumber District, South Branch Chicago River, Proposed Sun-Times Printing & Distribution Center, Marquette Memorials, Former West Fork of, South Branch, David Lee Animal Care Center, Chicago Terminus of the I & M Canal, East End Sanitary & Ship Canal, Santa Fe Elevator, Former Plants, International Harvester, (Filled) I & M Canal, Western Avenue, Domino Sugar & Refining, Sanitary & Ship Canal, Damen Avenue, Southern Pacific Piggy-Back Yards, Southern Pacific Inter-Modal Freight Yards, I-55, Stevenson Expressway, vz

MAP 45. Junction of the Sanitary Canal and Chicago River South Branch. Gray area shows the former channel of the Chicago River West Fork, filled-in slips, and the eastern end of the I & M Canal.

covered barges that have made the trip from the lower Mississippi to Chicago. They bring granulated sugar for the city's food processing, ice cream, and candy-making industries, and for pharmaceutical manufacturing.

Each year, about forty-five thousand tons of sugar arrive at this facility. The sugar is melted down into liquid form and shipped out to industrial customers by tank trucks. Although no packaging of sugar products is done here, the plant warehouses package sugar products that are manufactured elsewhere for commercial and home use throughout the Midwest.

From the 1870s until the 1950s, sites on both sides of Western Avenue along the canal's north bank were occupied by the giant **McCormick reaper plant.** When McCormick and Deering Harvester merged in 1902, it became part of the **International Harvester Company.** After the main plant was demolished in the 1950s, the only remaining Harvester operations left in Chicago were the Tractor Works and the Wisconsin Steel Mill.

Beyond the sugar terminal is a sizable area devoted to trailer truck storage. Even though users of bulk materials require water for transport, many other industries have no direct need for a waterfront location. As fewer industries require waterfront sites, the properties become available at relatively low prices. Then trucking and other space-hungry firms seeking inexpensive land are attracted to waterside locations. As a result, many Chicago truck terminals are situated on or close to the waterway.

An extensive parcel of land on the south bank holds the Southern Pacific Intermodal Facility, an operation where truck trailers and standard containers are placed on railroad cars for long haul shipping. Economy and flexibility are the key benefits of such operations and many similar intermodal yards are now active in the Chicago area.

Finally, on the right bank is another outdoor salt storage yard. At the end of the sheet steel piling wall on the left is the eastern end of the Sanitary and Ship Canal. East of this point, the tour is back in the modified course of the natural South Branch of the Chicago River.

The large basin west of the Damen Avenue Bridge was the place where the west fork, the principal channel of the Mud Lake marsh, flowed into the South Branch from the city's West Side. It was also the eastern end of the Chicago Portage. A **wooden cross** and **plaque** marks the approximate place where **Father Jacques Marquette** endured the winter of 1674–75 on the wet prairie. His winter sojourn is also memorialized on a bronze tablet on the northeast bridge tower. Although Marquette has been more celebrated, it was **Louis Joliet** who more truly foresaw the potential of the portage to the commercial future of the area.

A wooden cross marks the approximate place where Father Marquette wintered in 1674–75.

A commemorative plaque on the northern bridge house of the Damen Avenue Bridge honors Pere Jacques Marquette.

THE CHICAGO RIVER

Damen Avenue

The bridge at Damen Avenue is a high fixed span, and just east of it is the area that became the largest lumber market in the world by the 1870s. To this area came wood cut from the virgin white-pine forests of the northern lakes, forests erased by Chicago's voracious appetite for lumber. For the last three decades of the nineteenth century, lumberyards lined the river from its mouth up the North Branch and down the South Branch. But the South Branch from Damen Avenue east to Halsted was the principal lumber district. Hundreds of lumber ships arrived daily.

Chicago's skyrocketing population needed lumber to build houses. And despite the development of the balloon frame, a lumber-saving form of construction, lumber requirements continued to climb. Not only was it needed for housing but also to make wagons, furniture, pianos, tools, and other manufactured items that the city supplied to its expanding markets.

Railroads stretched Chicago's vast market westward into the dry unforested prairies where, "before 1850, wood was so scarce . . . that farmers heading home from the Chicago market would tear up pieces of plank board from the toll roads . . . and load them in the backs of their wagons" (Miller 1996, 113).

The lumber that arrived in Chicago by three-masted schooners from the northern lakes was, at first, shipped west via the Illinois and Michigan Canal. Later, as the railroads expanded, Sears Roebuck and other firms offered prefabricated farmhouses and other buildings, even *entire towns,* that were built in Chicago and then shipped west by rail.

Until the early 1990s, a few lumberyards lingered in the area east of Damen Avenue. Now, more than a century after Chicago was the largest lumber market in the world, there are no more lumberyards remaining along the Chicago River.

Today truck terminals and scrap yards line the north bank of the South Branch, where 120 years ago slips filled with lumber schooners dominated the scene. Overall, as many as eighteen slips were cut into the banks to park the sailing vessels, which jostled for position in the crowded waterway. A few of the slips remain, but most have been partially or completely filled in. Now scrap yards sit on the bank, steadily separating ferrous from nonferrous scrap and crushing some of it into solid metal bales.

The view is extraordinary here. In the foreground, craggy, noisome, metal-reclaiming activities sit at the water's edge, with barges tied alongside. In the middle ground, standard containers are piled up in storage, and church spires rise above neighborhoods that sheltered one group after another of industries and immigrants. In the background, the tower skyscrapers of the Loop reach for the sky with service, trading, and information activities. The view is almost like a geological cross section of different eras and different life-forms.

The river widens greatly east of Ashland and forms the **U.S. Turning Basin.** The turning basin was created by dredging out a triangular piece of land between the South Branch of the river and the river's south fork, known as Bubbly Creek. In the process several streets and many houses were removed from the landscape. **Bubbly Creek,** which flows for about 1 1/2 miles, was part of the original river system and has

Opposite:
Map 46.
Chicago River
South Branch,
Bridgeport.
Gray area
indicates
former west
and east
arms of the
South Fork.

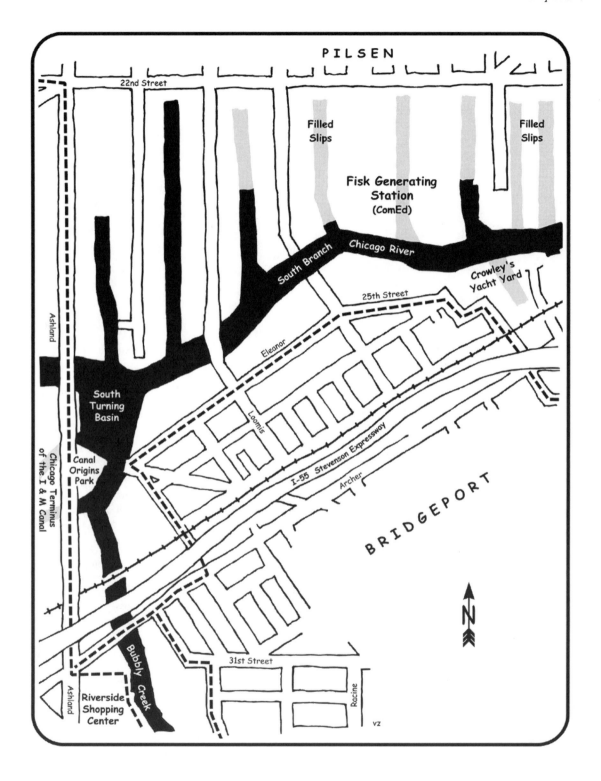

a rich, colorful, and highly aromatic history. The west bank of the turning basin was the point of origin for the Illinois and Michigan Canal, which transformed Chicago and impelled its growth.

Riverbank cleanup efforts by area young people along with work parties from Friends of the Chicago River have made it possible for a **Canal Origins Park** to be planned for the site. A pumping station was erected nearby in 1871 to force water through the canal so that it would reverse the flow of the Chicago River. Although this effort worked minimally at first and then not at all, the area is of historic significance, and the proposed park would greatly benefit this inner-city neighborhood.

At Ashland Avenue a bridge spanned the canal, which forced barges to unload and transfer cargo. This area came to be known as **Bridgeport.** Bridgeport's beginnings hark back to the early nineteenth century, when Charles Lee carved out a farm east of the present Throop Street on the river's north bank. The farm developed into a fur-trading post and was named **Hardscrabble.** Irish settlement began as slums on the opposite bank, and Bridgeport began its colorful history.

CHICAGO RIVER FACT: BUBBLY CREEK DE-RIVES ITS NAME FROM THE BUBBLES THAT RISE TO THE SURFACE OF THE STREAM FROM ORGANIC MATTER ON THE RIVER'S BOTTOM. CHICAGO'S MEATPACKING INDUSTRY, WHICH UPTON SINCLAIR DESCRIBED SO FORCEFULLY IN *THE JUNGLE*, ONCE USED THIS SECTION OF THE SOUTH BRANCH OF THE CHICAGO RIVER AS ITS SEWER.

Bubbly Creek

Bridgeport lay not only on the South Branch of the Chicago River, but also along the south fork, known as **Bubbly Creek.** By the 1860s, when the **Union Stockyards** were established, a large canal was cut eastward from the south fork toward the yards. It quickly became such a sewer that other portions of the river look good by comparison.

This infernal stream became filled with the refuse of the slaughterhouses before the great meatpacking barons learned to use "everything but the squeal." Offal, carcasses, and manure filled the south fork, which occasionally crusted over. At such times chickens walked across it, and strangers, unaware of the stream's true character, fell through and temporarily disappeared into the hellish brew. From time to time the surface of the vile creek even caught fire and burned.

Eventually, not knowing what else to do, the city filled in the eastern arm of the south fork; much later, the western arm met the same fate. As late as the 1960s, the Iron Street Bridge sat high and dry, although the channel it once spanned was a dimming memory. Even today, decaying matter on the

PANORAMIC VIEW OF UNION STOCKYARDS CHICAGO.

Copyright 1909 by

Union Stockyards, 1909. (Photo by Max Riott. Courtesy, Chicago Historical Society.)

stream bottom causes the water to bubble.

But the pollution of this reach of the river did not end with the demise of the stock-yards in 1971. A huge pumping station stands at 38th Street at the end of the remaining channel. Virtually all of the water from the city's South Side feeds through this facility. When the flow is too great for the sewer system, the effluent is turned into the channel. This flow is not negligible: it represents the outflow of fourteen sixty-inch-diameter pumps which, when they were installed in 1951, made up the largest pumping station in the world.

When all fourteen pumps are in operation, their two-billion-gallon capacity causes the surface of the river to rise dramatically. A dark tide of effluent can then be seen moving against the current from the station toward Lake Michigan. On a few occasions, water is actually allowed to escape through the lock into the lake. The last time this happened was in February 1997. Fortunately, the Deep Tunnel Project has worked well, so these discharges into the lake are becoming more unusual and infrequent.

In the past, the **Armour and Company Glue Factory** was located on the east side

of Bubbly Creek, and lumberyards and heavy industry lined the banks. The **Union Rolling Mills** were founded in 1862 along the south fork, at the corner of Ashland and Archer Avenues. The firm was originally a rail mill that made fifty tons of rail per day. In 1879 the name of the firm was changed to the Union Iron and Steel Company, and after blast furnaces were installed, the company increased production to five hundred tons of steel rails daily as well as seventy tons of other types of steel. In 1889 the firm merged with the North Chicago Rolling Mills and other plants to become part of the Illinois Steel

Company. The new firm ultimately was absorbed by the giant United States Steel Company.

Today only **Aztec Building Materials** on the east bank still uses the waterway for transport. The **Riverside Shopping Center** on the west bank is dedicated to cleaning up the environment and has organized numerous cleanups along the banks. Only a short stretch of Bubbly Creek is still navigable by barges.

Virtually all of Bubbly Creek is accessible for canoes, though, and a canoe-launching facility is planned for the area under the bridge that carries the Stevenson Expressway (I-55) over the stream. Surprisingly, canoeing on this stretch of the waterway is very pleasant—except for the occasional whiff of history. But there is essentially no other water traffic and, surprisingly, many waterbirds such as herons and ducks favor this stream. There are, however, three rules for those who canoe the south fork: stay away from the pumping station, don't fall in, and don't go swimming! This is still the most polluted section of the area's improving waterways.

The remaining section of the Fisk Street Power Station. The oldest portion of the station was made from limestone blocks and was dismantled some years ago.

Construction of the Illinois and Michigan Canal provided jobs to many Irish immigrants who had come to America with little learning and few marketable skills. They were little appreciated and virtually unemployable except for the harshest manual labor. For them, the canal project was a godsend. Many Irish worked on the canal, digging the ditch by hand. Such men were human digging machines who labored six days-a-week for whiskey and a-dollar-a-day. They even dug in their own backyards on Sunday after church so their muscles wouldn't tighten up and prevent them from working. As we have seen, many of these laborers who died digging the canal

are buried at **Saint James of the Sag Church** near Lemont.

Irish and German immigrants made up the largest share of foreign-born settlers in Chicago's early history. Eventually, the Irish established a political presence that had its power base in Bridgeport. The neighborhood produced many Chicago mayors, including the current mayor, Richard M. Daley, and his father, the famed Richard J. Daley.

East of Bubbly Creek, homes of industrial workers crowd the river on the south, and industrial activities line the banks. Truck yards and warehouses also are frequent sights. The attractive double-leaf bascule span at Loomis Street dates from 1975. It was given an engineering award for pleasing and functional design.

To the east is the complex of the **Brandenburg Industrial Service Company,** one of the largest demolition and dismantling firms in the nation. This firm occupies a site where for many years Peoples Gas stored natural gas in huge, aboveground, expandable tanks. Heavy trucks and equipment painted in Brandenburg's colors form neat rows all along the waterfront. The city requires both builders and wreckers. As Carl Sandburg wrote: "Build the city up, tear the city down, let us have a city."

The north side of the stream still features useable slips in which coal barges are often parked. The coal is intended for use by the **Fisk Street Station of Commonwealth Edison,** the city's oldest power station. When the plant opened in 1903, it could generate five thousand kilowatts of electric power and was the world's largest coal-fired power plant. Nine more generating units were added to Fisk by 1910. A few years ago the oldest limestone-jacketed section of the plant was demolished. Gone is the building's almost castlelike appearance and the remaining section has a rough unfinished look where the old section was removed.

Today the Fisk Street Station can be operated by either coal or natural gas. It uses the waterway for coal transport and for cooling water, as does the Crawford Avenue Station farther to the west. It is very common for river travelers to see coal barges being unloaded by the large bridge crane that overhangs the river. In fact, this power plant is one of the destinations for the "six packs"—six coal barges in a tow—that carry coal from the Calumet.

In the past, the police districts that serve the two sides of the river used the

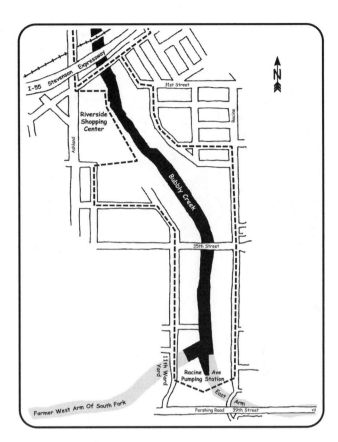

MAP 47. Chicago River South Branch, Bubbly Creek.

center of the channel as their boundary. In a number of grisly instances when a body was discovered floating in the stream, police from one district would push the corpse with long poles so that it would become the problem of their adjoining district. Nowadays the police district boundary runs across the river and includes both banks, so jurisdictional disputes are avoided.

On the south bank across from the power plant is **Crowley's Yacht Yard,** another pleasure-craft marina. Located on the site of the former J. M. Corbett Company, Crowley's sells, repairs, and stores recreational boats and equipment. One thousand boats are stored here during the winter season. Crowley has discovered more than one hundred

automobiles in the river. They are slowly being removed.

Halsted Street

Now the high fixed bridges of the Dan Ryan Expressway (I-90 and I-94) span the Chicago River, framing the historic industrial area south of the Loop. The height of these bridges was set at sixty feet as a compromise so that large lake ships could bring paper to nearby warehouses if they were equipped with folding masts. Standard mast heights of 120 feet would have required a drawbridge, but interstate highways must be free of such interruptions.

In times past, huge self-unloaders delivered coal to the power station on the South Branch. Unfortunately, the high bridge is no longer necessary: the river is too shallow to allow large vessels passage, and toxic bottom sediments have made dredging unlikely.

Development along this portion of the South Branch during the early twentieth century embraced nearly all the industries that made Chicago one of the world's leading industrial cities. Here were found grain elevators, printing establishments, coal yards, and packinghouses. Nearby were lumberyards, glass companies, electric utilities, furniture manufacturers, and metalworking industries. The Warfield Chocolate Company sat sandwiched between Sterling Glass Company and the Chicago Retort and Firebrick Company, which made equipment for the steel industry.

Many of these diverse industrial operations received raw materials by water. Evidence of this is still to be found in some of the older buildings along the river. For example, one can easily see the extra-large loading doors at odd heights facing the river. These were designed so that lake vessels could tie up alongside and unload their cargoes directly into the buildings.

The area's streets break the iron hold of the grid pattern and takes its direction from the wandering course of the river and the slips that were cut into the banks. **Lumber Street,** for instance, still parallels the river just north of the operations next to the stream.

Today the raised roadway of the Dan Ryan Expressway cuts through this old industrial district. Many of the industrial loft buildings and grain elevators have been razed and replaced by new, less-intensive activities. An Ozinga cement terminal sits on the north bank next to a pleasure-boat marina, and just past the Cermak Road Bridge an industrial loft building has been adapted for use by advertising offices, photo studios, and other businesses.

Across the river on the south bank is an empty area that was the home of **Cuneo Press,** a large Chicago job-printing operation. After Cuneo moved its operations, the loft building was used as a warehouse for old automobile tires. When a tremendous fire broke out and burned for more than a week, most of the building was rendered unusable except for one relatively strong section, which was used in the film *Backdraft.* Ultimately, the huge, dangerous building was dynamited so that it fell in upon itself. To date, this is the only time that this method of demolition has been used in Chicago.

A small residual fishing operation sits on the south bank just west of the Canal Street Bridge. At one time commercial fishing in Lake Michigan was a sizable business, but today environmental pollution, changing ecosystems, and overfishing have depleted the resource

Opposite:
(*top photo*)
A typical river towboat travels down the channel.

(*bottom photo*)
Crowley's Yacht Yard.

The bridge at Cermak Road is being raised and rebuilt. It is Chicago's only surviving example of a rolling-lift bridge designed by Chicagoan William Scherzer.

The Cermak Road Bridge

The double-leaf **Cermak Road Bridge** dates from 1906 and is the only surviving example of the Scherzer rolling lift bridge invented by **William Scherzer,** a Chicago engineer. A Scherzer bridge carries its counterweights above the roadway. Instead of turning on a fixed pivot, like the trunnion bascule bridge, it rocks and rolls. That is, it literally rolls open along a curved metal sector, rather like the rocker on a rocking chair. Holes in the rocker match teeth in the bridge abutments to prevent the span from slipping when the bridge is open.

The Cermak bridge was built low over the river, so it has been a busy span that demands round-the-clock tending. Now it has been dismantled and will be completely rebuilt on new elevated piers that will raise the entire bridge structure to greatly reduce the required number of openings. This historic bridge is another key element of Chicago's living museum of bridges which, with the city's other architectural wonders, are a source of pleasure and interest for locals and an attraction for tourists.

and limited its usefulness for food. At this time, yellow perch are in severe decline and so even sport fishing limits have been greatly restricted.

In short order the river traveler passes under the double-leaf bascule bridge at Canal Street. This attractive bridge was completed in 1941, and it includes a number of innovations. Roller bearings were used in place of the sleeve bearings that were then standard, and hydraulic motors are used to operate the gear train.

Now a short section of the river takes the traveler to the **Amtrak vertical lift bridge.** The bridge carries Amtrak passenger trains arriving from the south over the Chicago River enroute to Union Station. This low bridge spans the water at 10 1/2 feet when closed. Although small pleasure boats can easily pass under, most larger vessels, such as tour boats, cannot. The bridge must open to allow such vessels to pass along the channel. Complicating matters, federal law prohibits opening the bridge if a train is approaching from either side and is scheduled to arrive in ten minutes or less. Hence, river tourists often have plenty of time to inspect this part of the stream and to meditate on what they have seen.

To the right (south) one may see the trestle that carries the city's newest elevated trains, the CTA Orange Line, to the Southwest Side and **Midway Airport.** Improved access usually spurs development, and there is ample evidence of this in the old Southwest Side communities, such as Bridgeport. The provision of rapid transit service to Midway has had a similarly beneficial effect on traffic at the city's old airport, once the world's busiest.

Visible to the south are the red-roofed pagodas adjoining the new exten-

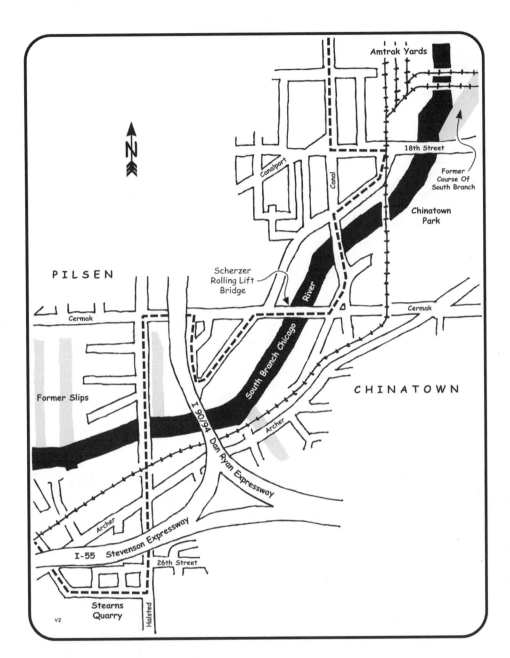

MAP 48.
Chicago River South Branch, Chinatown. The gray area indicates filled former slips and a part of the original river channel.

sion of **Chinatown** called **Chinatown Square.** For many years, Chinatown was hemmed in by rail yards with little room for expansion. Chicago's first Chinatown was at the south edge of the Loop. Since few would sell to them, the Chinese purchased land on the Near South Side through a non-Chinese intermediary.

At last a siren sounds, the signal that the bridge is finally about to open.

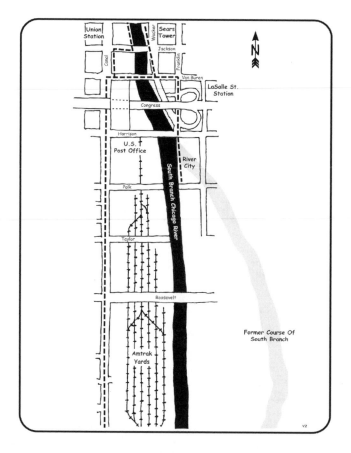

The wheels begin to turn and the cables jump to taut attention. Slowly, the great weight of the center span begins to rise. Looking up from below, it seems not so much that the bridge is rising, but rather that the river traveler is sinking down. With this obstacle now over, the way lies open to complete the Great Circle Tour.

Now the river makes a bend to the left and a warehouse building comes into view. Originally, the building was a warehouse for **Carson Pirie Scott and Company.** Later it was rented out to a variety of small businesses. The building's basement once was used for a farming operation. It was sealed tight with plastics and tapes, and horse manure was brought in and placed on shelves where Chinese entrepreneurs grew cloud's-ear mushrooms for Asian restaurants. Alas, this experiment is over, and farming has once again retreated to rural areas.

At 18th Street there is a single-leaf bascule bridge, built in 1967 and one of

MAP 49.
Chicago River South Branch, River City. The gray area indicates the original river channel.

An Amtrak passenger train approaches Union Station from the south, crossing the Amtrak lift bridge over the Chicago River.

the longest in the world. The bridge was recently painted and repaired as part of a citywide bridge restoration project.

On the left, beyond the 18th Street Bridge, is another warehouse that once belonged to Carson Pirie before Scott came along. One of the older buildings along the river, its style of construction and large loading doors fronting the river speak of the days when the river carried all types of cargo for the retailers of the central city.

A short distance beyond is a pair of rail bridges that give the appearance of

calipers measuring the **Sears Tower** one mile ahead. This giant in the city where the skyscraper is said to have been born, recently lost its title of the world's tallest to a building in Malaysia. To be sure, the title changed on a technicality—the height of built-in towers. Nevertheless, construction of a huge building in a developing country signals a new world in which economics, trade, and ideas are global.

The two rail bridges, bascule structures, are giant industrial sculptures. The northern bridge, built in 1929 and

Bridges up, the Sears Tower looms in the distance.

Marina City

but also one of the most complicated real estate transactions in the history of the United States. Twenty-two railroads and the federal, state, and city governments traded property to accomplish the task.

The northern bridge was built on dry land. Then the new channel was cut beneath it straight as an arrow, and when it was complete, the old channel was filled in. But there remained the small problem of moving the southern rail bridge. It was accomplished in 1929, when the bridge was moved seven hundred feet to the west to span the new river channel (*Chicago Public Works* 1973).

On the left bank are the coach and engine yards of **Amtrak,** and the complex holds the commissary facility as well. Although the rails that converge along the river are vast and complex today, they pale in comparison to the incredible strands of iron that bound Chicago to other destinations in past years. Those tendrils stretched across the continent and held fast the overland trading network that solidified Chicago's transport dominance.

The right bank holds much unused land left over after the passenger rail operations moved out. Land near the 18th Street Bridge is set aside for a much-needed park for Chinatown. Plans call for work to begin soon. Among the interesting features of the now-vacant rail land are the scars left by the original river channel. Although they cannot be seen directly from the river, they are obvious when the land is viewed from one of the Loop skyscrapers.

This precious 286-acre parcel, the largest piece of undeveloped land near the Loop, has just been designated a new Tax Increment Financing District (TIF). Plans include a two-mile riverwalk that will help transform the south Loop. First

owned by CSX Corporation, is permanently deactivated and may not long adorn the cityscape. The southern bridge, built in 1916, is owned by the St. Charles Air Line Railroad. Both spans have borne the weight of many trains over their long lives. And the southern bridge has done what few bridges have ever done: it has traveled!

In 1926 a project was undertaken to eliminate a wide river bend that blocked access to the Loop from the south. This was not only a major engineering effort

River City is the first of a number of developments scheduled for the South Branch near the Loop. Beyond is the Roosevelt Road Bridge and two old rail bridges. A new park is planned for Chinatown at the river bend in the distance.

on the block is the **River City** develop-ment, where twelve acres of a planned forty-five-acre site have been turned into fifteen hundred dwellings ranging from small apartments to three-bedroom townhouses. The lyrical reinforced-concrete design is by the late **Bertrand Goldberg** whose attention to the improv-ing river was previously demonstrated at **Marina City**. Like the earlier building, River City has a marina where it meets the river. The popular music club, **House of Blues**, is located where once stood the Marina City Cinema complex.

At Polk Street, the Chicago River resumes its original bed, departing from the unnatural straightness of the altered channel. On the west bank, a new **post office** has risen to replace the huge, but outdated one. As of this writing, no plan has been advanced for the former post office. It continues to straddle the Eisen-hower Expressway (I-290), following the lead of the Burnham Plan, which called for a post office astride a "double carriageway."

The new post office contains nearly three million square feet of space and fea-tures twelve active railroad tracks. The sixteen-acre, two-floor main workroom is heavily automated with optical scanners and other high-tech mail-handling de-vices. The eight-story office building fronting on Harrison Street includes other federal offices. After a struggle, the federal government has agreed to land-scape the river edge in accordance with city guidelines.

A double-leaf bascule bridge com-pleted in 1956 conveys the Eisenhower Expressway across the river. The heart of the city, which has been seen ahead of the tour vessel for two miles, now leaps up and engulfs it. It is an unforgettable sight. In the 1920s all of the land on the

west bank and much on the east bank of the river was in transportation-related uses. Freight houses, warehouses, and rail stations filled the area. Before this time, lumberyards ran for nearly ten miles along the banks, and grain elevators ac-cented the riverscape.

Few commercial office buildings sat along the Chicago River, and those that did, like the **Civic Opera House**, turned their backs on it. From the beginning of the Chicago settlement, the river was scarcely more than an open sewer. Even after the sanitary canal transported the sewage away from Lake Michigan and the Stickney Works treated it, the city's combined sewers carried overflows of storm water and sewage into the river.

Since then the river gradually has been growing cleaner, especially since the Tunnel and Reservoir Plan began opera-tion. Even though this project of the Water Reclamation District is still not fully completed, the tunnels are virtually finished, and some of the reservoirs are coming onstream. The improved water quality has been indicated by greater numbers and varieties of healthy river or-ganisms and by increases in fish and bird populations. As the river has grown cleaner recreation on the water has in-creased. Now that the river is healthier, buildings are being designed with the river in mind.

An esplanade stretches for many blocks on the river's west bank in the **Gateway Center** development, on air rights over the tracks leading to **Union Station**. A "vest-pocket" park adorns the river's edge between Adams and Monroe Streets on the east side of the channel. It sits beneath Harry Weese's ingenious, double-triangular **222 South Wacker Drive Building** and features a fifteen-foot waterfall and honey locust shade

trees. It is a lovely place for lunch in warm weather.

Chapter 3 discusses the history of bridges in some detail, but one especially interesting structure spanned the Chicago River South Branch between Van Buren Street and Jackson Boulevard. It was the **Metropolitan West Side Elevated Railway Bridge,** which carried both rapid transit lines and the now-abandoned Chicago, Aurora, and Elgin interurban railroad. The only four-track bridge ever constructed over area waterways, this bridge was of the Scherzer rolling lift design. It served until June 22, 1958, when the new Congress Parkway Bridge opened.

Many distinguished buildings look down on the river, which serves as

needed open space in the rapidly developing westward expansion of the city's commercial core. The Sears Tower, mentioned earlier, rises 1,454 feet and 110 stories and is still the largest private office building in the world. Its daytime population exceeds 12,000.

The Sears Tower and the other modern buildings along the river house a wide and increasing variety of information-based activities that range from stockbrokers and trading exchanges to corporate offices, insurance brokers, and publications detailing the flow of commodities worldwide. To accommodate the myriad forms of electronic apparatus linked by fiber-optic networks, these glass-and-steel towers contain a great deal

When the Civic Opera House was built in 1929, the Chicago River was basically an open sewer. Today, the river is on the mend and increasingly is seen as an amenity for the buildings that line its banks.

Subterranean Chicago

9182 Illinois Telephone & Telegraph Co. Sherman & Van Buren Sts. looking South.

Subterranean freight tunnel junction beneath Sherman and Van Buren Streets, looking south. A maze of freight tunnels runs under the central city. Originally built in 1901 to carry telephone cables, the tunnels now serve as pathways for fiber optic networks through the central business district. (Courtesy, Chicago Historical Society.)

In addition to a procession of bridges and bridge types, two tunnels once carried vehicles and pedestrians beneath the Chicago River. Located at Washington Street on the South Branch and at LaSalle Street on the main stem, these tunnels were a blessed escape route for people trapped by the Great Fire in 1871. They no doubt saved many lives in the conflagration.

The Washington Street traffic tunnel was begun in July 1867 and was completed January 1, 1869. It cost $517,000 and was 1,606 feet long. This tunnel was in active use until 1953. The 1,890-foot LaSalle Street tunnel was begun November 3, 1869, and opened on July 4, 1871. It was in use until November 1939, when it was closed because of the construction of the Dearborn Street subway.

Tunnels for carrying telephone cables were built beneath the Loop and central city in 1901. They began to be used also to transport packages and freight in 1903, and by 1914 extended for sixty-two miles beneath the central city. At that time, 117 electric locomotives and 3,000 freight cars scurried through the city's nether regions, bringing coal and packages and carrying away ash. Actress Mae West joined some of the city's social leaders to dedicate the little railway with a sumptuous dinner down in the tunnels.

During the Vietnam War, rumors flew that radicals intended to place bombs in the old freight tunnels, which by that time had been abandoned because of competition from trucks. But Chicago needed no terrorists to create chaos in the tunnels. In April 1992, pilings next to the Kinzie Street Bridge on the North Branch accidentally broke through into the old tunnel system and allowed river water to surge into the tunnels. The resulting underground flood caused millions of dollars in damages and untold grief for thousands.

Interestingly, these tunnels, originally planned to carry telephone cables, now carry fiber-optic networks through the central business district.

of space allocated to computer and communications equipment. As a result, the numbers of people working in these buildings, although large, is smaller than one might expect based solely on building size. The trading floors of Chicago's exchanges are electronically linked to similar operations around the world.

To the south of the Sears Tower is the **311 South Wacker Building,** the tallest reinforced-concrete building in the world. It was designed by Kohn, Pedersen, Fox and is intended as the first of three similar buildings. A curious lighted glass cylinder tops the structure and has given it a nickname—the White Castle.

The **Mid-America Commodities Exchange,** a low, green-glass building at Jackson Boulevard on the west side of the river, is cantilevered over the commuter entrance to Union Station. Its crisscross supports refer architecturally to the crossbraces of the John Hancock Center on North Michigan Avenue.

The twin towers of the **Chicago Mercantile Exchange Center** occupy the east bank of the river between Madison and Monroe Street. Serrated corners increase the number of prized corner offices in these 1.1-million-square-foot buildings, designed by Fujikawa, Johnson and Associates. The ten-story Mercantile Exchange offers a 40,000 square-foot trading floor with no internal columns. This vast open space is made possible by 140-by-35 foot trusses that provide ceiling support. The two framing towers are cantilevered over the exchange to generate more leasable space (McBrien 1991, 27).

Modern bascule bridges cross the river at Van Buren, Jackson, Adams, Monroe, Madison, Washington, Randolph, and Lake Streets. The Randolph Street Bridge was recently replaced with a very clean, simple bascule span.

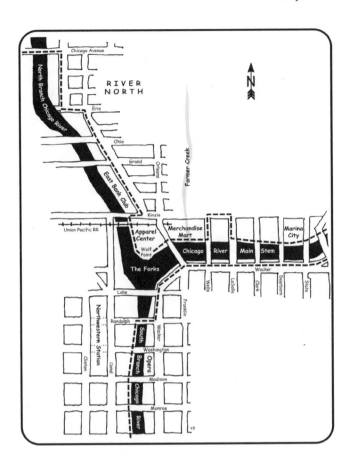

Work is progressing on repair and replacement of a number of the other bridges, and the double-decker Lake Street Bridge that carries the CTA Green Line elevated train over the river has been completely rebuilt.

The 1987 **Northwestern Atrium Center** (now **Citibank**) designed by Helmut Jahn in postmodern style rises above the **Northwestern Railroad Station** and takes its form from waterfall lamps in the **Chicago Board of Trade.** This Art Deco inspiration helps the building relate to the nearby **Riverside Plaza** (formerly the **Chicago Daily News Building**), which is a noted Art Deco design. Riverside Plaza was the first

MAP 50.
The forks of the Chicago River. Here the North and South Branches of the Chicago meet at the Main Stem.

Riverside Plaza Building, the first Chicago building to use air rights over railroad tracks, is a notable example of the Art Moderne style.

Chicago building built on air rights over the rail tracks below. It has a special ventilation system that collects fumes from the railroad operations and dissipates them above the roof.

Morton International Corporation completed an interesting new headquarters building in 1990 on the west bank, opposite its old offices. It features what is said to be the highest clock tower on the planet, and the southwestern corner of the building is cantilevered over rail tracks that prevent a more usual method of support. Ralph Johnson, the building's architect, left the support trusses exposed to

serve as a reminder of Chicago's bridges and to help integrate the building with its surroundings. The garden at the building's river-edge park was installed and is cared for by the Garden Club of Illinois.

As the tour vessel approaches the Lake Street Bridge an old warehouse building that has been adapted for modern office use appears on the right bank. It is quite attractive and serves both as a reminder of the past and as an accent to the modern structures that surround it. East of this building, across West Wacker Drive, is the place where, in 1860, almost on the site of the old Sauganash

Hotel, a frame building was thrown up in just five weeks to house the Republican National Convention of that year. Ten thousand delegates crammed into the hastily built wooden structure called the **Wigwam,** and there, on the third ballot, Abraham Lincoln was nominated for the presidency.

The Forks

As the tour passes under the Lake Street Bridge, it leaves the South Branch, the River of the Portage, and arrives at the Forks, where the river's North and South Branches join. This area was early Chicago's center, and the "Y" form of the forks was adopted as Chicago's emblem. The design of a "Y" in a circle was developed in 1892 by R. Roewood as his entry in a competition sponsored by the *Chicago Inter-Ocean* newspaper. First used at the World's Columbian Exposition in 1893, it now appears in many contexts, ranging from decorations on the Division Street canal bridge and the east towers at Navy Pier to the neon marquee of the Chicago Theater as well as in the elevators and ceilings at the Chicago Cultural Center and CTA tokens.

In the early days, each of the three riverbanks had its own tavern. They not only sold whiskey but also served as hotels, public meeting places, and even as temporary churches. The **Sauganash**

Hotel on the south bank was run by Mark Beaubien, a French Creole from the Detroit area and one of the early settlement's most colorful characters. He was an innkeeper, fiddle player, and bon vivant who said, "I plays de fiddle like de debble, an' I keeps hotel like hell." His establishment held the meeting in which the town of Chicago was incorporated (Miller 1996, 57).

Between those early times and the present, the Forks were inundated by industrial and transport activities and held docks, boatyards, warehouses, grain elevators, and the city's first railroad station. Now, almost two hundred years later, relative quiet has returned to the confluence, and grassy lawns and trees front the river on the north bank. Once again, as in Indian days, ducks, herons, gulls, and other birds grace the scene, and an industrious pair of beavers had to be moved to a new home in the forest preserves to protect the trees along the banks.

Chicago boatyards were famed, and many distinctive vessels were born along the Chicago River. One such yard under the Randolph Street Bridge was operated by a fellow named Bagley, a sailor who had jumped ship in Chicago. We remember him today because he built the four special rowboats John Wesley Powell used for his daring and successful 1869 expedition through the Grand Canyon.

CHICAGO RIVER FACT: The "Y" on the City of Chicago seal represents the joining of the North and South branches of the Chicago River with the Main Stem at Wolf Point.

The 333 West Wacker Drive Building sits on the south bank of the river at the forks.

today the site of the **Apparel Center.** The center was designed to provide hundreds of showroom-offices for manufacturers and distributors of apparel, and it served that function for many years. However, buying patterns for these businesses gradually changed, so that many of the former showrooms have been converted to regular commercial offices. A Holiday Inn occupies the uppermost floors of this mixed-use building, and a park and esplanade face the water.

The **park at Wolf Point** is one of the best places to watch the city at work and play. Rowing skulls, canoes, and sailboats glide quietly by and barge tows move up and down the river. Elevated trains roar across double-deck bridges on both the North and South Branches. Pedestrians throng while traffic flows or snarls on upper and lower Wacker Drive. Overhead, jet planes streak to cities around the globe. Day and night, sun and shadow, storm and calm, play across the river and the architectural treasures of the city center.

One of the Chicago's most distinguished modern buildings, **333 West Wacker,** graces the curving south bank of the river and mirrors the gestures of the changing scene. William Pedersen of the New York architectural firm of Kohn, Pedersen, Fox created this unique, emphatic, and remarkably fitting design.

Powell took about three months to run the canyon in Bagley's boats and became the first explorer to accomplish this feat.

Wolf Point was the name given by the locals to a small projection from the west bank at the Forks; the **Wolf Tavern** sat near this point. After the little peninsula was cut away to clear the channel, its name was transferred across the river to the north bank. This new Wolf Point is

The tumult of trading that marked commerce at the Forks in the early days has been supplanted by an even greater volume of trading. Today, however, the trading is done electronically and globally in cyberspace. And, the firms that fill the glass-walled towers along the river regularly deal worldwide with volumes of commodities and floods of capital that would have been inconceivable to those who came before.

A stereograph image of the river forks in 1875. Canal barges are moored along the west bank and sailing schooners clog the turn into the forks. Piles of lumber are stacked on what is now called Wolf Point, and a large grain elevator occupies the current site of the Merchandise Mart. (Courtesy, Chicago Historical Society.)

The classically designed 41-story Jewelers Building (35 East Wacker Drive), completed in 1926, takes its inspiration from the 15th-century chapel for the Certosa of Pavia. At one time it had an interior garage served by elevators to allow jewelers to enter and leave without risk.

On the north bank, east of the double-leaf bascule bridge at Orleans Street, rises the powerful presence of the **Merchandise Mart.** The massive building provides a massive counterpoint to the mirrored lightness of the 333 Wacker Building.

Marshall Field and Company built this four-million-square-foot behemoth in 1931 to consolidate its warehouse operations. The Mart was constructed on air rights over the North Western train tracks and was the world's largest building until the Pentagon took over that title. Later, after space was leased to other distributors, the building was sold to Joseph P. Kennedy, the scion of the great political family. Until recently, it was the crown jewel in the family's holdings. In early 1998 the Kennedy family sold the Mart, the Apparel Center, and related properties to a New Jersey-based public real estate firm.

Chicago's rich design heritage makes it a museum of architecture and one of the world's most interesting cities. The main stem of the river is an architectural showplace. From the giant Merchandise Mart and the curved glass facade of 333 Wacker to the gleaming terra-cotta facade of the Wrigley Building, the varied designs of the bridges and buildings make an unforgettable impression.

Building styles along the river are very diverse and range from classical to postmodern. The design of the **Jewelers Building** was based on the fifteenth-century chapel of the Certosa of Pavia, a monastery in Italy. Nearby, the **Tribune Tower** reflects gothic cathedrals, and the **R. R. Donnelly Building,** world headquarters for one of the largest printing and information services companies on earth, incorporates classical Greek elements in its postmodern skyscraper

Along the Chicago River, industry and commerce come together.

The IBM building epitomizes the less-is-more philosophy of noted architect Ludwig Mies van der Rohe.

design. Similarly, the world headquarters for the **Leo Burnett** advertising agency is in the form of a classical Greek column, and the design of the famed **Wrigley Building,** which inspired many Russian buildings built under Joseph Stalin, reflects elements from the Spanish renaissance. Classical elements also motivated the 1923 **London Guarantee Building,** which was designed by Alfred S. Alschuler and built on the site where **Fort Dearborn** once guarded the portage · on the advancing frontier.

Some of the older buildings, such as the **LaSalle-Wacker Building** and the **333 North Michigan Avenue Building,** reflect Art Moderne/Art Deco traditions, while others break with tradition to create new styles. **The Mather Building,** Harry Weese's **Seventeenth Church of Christ Scientists,** and Bertrand Goldberg's **Marina City** are included in this group.

The less-is-more, glass-box outgrowth of the Bauhaus school is epitomized in Mies Van der Rohe's last work, the **IBM Building.** This unornamented, starkly beautiful structure sits at a particularly prominent spot where the river curves, so it has an unimpeded view of the modern rivermouth and Lake Michigan. The minimalist style is also represented by a small, elegant park on the south riverbank, opposite the **Westin Hotel.** Its design reflects a medieval Japanese temple garden.

Just as amazing as the quantity of architectural riches along the Chicago River main stem is the fact that these treasures have emerged within the lifetimes of many still living. At the beginning of the twentieth century, schooners still competed with steel-hulled vessels and boats from the Illinois and Michigan Canal along the crowded wharves of the

Chicago River. Grain elevators, produce terminals, and warehouses thronged the riverbanks with no hint of the architectural glories to come.

So many activities and industries lined the riverbanks when Chicago was the greatest port in the United States that there is really no way—short of another complete book—to list them all. But throughout the nineteenth century, the river was Chicago's main port. And goods of all kinds continued to come into the city by water, even though, by the 1870s, railroads dominated freight transfer.

From the middle of the nineteenth century onward, entire shiploads of lumber were sold at the wholesale docks at the foot of Franklin Street, probably the only place in the United States where such sales were possible. After the sale, the lumber schooners were towed to the South Branch lumber district and unloaded at the purchaser's yard. The city's insatiable appetite for wood was so great that all of the reaches of the Chicago River were inundated in wood; by 1874, the concentrated demand in Chicago's lumberyards "could dispose of an average of three million feet per day . . . for nearly seven months each year" (Cronon 1991, 170–71). And despite the gradual reduction of the lumber trade, the riverbanks were still filled with lumberyards as late as 1935.

In the late 1880s Chicago became the world's busiest port; on average, two lumber schooners passed through the downtown bridges every minute. This led to constant traffic backups and the custom of opening swing bridges while people and wagons were still on the spans. An earlier collapse of the Clark Street Bridge occurred when a herd of cattle on the opening bridge was spooked by the whistle of a tugboat and the frightened

animals stampeded to one unsupported end of the bridge.

Since the river was the reason for the founding of the city, and since it became the focus of commerce and industry, it was also the focal point for many of the triumphs and tragedies that marked Chicago's history. Paramount among the disasters was the Great Chicago Fire of October 1871. Walls of flame leapt the Chicago River as if the stream were nonexistent. Flaming brands blown high into the air were carried over the river, igniting ships in the water as well as structures on the far bank.

The magnitude of the fire may be better understood when it is realized that the wind-blown embers were thrown two miles out in Lake Michigan and repeatedly set the water-intake crib ablaze. Except for the heroic actions of a worker who put out each new fire, the crib, too, would have burned (Andreas 1884–86, 742).

"Within an hour, planing mills and furniture factories astride the river were on fire, and then the towering grain elevators . . . began burning from top to bottom. . . . Around eleven-thirty, a flaming mass of material was blown across the river and landed on the roof of a horse stable, and another . . . struck the South Side Gas Works. From these two places, a new and larger fire center started. Even the grease-and-oil-slicked river went up in flames" (Miller 1996, 151).

Explosives were used to destroy buildings that lay in the path of the onrushing fire. The hysteria of the rushing crowds before the walls of flame was compounded by a cacophony of sounds: the moaning wind, the roar of the racing fire, screams, collapsing buildings, and the "shrill whistling of the tugs" as they moved ships filled with lumber out of the river

Historic Plaques along the Wacker Drive Riverwalk

The stretch of Wacker Drive from Michigan Avenue to Franklin Street bears the honorary name of the **Ira J. Bach Walkway.** Bach, who died in 1985, was a city planner and author as well as chairman of the Chicago Commission on Historical and Architectural Landmarks. The walkway follows the path of the main stem of the Chicago River and is studded with several historic plaques, which the average pedestrian probably doesn't even know are there. The following is an informal tour of some of the most prominent and historically interesting memorials.

At the southwest corner of the Michigan Avenue Bridge are two plaques:

CHICAGO LANDMARK
MICHIGAN AVENUE BRIDGE AND
WACKER DRIVE ESPLANADE
EDWARD H. BENNETT, ARCHITECT
1918–28

Conceived as part of Daniel Burnham's 1900 Plan of Chicago, the Michigan Avenue Bridge and Wacker Drive were designed to improve transportation and to enhance Chicago's river front. The opening of the bridge in 1920, followed by the esplanade in 1926 and the monumental sculptures of 1928, provided an impressive gateway to North Michigan Avenue and led to its development as one of the city's premier thoroughfares.

Designated October 2, 1991

CHICAGO LANDMARK
SITE OF FORT DEARBORN
1803
Fort Dearborn served as the major western garrison of the United States until destroyed during an Indian uprising in August of 1812. A second fort, erected on thet same site in 1816, was demolished in 1856.

Designated September 15, 1971

Continue west along Wacker Drive. Near State Street are two rather weathered plaques:

SOUTH WATER STREET

This was Chicago's main business street in 1834 connecting the village with Fort Dearborn. Years before this also was the site of a trading post with the Indians.

Erected 1937

Near this spot, April 3, 1848, was held the first session of the Board of Trade of the city of Chicago, now the world's largest grain exchange.

Erected March 24, 1948

The tragic capsizing of the *Eastland* in 1915 warrants a large plaque situated in its own courtyard on the river:

THE *EASTLAND* DISASTER

While still partially tied to its dock at the river's edge, the excursion steamer *Eastland* rolled over on the morning of July 24, 1915. The result was one of the worst maritime disasters in American history. More than eight hundred people lost their lives within a few feet of shore. The *Eastland* was filled to overflowing with picnic bound Western Electric Company employees and their families when the tragedy occurred. Investigations following the disaster raised questions about the ship's seaworthiness and inspection of Great Lakes steamers in general.

Erected 1988

Gurdon S. Hubbard's grand building, or "folly," is commemorated near Wacker and LaSalle:

"HUBBARD'S FOLLY"

On this site about 1834, Gurdon S. Hubbard built Chicago's first warehouse for storing pork and other pioneer produce. Because of its size and substantial construction, early skeptics called the building "Hubbard's Folly."

Erected 1937

Markers on the Michigan Avenue Bridge

The Michigan Avenue Bridge contains additional river-related memorials.

On the west side of the bridge

- A brown rectangular plaque on the southwest corner explains the strategic importance of the river.
- On the northwest corner of the bridge is a small, green plaque commemorating **Green Bay Road,** which ran northwesterly to Clark Street and North Avenue and connected Fort Dearborn with Fort Howard in Green Bay, Wisconsin.

On the east side of the bridge

- A plaque for "Outstanding Civil Engineering Achievement of 1986" honors the Tunnel and Reservoir Plan.
- A small plaque erected on June 22, 1990, by the Friends of the Chicago Public Library designates the site as a "literary landmark in recognition of the use of BRIDGES AS SYMBOLS by such authors as Carl Sandburg, Theodore Dreiser and

Upton Sinclair in Chicago's Literary Tradition."
- A plaque erected in 1925 honors Joliet and Marquette.
- An above eye level plaque erected in 1977 commemorates the reversal of the Chicago River as a national civil engineering landmark.

Pioneer Court

Continue walking north to Pioneer Court, under the shadow of the Tribune Tower. Along the banks of the river on the east side of Michigan Avenue are several plaques:

- Kinzie Mansion. "Near this site stood Kinzie Mansion, 1784–1832, home of Pointe du Sable, Le Mai, and John Kinzie, Chicago's 'first civilian.'"
- "On December 4, 1674 Pere Jacques Marquette, S.J. and two voyageurs built a shelter near the mouth of the Chicago

River. They were the first Europeans to camp here, the site of Chicago."

- "Jean Baptiste Point DuSable Homesite has been designated a National Historic Landmark"

A seven-foot-high, free-standing sign, part of the city's Tribute Markers of Distinction Program, honors DuSable and his wife Catherine and stands at 401 North Michigan Avenue, just south of the Tribune Tower.

Marina City

Two historic markers are located outside Marina City. On the Dearborn Street side, outside the West Tower entrance, is a large plaque commemorating Chicago's first movable bridge.

> Chicago's first movable bridge was constructed at this site in 1834. The timber span provided only a 60 foot opening for the passage of vessels. So dangerous to ships was this narrow draw, that the bridge was ordered removed by the Council in 1839. The present bridge is the fourth at this site.

On the State Street side, a few yards from the East Tower entrance, is a memorial to the Norwegian brig *Sleipner.*

> FIRST VESSEL DIRECT FROM EUROPE DESTINED FOR CHICAGO
>
> THE NORWEGIAN SAILING SHIP
> *SLEIPNER*
> LEFT BERGEN, NORWAY
> MAY 23, 1862
> ARRIVED IN CHICAGO—
> AUGUST 2, 1862
>
> This ship carrying 107 passengers and 350 tons of cargo moored at this location in the Chicago River. The *Sleipner* called again in 1863, 1864 and 1865 thus paving the way for overseas-Great Lakes transportation by water.
>
> *Erected August 2, 1962*

A Sunken Submarine

As terrible as the *Eastland* tragedy was, it was compounded by news of an earlier, smaller, and even stranger calamity. It seems that while a diver named **William Deneau** from Michigan City, Indiana, was recovering bodies from the *Eastland* and preparing to refloat the ship, he came upon a sunken submarine vessel at the bottom of the Chicago River. Deneau applied to the federal government for permission to remove and exhibit the craft, and the submarine named the *Foolkiller* was placed on exhibit at 208 South State Street in February 1916.

To make the tale even more incredible, the bones of a man and a dog were discovered aboard the little submarine when it was lifted. These, too, were exhibited when the submarine went on display. It is believed that the submarine was the handiwork of **Lodner Darvontis Phillips** (1825–69), who also came from Michigan City, Indiana, and later lived in Chicago. Phillips began experimenting with submarines at an early age, eventually perfecting craft that were capable of carrying his wife and children on afternoon-long expeditions below the surface of Lake Michigan.

The submarine in the Chicago River was apparently an earlier, flawed version that Phillips lost to the river during an experiment. It was subsequently raised in 1890 and sold to William Nissen of Chicago who may have been the unfortunate fellow found when the vessel was discovered after the *Eastland* disaster.

Phillips went on to devise submarines that were practicable for warfare and salvage operations and for which he received various patents. His designs incorporated many features that are found aboard modern submarines, and his methods of purifying air within such vessels were novel and effective. Phillips also developed and patented a diving suit, which he tested himself in the Chicago River while newspapers proclaimed that, "a crazy man is going to dive in the Chicago River with an iron suit on" (Harris 1982).

and away from the fire. Crowds on the riverbank begged bridge tenders to swing the bridges closed so they could escape instead of opening the bridges for tugs and their tows of lumber schooners (Ibid.).

Chicago recovered from the fire's devastation in remarkably short time. The riverbank once again filled with the grain elevators, warehouses, and terminals that relied on water-borne trade. Within five years the city rose phoenixlike from the ashes. Not only did commercial cargo vessels use the river docks but also a variety of excursion ships and passenger vessels docked along the riverbanks.

It was between Clark and LaSalle Streets on the river's south bank that the most horrific river tragedy in Chicago history occurred: the capsizing of the *Eastland* on July 24, 1915. The *Eastland* was an excursion vessel that had been chartered to carry twenty-five hundred workers from Western Electric to an outing at the Indiana dunes. Apparently, the ship was overloaded, and there was some evidence that it had not been ballasted correctly. As a result, when most of its passengers crowded the shoreside rail to wave to friends, the unstable vessel capsized.

In a moment the vessel lay grounded on its side on the river bottom. Passengers on the main deck were pitched into the filthy river, and some of those trapped below decks pounded on the hull until they were cut free. But many of those below drowned or were crushed. All told, 812 people lost their lives. Most were young people between the ages of fifteen and thirty, but many younger children were also killed. Twenty-two entire families perished, and some bodies lay unclaimed because no one from their families survived.

Many of the *Eastland* victims were buried at the **Bohemian National Cemetery** on the North Branch of the river. Today a **plaque on Wacker Drive** marks the place where the tragedy occurred.

The story of the *Eastland* does not end in the Chicago River. It was refloated, rebuilt, and eventually recommissioned as the Navy gunboat *USS Wilmette*. Under this new name, it served the U.S. Navy in World War I. After the war it played a role in another drama involving a submarine.

A German submarine, the UC-97, was among many captured during World War I. After the war, it and five other German submarines toured around U.S. waters to promote Liberty Bonds. The UC-97, in particular, was ordered to tour the Great Lakes, and it called at many U.S. and Canadian ports.

The Treaty of Versailles mandated that confiscated war matériel be destroyed within three years. To comply with these terms, the old sub was used for target practice, and the gunboat ordered to sink the vessel was none other than the former *Eastland*. So it was that the UC-97 came to an end in Lake Michigan, far from the ocean and twenty miles off the Chicago shoreline, sunk by a four-inch cannon aboard the *USS Wilmette* (Wise 1989, 12–17).

It is strange that Chicago should be associated with any submarines at all. Yet, the Chicago River was the tomb of Phillips's early experimental craft, and two German submarines, one from each world war, are located in or near Chicago. To this day, the Museum of Science and Industry continues its popular exhibit of the German U-boat 505, which was captured during World War II.

The River's Wearin' O' the Green

Happily, not all of the strange happenings involving the Chicago River are tragic. In 1962 city crews investigating sources of river pollution began using dyes to trace discharges into the river. Apparently, a city plumber working with the crew got his overalls stained green with the dye. This mishap inspired

Stephen Bailey, a labor leader and close friend of Mayor Richard J. Daley, to suggest that the city dye the river green on Saint Patrick's Day.

That first year 100 pounds of vegetable dye were dumped into the stream, and it remained unnaturally green for a week. Nowadays, forty pounds of (we hope) vegetable dye stain the river for only a few hours.

Only after the Michigan Avenue Bridge was completed in 1920 did sleepy Pine Street on the river's north side become **The Magnificent Mile,** Chicago's most elegant shopping street. Slowly the clutter and clamor of the riverbank yielded to new commercial offices, and the lake and river traffic abandoned the crowded frenzy of the restrictive river to call at Navy Pier and the more-spacious industrial areas along the Calumet River.

Double-decked **Wacker Drive,** completed in 1926, brought to an end the grand and colorful chaos of the produce markets that hugged the river's south bank. It also utterly changed the character of South Water Street, which had been Chicago's first street when the town was nothing more than a brawling wilderness outpost. Edward H. Bennett, Daniel Burnham's collaborator on the 1909 Plan of Chicago, designed the Michigan Avenue Bridge and oversaw the implementation of many of the plan's proposals. It was Bennett and Charles H. Wacker, first chairman of the Chicago Plan Commission, who propelled the Wacker Drive project.

To make way for the gargantuan project, every building between South Water Street and the river was demolished. Then the extraordinary new boulevard was erected over the objections of produce traders and the nearly eight thousand property owners who complained that they were there first, and had no place else to go. Their complaints fell on deaf ears, although ultimately they did receive some compensation for their dislocation. The entire project exhibited the same kind of unsentimental "I Will," commercially motivated spirit that has characterized Chicago from the day they cut the sandbar to the present.

An aerial view
of Wacker
Drive, the
Stouffer
Hotel, and
the Leo
Burnett and
R.R. Donnelly
buildings.

CONCLUSION

. . . those damn bridges. . . . When up they go and all traffic stops, you lean against the railing and watch the boats. . . . You may not feel particulary chesty, yet there's a slight stirring, a feeling of Chicago's connection with elsewhere.

Studs Terkel, *Chicago* (1985)

A s CHICAGO APPROACHES THE TWENTY-FIRST CENTURY, plans are afoot to tear down worn-out Wacker Drive and replace it with a completely new version. The nature and volume of traffic in the 1990s so exceeds that of the 1920s that only a complete re-building of the structure will cure its ills and be both prudent and cost-effective.

The city changes, and change is the one constant in Chicago. Familiar buildings are torn down and replaced by others. Streets are moved, people stream in, people move out, bridges are erected or removed, whole neighborhoods change character, Lake Michigan grows smaller as the shore pushes out. Before we quite realize it, the city of our child-hood and the city of our youth melt away and are replaced by a new city. Yet, try as we might, watch as we will, we cannot fully compass the changes. Chicago keeps surprising us, and we are surprised after our long voyage of the imagination to find ourselves back where we started—perhaps "to know the place for the first time."

So, at last, our imaginary tours of Chicago's waters reach their end where Chicago began, and the circle closes at the dock just west of Michigan Avenue. Fatigue and exhila-ration mingle as the imagination reels over the flood of impressions, ideas, and facts. Yet the river flows placidly on—albeit backwards—and tomorrow's tours would show new details and circumstances that were not present today. For the river is not static, but ever changing and ever fascinating: a living presence.

As we have seen on these journeys of exploration and discovery there are many Chicago rivers. There is the original stream, the wild river—the river of trees and grasses, of birds and fish and animals. There is the historic river—the river of the Indians, voyageurs, and explorers. There is the river of commerce and industry—of lumber, grain, and steel—and the engineered river of locks and docks and dams and canals. There is the recreational river of boating and fishing. Finally, there is the spiritual river—the river of contemplation and meditation. Our tours have touched aspects of all of these rivers, yet it is clear that more has been omitted than described. At the end of my waterway tours, I often remark that there is so much to see and so much to say that the boat should not stop, but go around again.

My chagrin at leaving out so much is tempered by the happy realization that there will always be more to see, more to learn, more to understand. As an old piano teacher once said to me, "I envy you—you have so much to learn." In the constant flux of inevitable change a new Chicago River is emerging—the river of the future. This river will, we hope, be cleaner, more inviting, and even more useful than the river of the past. We can help this river to emerge. We can use the river, we can protect the river, we can befriend the river.

From the Forks eastward to the lake, ten bascule bridges span the river's main stem. Their graceful and silent movements alternately delight and dismay pedestrians and motorists rushing about doing the city's business. In the fall and spring, when flotillas of sailboats pass along the river going into or coming out of winter storage, the lifting bridges rise like arms signalling a touchdown, rising in triumph.

Who, in his right mind, could have come to this place two hundred years ago and imagined the metropolis that rose like a dream from a swampy river on the shore of a freshwater sea? Who could have imagined how the resources of seventeen states have been transmuted through the alchemy of human energy, hustle, and imagination into this world city, this city of the spirit? Who could have imagined Chicago, the gift of the river?

APPENDIX A

ORGANIZATIONS OF THE CHICAGO REGION

Brookfield Zoo
3300 Golf Road
Brookfield, Illinois 60513
(708) 485-0263

Canal Corridor Association
220 S. State Street, Suite 1880
Chicago, Illinois 60604
(312) 427-3688

Chicago Botanic Garden
Lake Cook Road
P.O. Box 400
Glencoe, Illinois 60022-0400
(847) 835-5440

Chicago Park District
425 E. McFetridge Drive
Chicago, Illinois 60605
(312) 747-2200

City of Chicago, Department of Environment
30 N. LaSalle Street #2500
Chicago, Illinois 60602-2505
(312) 744-7606

Forest Preserve District of Cook County
536 N. Harlem Avenue
River Forest, Illinois 60305
(708) 366-9420

Forest Preserve District of DuPage County
185 Spring Avenue
P.O. Box 2339
Glen Ellyn, Illinois 60138
(630) 790-4900

Forest Preserve District of Will County
22606 Cherry Hill Road
Joliet, Illinois 60433
(815) 727-8700

Friends of the Chicago River
407 South Dearborn Street #1580
Chicago, Illinois 60605
(312) 939-0490

Illinois Department of Natural Resources
524 South Second Street
Springfield, Illinois 62701
(217) 782-6302

Illinois Natural History Survey
607 East Peabody Drive
Champaign, Illinois 61820
(217) 333-5986

Illinois Nature Preserves Commission
524 South Second Street
Springfield, Illinois 62701
(217) 785-8686

Kane County Forest Preserve District
719 South Batavia Avenue
Geneva, Illinois 60134
(630) 232-5980

Lake County Forest Preserves
2000 North Milwaukee Avenue
Libertyville, Illinois 60048-1199
(847) 367-6640

Lake Michigan Federation
59 East Van Buren Street #2215
Chicago, Illinois 60605
(312) 939-0838

Lincoln Park Zoo
2200 North Cannon Drive
Chicago, Illinois 60614
(312) 742-2353

Little Red Schoolhouse Nature Center
Willow Springs Road at 104th Avenue
Willow Springs, Illinois 60480
(708) 839-6897

McHenry County Conservation District
6512 Harts Road
Ringwood, Illinois 60072
(815) 678-4431

**Metropolitan Water Reclamation
District of Greater Chicago**
100 East Erie Street
Chicago, Illinois 60611
(312) 751-6634

Morton Arboretum
Route 53
Lisle, Illinois 60532
(630) 968-0074

The Nature Conservancy
8 South Michigan Avenue #900
Chicago, Illinois 60603
(312) 346-8166

**Northeastern Illinois Planning
Commission**
222 South Riverside Plaza #1800
Chicago, Illinois 60606
(312) 454-0400

Openlands Project
220 South State Street #1880
Chicago, Illinois 60604-2103
(312) 427-4256

River Trail Nature Center
3120 West Milwaukee Avenue
Northbrook, Illinois 60062
(847) 824-8360

Edward L. Ryerson Conservation Area
21950 North Riverwoods Road
Deerfield, Illinois 60015
(847) 948-7750

Sierra Club, Illinois Chapter
1 North LaSalle Street #4242
Chicago, Illinois 60602
(312) 251-1680

Urban Resources Partnership
c/o U.S. Department of Housing and
Urban Development
77 West Jackson Boulevard
Chicago, Illinois 60604
(312) 353-2473

U.S. Army Corps of Engineers
Chicago District
111 North Canal Street 3600
Chicago, Illinois 60606
(312) 353-6400

U.S. Environmental Protection Agency
Region 5
77 West Jackson Boulevard
Chicago, Illinois 60604-3590

**U.S. EPA Great Lakes Nation Program
Office**
77 West Jackson Boulevard
Chicago, Illinois 60604-3590
(800) 621-8431

U.S. Fish and Wildlife Service
1000 Hart Road #180
Barrington, Illinois 60010
(847) 381-2253

USDA Forest Service
845 Chicago Avenue #225
Evanston, Illinois 60202-2357
(847) 866-9311

Source: Biodiversity Council

USDA Natural Resources Conservation Service
603 East Diehl Road #131
Naperville, Illinois 60563-1476
(630) 505-7808

USDI National Park Service
1709 Jackson Street
Omaha, Nebraska 68102
(402) 221-3471

Museums

Chicago Academy of Sciences
2060 North Clark Street
Chicago, Illinois 60614
(773) 871-2668

Chicago Historical Society
Clark Street and North Avenue
Chicago, Illinois 60614
(312) 642-4600

The Field Museum
Roosevelt Road at Lake Shore Drive
Chicago, Illinois 60605-2496
(312) 922-9410

John G. Shedd Aquarium
1200 South Lake Shore Drive
Chicago, Illinois 60605
(312) 939-2438

Isle a la Cache Museum
501 E. Romeo Road
Romeoville, Illinois 60446
(815) 886-1467

Illinois and Michigan Canal Museum
803 South State Street
Lockport, Illinois 60441
(815) 838-5080

Appendix B

Tours and Recreation

I. Tours of the Chicago River, the River System, and Lake Michigan

A. Tours of the Chicago River and Lake Michigan Shore
1. *Chicago Architecture Foundation.* Architecture River Cruise. One and one-half hour tours of the river's role in the evolution of Chicago and landmarks along the stream. Three times daily and four on weekends. Cost: $18.00. Reservations required. For information call: (312) 922-3432.
2. *Friends of the Chicago River.* River tours by boat and walking tours along the Chicago River. 407 South Dearborn, Suite 1580, Chicago, IL 60605. (312) 922-0490.
3. *Chicago from the Lake.* One and one-half hour architecture tours on the river and history tours on the lake. Tours leave from North Pier. Cost: $18.00 adults, $16.50 seniors, $12.00 children 7 to 18. Architecture tours on weekends feature Japanese, German, and French interpreters. Call (312) 527-1977.
4. *Shoreline Sightseeing.* Thirty minute tours from Shedd Aquarium, Buckingham Fountain, and Navy Pier. Tours leave at fifteen minutes before and past the hour from morning through evening hours. Reservations not required. Cost: $9.00 adults, $8.00 seniors, $4.00 children. For information call: (312) 222-9328.
5. *Canoe Trips*
   a. Friends of the Chicago River
      (312) 939-0490
   b. Chicagoland Canoe Base (773) 777-1489
      4109 N. Narragansett, Chicago, IL 60634

B. Tours of the River System: Circumnavigation of the southern half of Chicago via the Chicago River, south lakefront, Calumet, Cal-Sag, Sanitary Canal, South Branch Chicago River, Main Stem.
1. Graham School of General Studies (formerly the University of Chicago Center for Continuing Studies) (773) 702-0539
2. The University of Illinois Alumni Association
   (312) 996-8535
3. The Field Museum
   (312) 322-8854
4. Mercury Cruise Lines; many cruises.
   (312) 332-1353
5. Wendella Boat Lines; many cruises.
   (312) 337-1446

C. Recreational Tours
> Dining and dancing on the lake
>> 1. *Spirit of Chicago.* Departs south side of Navy Pier, various cruises. Reservations necessary. (312) 836-7899.
>> 2. *Odyssey.* Departs south side of Navy Pier, various cruises. Reservations necessary. (312) 321-7600.
>> 3. *Windy.* Various cruises. Reservations necessary. Call: (312) 595-5555.
>> 4. *Chicago's First Lady.* Sunset dinner cruises, 7 P.M., Wednesdays. Cost: $41.50 adult, $31.50 children under 11. Other cruises are available. Call: (708) 358-9900.
> Fishing: Call city's fishing hotline: (312) 744-3370.

II. Tours of the Metropolitan Water Reclamation District Facilities

Group tours for ten or more visitors to wastewater treatment facilities are offered Monday through Friday at 10 A.M. or 12:30 P.M. Tours are approximately two hours. All visitors must be 10 years of age or older. Tours may be arranged by contacting the district's public information office at (312) 751-6634. Advanced reservations are required.

Tour Highlights:

Calumet Water Reclamation Plant and TARP
Guests may descend into the actual pumping room of the Calumet TARP System, approximately 350 feet below ground. Visitors also see the highly technical, state-of-the-art research and development laboratory.

John E. Egan Reclamation Plant
Guests will see a room-size scale model of the plant, the control room where the plant is operated from a 24-hour computerized system, the blower facility, settling tanks, and the sludge-drying fields.

Hanover Park Water Reclamation Plant and Tree Nursery
The Tree Nursery sets the Hanover plant aside from all others. It is a nature lover's delight.

Lemont Water Reclamation Plant
Tours of Lemont are approximately 30 minutes in length. Visitors are taken through the main building and digester building and then given a step-by-step picture of the plant process.

Lockport Powerhouse
The Powerhouse offers visitors the opportunity to walk through a turn-of-the-century building that houses old but still serviceable equipment such as turbine wheel generators.

North Side Water Reclamation Plant
Visitors follow the path of sewage treatment from the pump and blower house and primary settling tanks to aeration tanks and final settling tanks.

James J. Kirie Water Reclamation Plant and TARP
Visitors are guided through the different stages of treatment—primary, secondary, and tertiary—and then shown how coarse and fine screens separate solid and liquid matter during pretreatment.

Stickney Water Reclamation Plant
A sophisticated computerized process monitoring and control system is used by plant operators to operate the facility at peak efficiency around the clock with minimum staff.

Mainstream Pumping Station
Visitors are invited to descend 350 feet below ground to the pumping room, view a miniature replica of the colossal boring machine used to construct the tunnel, and see a model of the plant grounds on a hydraulic lift designed to illustrate the underground workings of the tunnel system.

III. Dining and Entertainment along or Near the River

Bacino's, 75 E. Wacker Drive; (312) 263-0070.
Caffe Baci, 225 W. Wacker Drive; (312) 251-1234 and
    77 W. Wacker Drive; (312) 629-2224. Cafe/bar.
Catch 35, Leo Burnett Building, 35 W. Wacker Drive; (312) 346-3500.
Celebrity Cafe, 320 N. Dearborn Street; (312) 836-5499.
Coogan's Riverside Saloon, 180 N. Wacker Drive; (312) 444-1134.
Dick's Last Resort, North Pier Terminal, 435 E. Illinois Street; (312) 836-7870.
Green Dolphin Street, 2200 N. Ashland Avenue; (773) 395-0066.
House of Blues, Marina City, 329 N. Dearborn Street; (312) 923-2000. Lunch and
    Sunday Gospel brunch served.
Lizzie McNeill's Irish Pub and Restaurant, 400 N. McClurg Court; (312) 467-1992.
Nick and Tony's, 1 E. Wacker Drive; (312) 467-1992.
Quincy Grille on the River, 200 S. Wacker Drive; (312) 627-1800.
    Located in the Harry Weese and Associates building and adjacent to Quincy
    Park, an urban park with seasonal seating and waterfall at the river's edge.
    Breakfast, lunch, and dinner.
Rivers, 30 S. Wacker Drive; (312) 559-1515.
Sorriso Ristorante and Pub. River Level. 321 N. Clark Street; (312) 644-0283.
The Venice Cafe, 250 S. Wacker Drive; (312) 382-0300.

IV. Miscellaneous

Schemel Marine Transit; (312) 669-1987. From early May to late October (weather
    permitting), water taxis leave every twenty minutes from Union Station to State
    Street (near Marina City) and Navy Pier. A single fare is $3 per person, round
    trip is $5 per person.
Wendella water taxis; (312) 337-1446. From late April to early-to-mid October,
    water taxis leave from Madison and Canal to 400 N. Michigan Avenue (Wrigley
    Building). $10 for a 10-ride pass, $1.25 single ride.

Appendix C

Canoeing Organizations

Illinois Paddling Council. An umbrella organization representing Illinois paddling clubs and Illinois paddler's interests.

> c/o Don Muggenborg
> 9 Peiffer
> Lemont, IL 60439
> (630) 257-7377

Chicago Area Paddling and Rowing Clubs

Chicago Area Sea Kayakers Association (CASKA). Informal paddling group established to encourage and promote recreational kayaking and related activities.

> Vic Hurtowy
> c/o Chicagoland Canoe Base
> 4019 North Narragansett
> Chicago, IL 60634

Chicago River Aquatic Center

> c/o Susan Urbas
> 400 E. Randolph
> Chicago, IL 60601

Chicago Whitewater Association

> c/o Marge Cline
> 1343 North Portage
> Palatine, IL 60067

The Lincoln Park Boat Club (rowing, paddling, and sailing since 1910)

> P.O. Box 146834
> Chicago, IL 60614-6834
> or call: Dave Woodman
> (773) 486-4265

Prairie State Canoeists (Midwest's largest canoe club)

> c/o Sherri Johnson
> 570 Trotter Drive
> Coal City, IL 60416

Northeastern Illinois Paddling Clubs

Illinois Downstreamers

> c/o Rich Burger
> 4638 Middaugh Avenue
> Downers Grove, IL 60515
> (708) 968-0828

St. Charles Canoe Club

> c/o Tave Lamperez
> 24 Roosevelt Street
> St. Charles, IL 60174
> (708) 584-6931

Voyageur Clubs

> *Illinois Brigade*
> 290 Lafayette Lane
> Hoffman Estates, IL 60195

> *Southwest Brigade*
> c/o Dave Anderson
> 15 Norton
> Lemont, IL 60439

CHICAGO RIVERS AND PADDLING INTERNET LINKS

Chicago Area Paddling/Fishing Pages

Extensive information on launch sites, rentals, river, and lake maps.
http://pages.ripco.com:8080/~jwn/

The Illinois Paddling Council (and other clubs)

http://www.prairienet.org/paddling

Illinois Department of Natural Resources

http://dnr.state.il.us/

Illinois Riverwatch Network

http://dnr.state.il.us/ildnr/offices/division/intro.HTM

CANOE ROUTES IN THE CHICAGO AREA

The canoe "season" generally begins in March and continues into November.

Chicago Portage Canoe Trail. A 14.4-mile trail that begins at Stony Ford and ends in Lemont. Part of the Illinois and Michigan National Heritage Corridor.

Skokie Lagoons. Near Glencoe. Includes seven miles of waterways.

Chicago River. Recommended routes: Begin at the control dam at Willow Road, down the East Fork of the North Branch, through Harms Woods, to Milwaukee and Devon Avenues; begin at Baha'i Temple in Wilmette to the Baha'i Beach Club at North Pier via the North Shore Channel to Foster Avenue, down the river to the main stem at Wolf Point, east through downtown to the inner harbor and the Ogden Slip.

Des Plaines River. Recommended: From the Chicago Portage National Historic Site at 43rd and Harlem to Lockport. Along the way, in Romeoville, is **Isle a la Cache Museum.** Located on an eighty-acre island in the Des Plaines River, the museum explores the early fur trade of the region and the activities of the seventeenth century French voyageurs.

OTHER

Chicagoland Canoe Base
4019 N. Narrangansett Avenue
Chicago, IL 60634
(773) 777-1489

Large selection of canoes, kayaks, inflatables, rowing craft, and related accessories. Also books, videos, and maps. Canoe rentals. They also help individuals or groups plan a trip.

REFERENCES

Achilles, Rolf. *Made in Illinois.* Chicago: Illinois Manufacturers' Association, 1993.

Algren, Nelson. *Chicago, City on the Make.* Reprint. Chicago: University of Chicago Press, 1987.

Andreas, A.T. *History of Chicago.* Chicago: A.T. Andreas, 1884–86. 3 vols. Reprint. New York: Arno Press, 1975.

Armstrong, Ken. "July 27, 1919: 38 killed after an invisible line is crossed." *Chicago Tribune,* May 8, 1997.

Atwood, W. W. *The Geology of Chicago and Its Region.* Chicago: University of Chicago Press, 1927.

Berry, Brian J.L., et al. *Chicago: Transformations of an Urban System.* Cambridge, Mass.: Ballinger Publishing Co., 1976.

Berton, Pierre, and Andre Gallant. *The Great Lakes.* Toronto: Stoddard Publishing, 1996.

Bretz, J. Harlen. *Geology of the Chicago Region. Part 2–The Pleistocene.* Urbana, Ill.: State Geological Survey, Bulletin no. 65, 1955.

———. *Geology of the Chicago Region. Part 1—General.* Urbana, Ill.: State Geological Survey, Bulletin no. 65., 1939. Reprinted, 1953.

Bukowski, Douglas. *Navy Pier: A Chicago Landmark.* Chicago: Metropolitan Pier and Exposition Authority, 1996.

Carter, Richard E. "A Preliminary Natural Area Management Plan for the North Shore Channel Lands." January 21, 1992.

Cassidy, Robert. "Our Friendless River." *Chicago Magazine,* August 1979.

Center for Governmental Studies, Northern Illinois University. *A Comparative Guide to Northeastern Illinois and 25 Other Metropolitan Areas: Factors Affecting Business Location.* Chicago: Northeastern Illinois Planning Commission, 1986.

Central Area Committee and the City of Chicago. *Chicago: Central Area Plan.* Chicago: Central Area Committee, 1983.

Chatfield-Taylor, H.C. *Chicago.* Boston: Houghton Mifflin, 1917.

Chicago Rivers Demonstration Project. *Resident Use and Perception of the Chicago and Calumet Rivers.* Milwaukee, Wis.: National Park Service, 1995.

City of Chicago. *Chicago Public Works: A History.* Chicago: Rand McNally, 1973.

City of Chicago. *Chicago Waterways: Background and Policies.* Chicago: Department of Planning, 1982.

City of Chicago. *Downtown Development, Chicago 1989–92.* Chicago: Department of Development, 1991.

City of Chicago. *Historic City: The Settlement of Chicago.* Chicago: Department of Development and Planning, 1976.

City of Chicago. *Life Along the Boulevards.* Chicago: Department of Planning, 1989.

City of Chicago. *The Movable Bridges of Chicago.* Chicago: Department of Public Works, 1979.

City of Chicago. *River North Urban Design Plan.* Chicago: Chicago Department of Planning, 1987.

City of Chicago. *The Straightening of the Chicago River.* Chicago: Department of Public Works, n.d.

City of Chicago. *Straightening the Chicago River.* Chicago: City of Chicago, 1930.

City of Chicago, Commission on Chicago Historical and Architectural Landmarks. *Site of the Beaubien Cabin,* 1975.

———. *Site of the Sauganash Hotel and the Wigwam,* 1975.

———. *Site of the Wolf Point Settlement,* 1975.

———. *Site of Camp Douglas,* 1976.

———. *Site of DuSable/Kinzie House,* 1977.

Cohen, Naomi. "The Unofficial Paddling Guide to the Chicago River." Chicago: Friends of the Chicago River, 1996.

Conzen, Michael P., and Kay J. Carr. *The Illinois and Michigan Canal National Heritage Corridor.* DeKalb, Ill.: Northern Illinois University Press, 1988.

Craig, Lois. "Federal Architecture: From Fort Dearborn to Dearborn Park." *Inland Architect,* vol. 28, no. 5 (September-October 1984).

Cromie, Robert. *A Short History of Chicago.* San Francisco: Lexikos, 1984.

Cronon, William. *Nature's Metropolis: Chicago and the Great West.* New York: W.W. Norton and Company, 1991.

Currey, J. Seymour. *Chicago: Its History and Its Builders: A Century of Marvellous Growth.* 5 vols. Chicago: S.J. Clarke Publishing, 1908–12.

Cutler, Irving. *Chicago: Metropolis of the Mid-Continent.* Dubuque, Ia.: Kendall Hunt, 1980.

Davidson, Alexander, and Bernard Stuve. *A Complete History of Illinois from 1673 to 1873.* Springfield, Ill.: Illinois Journal Company, 1874.

Dedmon, Emmett. *Fabulous Chicago: A Great City's History and People.* 2nd ed. New York: Atheneum, 1983.

Deep Waterway Committee. *From the Great Lakes to the Gulf of Mexico.* Chicago: Chicago Commercial Association, 1906.

Dennison, S.G., S.J. Sedita, D.R. Zenz, and C. Lue-Hing. *1985 Fish Survey of the Metropolitan Chicago Waterway System.* Report No. 92–7. Chicago: Metropolitan Water Reclamation District of Greater Chicago, 1992.

Dickenson, Paul R. *Great Lakes Dredge & Dock Company: A Century of Experience 1890–1990.* Oak Brook, Ill.: Great Lakes Dredge & Dock Company, 1990.

Draine, Edwin H., and Donald G. Meyer. *Port of Chicago: Unification Study.* Chicago: Chicago Association of Commerce and Industry, 1970.

Driscoll, Paul A. "Wieners or losers." *Chicago Tribune,* March 13, 1996.

Duis, Perry. *Chicago: Creating New Traditions.* Chicago: Chicago Historical Society, 1976.

Farr, Finis. *Chicago: A Personal History of America's Most American City.* New Rochelle, N.Y.: Arlington House, 1973.

Federal Writers' Project. *Selected Bibliography: Illinois, Chicago and Its Environs.* Chicago: Works Progress Administration, 1937. Reprint. Evanston, Ill.: Chicago Historical Bookworks, 1990.

———. *Illinois: Chicago and Its Environs.* American Guide Series. 1937, Reprint. Evanston, Ill.: Chicago Historical Bookworks, 1990.

Ford Motor Company. *75 Years in Chicago: 1914–89.* Chicago: Ford Motor Company, 1989.

Freese, Ralph. "Chicagoland Canoe Trails." Chicago: Chicagoland Canoe Base, n.d.

Friends of the Chicago River. "Chicago River Trail: A Walking Tour. North Branch Section." N.p., n.d.

Fryxell, F.M. *The Physiography of the Region of Chicago.* Chicago: University of Chicago Press, 1924.

Gale, Edwin O. *Reminiscences of Early Chicago and Vicinity.* Chicago: Fleming H. Revell Company, 1902.

Garreau, Joel. *The Nine Nations of North America.* Boston: Houghton Mifflin, 1981.

Gebhart, Richard. "Still Working—A Grand Old Lady of the Lakes." *Inland Seas,* vol. 47, no. 4 (winter 1991).

General Mills. "The South Chicago Story." *Big G Conveyor,* May 1, 1995.

Glibota, Ante, and Frederic Edelmann. *Chicago: 150 Years of Architecture, 1833–1983.* Paris: Paris Art Center, 1985.

Goddard, Connie, and Bruce Hatton Boyer. *The Great Chicago Trivia and Fact Book.* Nashville, Tenn.: Cumberland House, 1996.

Goldthwaites, Reuben, ed. *The Jesuit Relations and Allied Documents: Travels and Explorations of the Jesuit Missionaries in New France 1610–1791.* Cleveland, Ohio: Burrows Brothers, 1899.

Greeley, Andrew M. *Andrew Greeley's Chicago.* Chicago: Contemporary Books, 1989.

Hall, Jennie. *The Story of Chicago.* Chicago: Rand McNally and Company, 1911.

Hamilton, Henry Raymond. *The Epic of Chicago.* Chicago: Willett, Clark, and Company, 1932.

Hansen, Harry. *The Chicago.* New York: Rinehart and Company, 1942.

Harper, William Hudson, ed. *Chicago: A History and Forecast.* Chicago: Chicago Association of Commerce, 1921.

Harris, Patricia A. Gruse. *Great Lakes' First Submarine: L. D. Phillips' "Fool Killer."* Michigan City, Ind.: Michigan City Historical Society, 1982.

Hayner, Don, and Tom McNamee. *Streetwise Chicago.* Chicago: Loyola Press, 1988.

Hayner, Don. "Bridges Span History of the City." *Chicago Sun-Times,* September 22, 1982.

Heise, Kenan, and Mark Frazel. *Hands on Chicago: Getting Hold of the City.* Chicago: Bonus Books, 1987.

Hochgesang, Jim. *Hiking and Biking in Cook County, Illinois.* Lake Forest, Ill.: Root and Wings, 1996.

Holt, Glen E., and Dominic A. Pacyga. *Chicago: A Historical Guide to the Neighborhoods—The Loop and South Side.* Chicago: Chicago Historical Society, 1979.

Howe, Walter A. *Documentary History of the Illinois and Michigan Canal.* Springfield, Ill.: State of Illinois, Division of Waterways, 1956.

Hubbard, Gurdon Saltonstall. *The Autobiography of Gurdon Saltonstall Hubbard.* Reprint. Grand Rapids, Mich.: Black Letter Press, 1981.

Husar, John. "Maps unlock river's history." *Chicago Tribune,* December 12, 1996.

Jones, Peter d'A., and Melvin G. Holli. *Ethnic Chicago.* Grand Rapids, Mich.: William B. Eerdmans Publishing, 1981.

Kennicott, Robert. *Illinois Agricultural Society Report,* 1854. Cited in *Nature Bulletin,* no. 386-A, "Wildlife in Chicago," Forest Preserve District of Cook County.

Larson, John W. *Those Army Engineers.* Chicago: Chicago District, Corps of Engineers, 1979.

Lewis, Arnold. *An Early Encounter with Tomorrow.* Champaign, Ill.: University of Illinois Press, 1997.

Lindsey, Joan V. *Chicago from the River.* Chicago: Donneco International, 1995.

Linton, Cynthia, ed. *The Ethnic Handbook.* Chicago: Illinois Ethnic Coalition, 1996.

McBrien, Judith Paine. *Chicago's Riverfront: Where the Past Meets the Present.* Chicago: Perspectives Press, 1991.

McClellan, Keith. "A History of Chicago's Industrial Development." In *Mid-Chicago Economic Development Study.* Vol. 3. Chicago: Mayor's Committee for Economic and Cultural Development, 1966.

McClure, J.B. *Stories and Sketches of Chicago.* Chicago: Rhodes & McClure Publishers, 1880.

McIlvaine, Mabel. *Reminiscences of Chicago during the Forties and Fifties.* Chicago: R.R. Donnelly & Sons, 1913.

Mark, Norman. *Norman Mark's Chicago.* 3rd ed. Chicago: Chicago Review Press, 1987.

Mayer, Harold M. *The Port of Chicago and the St. Lawrence Seaway.* Chicago: University of Chicago Press, 1957.

————. "The Changing Role of Metropolitan Chicago in the Midwest and the Nation." Papers on Urban Problems. Report no. 2. Milwaukee, Wis.: Urban Research Center, University of Wisconsin-Milwaukee, 1975.

Mayer, Harold M., and Richard C. Wade. *Chicago: Growth of a Metropolis.* Chicago: University of Chicago Press, 1969.

Mayor's Committee for Economic and Cultural Development. *Mid-Chicago Economic Development Study.* 3 vols. Chicago: Mayor's Committee for Economic and Cultural Development, 1966.

Meeker, Arthur. *Chicago with Love.* New York: Alfred A. Knopf, 1955.

Mendes, Joel, and Theodore J. Karamanski. *The Maritime History of Chicago: A Guide to Sources.* Chicago: Chicago Maritime Society, 1990.

Miller, Donald L. *City of the Century: The Epic of Chicago and the Making of America.* New York: Simon and Schuster, 1996.

Miller, Hugh C. *The Chicago School of Architecture.* Washington, D.C.: Department of the Interior, National Park Service, 1973.

Nash, Jay Robert. *People to See.* Chicago: New Century Publishers, 1981.

National Park Service, Department of the Interior. *Illinois and Michigan Canal National Heritage Corridor,* n.d.

Northeastern Illinois Planning Commission. *1994–95 Water Quality Activities.* Chicago: Northeastern Illinois Planning Commission, 1996.

Northeastern Illinois Planning Commission and Center for Governmental Studies. *A Comparative Guide to Northeastern Illinois and 25 Other Metropolitan Areas: Factors Affecting Business Location.* Chicago: Northeastern Illinois Planning Commission, 1986.

Pacyga, Dominic A. *Polish Immigrants and Industries of Chicago.* Columbus, Ohio: Ohio State University Press, 1991.

Pacyga, Dominic A., and Ellen Skerrett. *Chicago: City of Neighborhoods.* Chicago: Loyola Press, 1986.

Petroski, Henry. "The Ferris Wheel on the Occasion of Its Centennial." *American Scientist,* vol. 81 (May–June 1993): 216–21.

Pierce, Bessie Louise. *A History of Chicago.* 3 vols. Chicago: University of Chicago Press, 1937.

Piety, James W. *Chicago-Historical Geographic Laboratory Guide.* 3rd ed. Champaign, Ill.: Stipes Publishing, 1983.

Port, Weimar. *Chicago the Pagan.* Chicago: Judy Publishing Company, 1953.

Quaife, Milo M. *Chicago's Highways Old and New.* Chicago: D.F. Keller & Co., 1923.

————. *Checagou 1673–1835.* Chicago: University of Chicago Press, 1933.

Redd, Jim. *The Illinois and Michigan Canal.* Carbondale, Ill.: Southern Illinois University Press, 1993.

Report of the Deep Waterway Committee. *From the Great Lakes to the Gulf of Mexico.* Chicago: Chicago Commercial Association, 1906.

Rice, Mary Jane Judson. *Chicago: Port to the World.* Chicago: Follett Publishing, 1969.

Sawyers, June Skinner. *Chicago Sketches: Urban Tales, Stories, and Legends from Chicago History.* Chicago: Wild Onion Books, 1995.

Schnedler, Jack. *Chicago.* Oakland, Calif.: Compass American Guides, 1996.

Sheridan Shore Yacht Club: A 60 Year History. Wilmette, Ill.: Sheridan Shore Yacht Club, 1969.

Siegel, Arthur, ed. *Chicago's Famous Buildings.* Chicago: University of Chicago Press, 1965.

Sinclair, Upton. *The Jungle.* New York: New American Library, 1960.

Solzman, David M. *Waterway Industrial Sites: A Chicago Case Study.* Chicago: University of Chicago, 1966.

Spear, Allan. *Black Chicago: The Making of a Negro Ghetto.* Chicago: University of Chicago Press, 1967.

Sullivan, Ann C. "Asia's Tallest Towers." *Architecture,* September 1996.

Sutton, Robert M., ed. *The Heartland: Pages from Illinois History.* Lake Forest, Ill.: Deerpath Publishing, 1975.

Terkel, Studs. *Chicago.* New York: Pantheon Books, 1985.

Tuttle, William M., Jr. *Race Riot: Chicago in the Red Summer of 1919.* Chicago: University of Illinois Press, 1996.

Vierling, Philip E. *A Self-Guided Loop Hiking Trail to the Chicago Portage National Historic Site.* Vol. 1, no. 1. Illinois Country Hiking Guide, 1973.

Walker, Ward. *The Story of the Metropolitan Sanitary District of Greater Chicago.* Chicago: Metropolitan Sanitary District, 1960.

Wallin, Dave. *Resident Use and Perception of the Chicago and Calumet Rivers.* Chicago Rivers Demonstration Project. Milwaukee, Wis.: National Park Service, 1995.

Wendt, Lloyd. *Swift Walker.* Chicago: Regnery Books, 1986.

Wille, Lois. *Forever Open, Clear and Free.* Chicago: Henry Regnery Company, 1972.

Willman, H.B. *Summary of the Geology of the Chicago Area.* Urbana, Ill.: Illinois State Geological Survey, 1971.

Wilson, William Julius. *The Declining Significance of Race: Blacks and Changing American Institutions.* Chicago: University of Chicago Press, 1980.

Wise, James E., Jr. "The Sinking of the UC-97." *Naval History* (winter 1989): 12–17.

Young, David M. "Pier Pressure." *Chicago Tribune,* October 25, 1992.

———. *Chicago Transit: An Illustrated History.* DeKalb, Ill.: Northern Illinois University Press, in press.

Zorbaugh, Harvey. *The Gold Coast and the Slum.* Chicago: University of Chicago Press, 1929.

Zotti, Ed. *Chicago River Urban Design Guidelines.* Chicago: Chicago Plan Commission, Department of Planning and Friends of the Chicago River, 1990.

INDEX

PHOTO CREDITS